GUY MARTIN

MY AUTOBIOGRAPHY

Virgin BOOKS

18

Virgin Books, an imprint of Ebury Publishing,
20 Vauxhall Bridge Road,
London SW1V 2SA

Virgin Books is part of the Penguin Random House group of companies
whose addresses can be found at global.penguinrandomhouse.com

Penguin Random House UK

First published by Virgin Books in 2014
This edition published by Virgin Books in 2015

www.eburypublishing.co.uk

A CIP catalogue record for this book is available from the British Library

ISBN 9780753555033

Career results compiled by Phil Wain

Penguin Random House is committed to a sustainable future for
our business, our readers and our planet. This book is made from
Forest Stewardship Council® certified paper.

FSC www.fsc.org MIX Paper from responsible sources FSC® C018179

Printed and bound in Great Britain by Clays Ltd, St Ives plc

CONTENTS

PROLOGUE:

GAME OVER

I'D JUST LEFT the pits after the fuel stop. Head down, wrestling the 210-horsepower Honda Fireblade through the outskirts of Douglas, the Manx capital, and out onto another 38-mile lap of the island. One of my mechanics, Cammy, had told me I was in the lead, but only by a second. I could hear a difference in his voice. He's normally as calm as if he was reading a shopping list, but there was an edge this time. He knew we could win.

It was the start of the third lap of the 2010 Isle of Man Senior TT, the last race of the fortnight, the race I have been desperate to win since 2004, and the last chance to get a TT win for another year. I was pushing hard.

I had already missed out on a win by three seconds that week. Three seconds in a race held over 150 miles. A race that lasts one hour and 12 minutes, or 4,300 seconds. That means the winning margin was 0.07 per cent. It's obvious that every second counts in modern real road racing.

Down Bray Hill, with a full tank of fuel and a new rear tyre.

The bike goes from nearly bone dry to brim full, and the extra 24 litres of unleaded always makes a difference to the handling, but I know how to deal with it.

Then, three miles from the pits, comes Ballagarey. This is the kind of corner that keeps me racing on the roads. It's a proper man's corner. You go through the right-hander at 170 mph or more, leant right over, eyes fixed as far down the road as it's possible to see, which isn't very far. Like so many corners at the Isle of Man, and most of the other circuits I specialise at, it's blind. I can't see the exit of the corner when I fully commit to the entry.

I'd been through Ballagarey 100 times flat-out, but this time something happened. This time the front end tucked, lost grip and started sliding. It's the beginning of a crash. That's not unusual. I'm saving slides regularly when I'm pushing for wins. Through the fastest corners the bike is always on the edge of crashing, just gripping enough to keep on going in the right direction. Go slightly too fast and the tyre shouts, 'Enough!' Go slightly too slow and you're no longer in the hunt for wins.

As the front tyre carried on skidding across the top of the road, I tried to save the slide. I thought, 'I've got it, I've got it, I've got it, I've got it ...' I can sometimes get away with front-end tucks, when the bike is leant so far over that the front tyre eventually loses grip and begins to slide. You can save them on your knee, or give it a bit of throttle and it'll come back to you. One thing's for sure, you don't do anything major, like grabbing a handful of brake, and you don't panic because that's when you come off.

I went through all that thought process, as the bike was steadily skating, increasingly out of control towards the Manx stone wall that lines the outside of this corner. Then the thought 'Game over' entered my head. At those speeds, on a corner like that, you're not jumping off the bike, just letting it go. I was leant over as far as a Honda CBR1000RR will lean, and a little bit more. I released my grip on the bars of the bike and slid down the road. I didn't think, 'This is going to hurt,' – just, 'Whatever will be, will be.'

CHAPTER 1

NO MIDDLE NAME

'The spaghetti measurer would be out and the chase would begin.'

I REGULARLY USED to say I was born and bred in Kirmington, because up until recently I always thought of the real town of my birth as a shithole. The truth is I actually arrived in the world in Grimsby, in 1981. I was born in the maternity hospital in Nunsthorpe, the roughest estate in the town. I was, and still am, Guy Martin – no middle name.

My dad missed my arrival. He was in the hospital for the birth of Sally, my older sister, but he had to stand outside because she was in breech and the father wasn't allowed in when things were getting complicated back in those days. When it was my turn to pop out, Dad was there with my mum waiting for me to appear, but at eight at night the midwife told them nothing would happen until midnight, so Dad went out to get some bits from Scanlink, the local truck part specialist, for a job he was working and missed me being born at just gone ten. He was there for Stuart's birth and Kate's, though. My little sister's was so quick she wrecked the interior of his Ford Granada on the way to Grimsby Maternity Hospital.

My mum, Rita, is nine years younger than Dad. She was only 16 when they met. I think the age difference caused some friction between Dad and his mates of the time, but when I see old photos of them together, even with the nearly ten-year age gap, they don't look wrong together. They always look dead happy.

Ian Martin and Rita Kidals married six years later when my mum was 22, and their first child, Sally, was born a couple of years later. Sally was only four months old when I was conceived. Mum says it all happened at the end of her first night out after Sally's birth.

On 4 November 1981, the Martin family, now with a 13-month-old girl and a day-old baby boy, left hospital, jumped in the car and drove the 12 miles to my very first home, a flat above the old Co-Op in Caistor. It was a second-floor flat with a nice, big garden that had a sandpit in it. Our entrance was around the back of the shop, off Bank Lane.

I don't have strong memories of the place because we moved, when I was still only three, to the house on Gravel Pit Lane, Kirmington, where my parents still live. Now the house is surrounded by conifers, but in those days it had a barbed wire fence.

My dad was a part-time motorcycle racer, a privateer, which meant he paid for his own way, and won a bit of prize money here and there. Though he was racing for fun, never a career, he lined up with some of the biggest names of the time, competing in the Shell Oils series, the British Superbikes of its time. He raced at

15 Isle of Man TTs. He was a top privateer. He didn't start racing until he was in his mid-twenties.

The window frames of Gravel Pit Lane had begun to rot and to have them repaired Dad eventually had to sell his P&M-framed Suzuki 1000, the race bike he finished twelfth on in the 1983 Isle of Man TT. He was the first privateer home that year. The bike had all the right bits on it and he still raves about it now, but double-glazing was more important. They must have been on the bones of their arse.

We didn't get a telephone until one of my granddads went into hospital, when I was ten, which makes it 1991. Up until then the family would use the traditional red phone box over the road if they needed to make, or take, calls. I remember when my dad was away racing he'd have a timetable for ringing home to tell everyone he was all right. Mum would go out, cross the road and wait by the phone box for it to ring.

Dad would often work seven days a week. Especially when he was saving up for a bike. He would fix trucks six days a week, well, five and a half really, then on Sundays he would sometimes drive trucks for another company, and me and Sally would jump in the cab with him, sitting on the bunk-bed in the back. The money earned on Sunday would go towards his racing or bike projects.

Dad has worked for himself since 1995. When I was born he was employed by R K Hirst, the hauliers, in the same yard in Caistor he works from now. After he met my mum, but before they were married, he was in Nigeria, working as a fitter for a crew of road builders. At the same time Mum was in Germany working in a hotel. They had a break from the relationship for a bit, and it was when they were thousands of miles apart that they realised how much they missed each other and that's when they decided to get married. One time Sally and I were in the garage and came across the love letters Dad sent from Nigeria. They both arranged to come back to England and were married three weeks later. That was over 35 years ago and they're still together now.

Even in his mid-sixties, and still not retired, Dad looks the same as he does in photos from when we were kids well over 20 years ago. I think this fact has gone a long way to shaping much of my view of work and life. Hard work never hurt him. The opposite, in fact. My dad has grafted on trucks for over four decades and he's as strong as a bull. He works in the pit, under Scania 4210s, with the 20-foot doors of the garage wide open whatever the weather and with nothing to protect him but his blue overalls, a few pints of stiff tea and cod liver oil. And he's fitter than a lot of men half his age.

If you met Ian Martin 30 years ago, you'd definitely recognise him now. He has always gone from having a full beard, to a goatee and then on to a porno-style handlebar 'tache. It's a three-yearly cycle, and I've never worked out what sets off the changes in the style of his facial hair. He has also worn spectacles as long as I've been alive, always the same size and style: big, rectangular ones, as thick as the bottom of a pint glass.

These specs were legendary in the Lincolnshire market town of Caistor. If Ian Martin's glasses came off there was going to be trouble, because my dad was a scrapper. I never have been, but he was a renowned fighter in Grimsby, Market Rasen and Caistor. If the glasses came off, stand back. I've heard the stories, but, I'm happy to say, I've never seen him in a fight. I think it was all part of a good night out for him: go out, get drunk, have a fight.

The famous Elton John song of 1973, 'Saturday Night's Alright (For Fighting)', was written about the rivalry between Caistor and Market Rasen, because Elton's co-writer, Bernie

Taupin, came from Normanby-by-Spital, 15 miles from Caistor. At the time there was a feud between lads of these towns just eight miles apart. It was the time of mods and rockers and anything went. One night the songwriter, then still unknown, was in the Aston Arms in Market Rasen when the Caistor mob came to town for a punch-up. Dad knows for a fact he was one of the Caistor lads causing bother that Taupin would write about.

It was good being Ian Martin's son, because it meant I rarely got in any bother. I've inherited a lot of Dad's traits, more than perhaps I'd like, but I've never been handy in a scrap. I've thrown the odd punch in self-defence, when I've had to, but I've never gone out looking for trouble. But those who did enjoy throwing fists around perhaps thought twice before picking on me. Another thing that helped me avoid the kind of trouble that kicks off every Friday and Saturday night in towns and cities all over Britain was that I've never been much of a boozer either, so I didn't go to pubs much. Still, I haven't escaped unscathed. I have no sense of smell after getting lamped on a night out in Lincoln when I was a teenager.

While he was lovey-dovey with my mum, buying her big Valentine's cards and all that, he wasn't a very cuddly dad when I was growing up. If everything was all right he'd give us a big thumbs up. He wouldn't say much and, as I've said, he seemed to be always working. Until I started working with him, part-time, we'd see him odd nights of the week, Saturday afternoon and some Sundays.

My mum, Rita, is a cracking lass, but awkward. Not socially awkward, more headstrong and stubborn. It must be where I get it from.

When I was young, I thought Rita Martin was the worst mum in the world, but I'm sure loads of people think that of their parents and only realise later how wrong they were!

Big Rita wouldn't take any nonsense, that's why I reckoned I was hard done by, but I look back now and think she did exactly the right thing. We learnt right from wrong. We weren't cheeky very often and we didn't have too much chelp. There definitely wasn't any naughty step in our house. She'd smack us to keep us in line if we weren't behaving. She would clip us with the spaghetti measurer, a flat piece of wood with rounded edges, basically a thin paddle about six inches long. It's the kitchen implement that has different-sized holes in it to help you judge how much spaghetti to put in the pan. She moved on to the spaghetti measurer, as a tool of child discipline, after realising wooden spoons weren't working. She was handy with it as well. It was thick enough not to snap, but not too thick, so it had a bit of whip to it.

The lead-up to a whack on the backside would follow a familiar pattern and develop like this: first we'd be cheeky or not pipe down after being told to, so Mum would put a hand on the cutlery drawer and look at us. That was the first warning. If we carried on, the next thing she'd do was close the kitchen window, so the neighbours couldn't hear us. Once the window was closed you knew you were getting it, and the spaghetti measurer would be out and the chase would begin. Until I learnt, my mum would spank my arse at least once a week, usually a quick whack while I was running away. It would come sharp, with a flick of the wrist.

Still, I got away lightly. My older sister Sally got it worse than me, and Stu got it worst of all. He was mischievous – a cheeky little bugger. He was suspended from school too, for mooning out of the bus window, throwing snowballs in class, breaking windows ... Kate is the youngest and never got a spanking as far as I can remember. She nearly died, from whooping cough, when she was still very young. She turned blue, was well on her way to going, according to my dad, and was rushed to Grimsby Hospital. She survived and, I reckon, played up to it too, even until she was 11 or 12, so she never got her spaghetti measured.

We'd often hear the threat, 'Wait till your dad gets home,' but he never did anything. Big Rita was the enforcer in Gravel Pit Lane. Of course, we weren't abused, I had a fantastic childhood. She was a great mum. She still is.

Rita had quite a tough upbringing herself. Once, when she was little, her school friends were all talking about Father Christmas. She raced home, all excited, to tell her mother, Double-Decker Lil, who then asked who had been filling her head with such rubbish! But Mum didn't pass that on to her own kids. Sally was 12 before she had any real doubts about the existence of Santa Claus, and Christmas time was mega at our house. On Christmas Eve my dad would have a few drinks and tell us to bring the pet rabbits into the house. It was the only day out of the whole year he'd do it, but it happened every year. He'd be as pissed as handcarts from the pub at lunchtime. It's the only time I remember seeing him drunk, but he'd be as daft as a brush, crawling around on the floor with our rabbits.

Rita laid down some weird rules. She wouldn't allow us to watch *Grange Hill* in case it led us down the wrong path. When we were playing out in the street with kids she regarded as a bad influence, Mum would shout, 'Your tea's ready,' even though we'd already had it. She wanted us to come in, but she wouldn't just say, 'Come in.' Perhaps she didn't want anyone thinking that she was looking down on anyone else in the village, even though that might have happened to us.

When Sally and I were very little, Mum had a trike, a pedal one, that she'd bought from a copper in Riby. She would pedal up to the Humber Bridge, with me and Sally sat in a basket behind her looking backwards at the traffic coming to overtake us. It was a good 20-mile round trip, with us two in the back. We had an old rusty length of chain across our laps to keep us in, but that was it! Helmets? You're kidding, aren't you?

It almost goes without saying Rita was the no-nonsense type. Once I fell off the monkey bars in the local playground and hurt my arm. I told her I thought it was broken, but she inspected the injury and said there was nothing wrong with it. I showed my dad when he got home and he agreed with me. So did the hospital he took me to. It was broken. By weird coincidence, on the day I broke my arm two other pupils from the 18-strong Kirmington Church of England Primary School, where I was a pupil, also broke their arms. It was so unusual, 17 per cent of the whole school breaking their arms in one 12-hour period, the local paper sent out a photographer.

When I was young we'd go to Butlin's in Skegness for holidays, and then when I was 13 or 14 we all went to Tenerife – our first foreign holiday. Eventually, when Sally was 16 and getting to the age where she wasn't keen to go on the big family holiday any more, the six of us all went for one last big blow-out together, to Florida. It is remembered, by all of us, as the best holiday ever. By that time, Dad's business was well established and he was earning a decent living thanks to his hard graft.

Rita is from Hull, but her dad was Latvian. After his homeland had been invaded by the Nazis, in 1941, Voldemars Kidals was conscripted to fight for the Germans in the war. He was one of 200,000 Latvians that were given the choice: fight or be shot. Voldemars fitted Hitler's bill perfectly. He was blond and six-foot-two, but because he wasn't German, he and all his fellow countrymen were treated as cannon-fodder. It's reckoned that half those Latvian conscripts died on the battlefield. Voldemars was sent straight to the Russian front, where he had to deal with the horrific winters that demolished Hitler's badly prepared and demoralised troops. Walter and his mate were manning a machine-gun post and realised that if, or when, the Russian army reached them they wouldn't be shown any mercy, so the pair of them deserted, escaping by clinging on to the bottom of a train for two days as it crossed Poland and into Germany. They were eventually captured by the Americans and put in a prisoner-of-war camp in Belgium. After that he was given the option of going to England or Canada, and he chose England. When the war ended a lot of Latvians were still housed at a camp near Leicester. After that Voldemars moved to another camp in Bransburton, just north of Hull. He learnt to speak a bit of English, but, even years later, when I was born, it was still only a bit. Everyone called him Walter.

Back in the years just after the war, Walter worked on the local farms and felt really well looked after. Lil lived in the same village, and they met at Hull Fair.

After they were married, the pair moved to Marmaduke Street in Hull. Then, in the late 1940s, they spotted a little place in a village called Nettleton advertised for sale in an estate agent's window. Walter cycled 18 miles from New Holland, after getting the ferry over from Hull, to look at the house. He and Lil moved to the village, near Caistor, and Walter ended up working in the Nettleton iron-mines. The iron ore mined there was some of the finest in the world, I've been told, and it was taken straight to the steelworks in Scunthorpe on a purpose-built railway line. Walter worked there for years, below ground, as a face-worker at a time when mules were pulling the rock to the surface. Later in his life he became a builder.

He was, like my mum and dad, a proper grafter. And Walter could make anything. He would re-sole shoes and make his own sweeping brushes. He had a map of Latvia made from iron, that he cast in sections to show the different regions. About the size and height of a large coffee table, it was a decorative feature of his back garden. He came from a time and place where people didn't automatically go to the shop and buy what they needed. Not if they could make it. When she was living at home, one of my mum's jobs was to rip up the newspaper and thread the pieces on to a string to use instead of toilet roll. That was a night's entertainment.

It was a long time before the Kidals bought a TV, but my dad's family were the first in the town of Caistor to have a television set, and proud that the mayor's son had to come to their house to watch it.

As kids we would love visiting Granddad and Granny Kidals because Walter had a smallholding with his own animals: mainly sheep, I remember one called Nancy, and rabbits, nothing too big. Walter wouldn't say much, but he'd show us things. Every now and then, when my mum was a little girl, a rabbit that she had become attached to would go missing. As they sat around the table that night little Rita would remember to ask, 'Where's my rabbit?' her mum, Lil, would reply, 'You're eating it.'

Walter had a load of sayings, but the most memorable for me was this, delivered in a broad Latvian accent: 'When you dead, you dead.' Perhaps it was memories of what he saw in the war that made him say stuff like that to his young grandkids. It was clear he didn't believe in heaven or hell. And thinking about it now, that attitude probably rubbed off on me.

Mum is one of five Kidals children, Rita and four brothers, and a lot of this make-do attitude of Voldemars and Lil obviously passed down to my mum. We had a cooked dinner every night, with a pudding to follow, but some of the meals were best described as concoctions. Very little went to waste. We'd have bubble and squeak on a Monday night, made from the left-over vegetables from Sunday dinner. I'd eat anything, but Sally was always more picky and dreaded Monday nights. I know most of my friends and schoolmates would turn their noses up at some of our meals: mashed swede and beans in gravy and stuff like that; anything really, because that's how my mum was brought up, just to get by. There was nothing wrong with it and it didn't do her any harm, or my mum's mum, Double-Decker Lil. She is 90 and going strong.

Why Double-Decker? It seems she was a big lass when she was younger. She had a stroke when Rita was 18, and Rita looked after her bed-bound mother. You wouldn't know now that she'd had a stroke, though. Lil has outlasted all my other grandparents. She's double hard. Around the time of the 2013 North West 200 race meeting, in the middle of May, my mum told me Lil was in hospital with cancer. When I got back from racing in Northern Ireland I spent quite a bit of time with Lil before I went away again to race at the TT. I wasn't sure what the future was going to bring for her, and being so busy at the time I hadn't been visiting her enough.

Lil had visited the doctors, and knew something was up, because she had some trouble with her plumbing or something. She was taken into hospital, where they told her she was pretty much riddled with cancer. She was 89 and still had all her marbles. When I visited her in hospital, she was telling me that she knew the doctors had got the diagnosis wrong because she felt fine. At the time, I didn't know if she was trying to convince me or herself, but she sounded pretty sure and she looked much the same as usual. Then, a few days later, a doctor came to see her and said, 'Sorry, Lil, we made a mistake.' It wasn't cancer, it was something else. So they let her out. She was right all along.

She knew there was nothing up. You don't mess with Double-Decker Lil.

The Second World War has had other influences on me. My dad was a baby boomer, born after all the surviving soldiers returned home and got back on the nest. And I was named after Guy Gibson, the Wing Commander of 617 Squadron, the Dambusters, who were based in Lincolnshire, not far down the road from Kirmington at RAF Scampton. When I was first told that, I didn't think much of it, but now I realise he's quite a man to be named after. It was my dad's decision, not Mum's. My dad has a lot of interest in the history of World War II. His dad was a Royal Marine; while Dad's father-in-law, Voldemars, was reluctantly fighting against the Allies. The only thing that was ever mentioned about this, was one time when both sets of grandparents were invited to Kirmington and, after a few drinks, Walter, in his broken English, said to my other granddad, Jack, 'Me and you on opposite sides.' When he said that, everyone burst out laughing.

Dad talked about the war so often – the Battle of Britain, Dunkirk etc. – that when I was little I once asked Mum, 'When is the war going to end?' Rita wrote it on a postcard and sent it to a 'Kids Say the Funniest Things' type competition in one of the weekly gossip magazines she read – and won!

My dad's father Jack was involved in the Normandy landings, one of the waves of servicemen who arrived on the beaches a day or so after D-Day. He drove a six-wheel GMC truck off the landing craft. On the trailer he was towing was the most advanced radar in the world at the time, one of only two in existence, my dad would tell us.

After VE Day, Jack came back to England and married May, my grandmother, but was then sent to South Africa to prepare for the invasion of Japan. The sea and ground attack on Japan never happened, though, because the two atomic bombs were dropped on Nagasaki and Hiroshima, ending the war once and for all.

Jack grew up in South Kelsey, less than a mile from where I bought my first house. The Martins never fall very far from the tree.

After leaving the Marines, Jack was the transport manager at T H Brown's, a haulage firm a stone's throw from the Moody International truck yard I now work at. They became the first Scania truck dealer in the country, and it was where my dad first started his training – working for his dad, like I later would. So Granddad Jack was in road transport, my dad is in road transport, and so am I. In fact, Jack's dad, my great-grandfather, was the road foreman for Lincolnshire County Council. He was involved in the building of the Caistor bypass. He had his then 14-year-old son Jack involved too, changing the points on the railway line that transported the rock to Nettleton to build the 20-per-cent incline to Caistor Top. Well, he had Jack involved until the boy forgot to change the points one time and the train, full of rock, crashed through the engine shed.

Four generations. It's in the breeding. My Granddad Martin was very much like my dad, because I remember he was all work, work, work, trucks, trucks, trucks. He was another stubborn one. He and my dad were close to scrapping no end of times, I'm told.

Grandma May Martin was always Nanny, while Lil was Granny. Nanny smoked like a damp bonfire. It was Nanny who first got me into tea. She would make it strong and always in a cup and saucer. I also remember her lifting the back of her skirt up to warm her bum by the fire.

Nanny was the first of my grandparents to die, but by then I was in my late teens. I was lucky to have had both sets of grandparents all through my growing up.

All my family lived close by when I was a child. Walter and Lil were in Nettleton, Jack and May in Caistor, us in Kirmington. With holidays in Skegness, it was rare for us ever to leave Lincolnshire, the county I've lived in all my life.

CHAPTER 2

THE KIRMINGTON BUBBLE

'We were all a bit thick, but we knew how to lift heavy things.'

KIRMINGTON. KIRMO. A one-pub village over the A18 from Humberside Airport. A couple of miles from Immingham, one of the busiest docks in Europe, and a bit further from Grimsby. Kirmington, a former World War II prisoner-of-war camp. Oh, and the centre of the universe.

I moved there when I was one, in 1983, and eventually left Kirmington, to move to Caistor, seven miles away, in 2010. For the last few of those 26 years I had lived with my girlfriend, Kate, on her parents' farm in the village.

The house on Gravel Pit Lane, where the four Martin kids did most, or all, of their growing up, is a three-bedroom bungalow. My mum and dad always talked about having a loft conversion, but never got around to it. I suppose they never had the money, and then when they did, there was no need, because we'd all left home.

There is 13-month age difference between Sally and me. My brother Stuart is four years younger than me, and then there's a two-year gap between him and Kate. So that made Sally six when Kate arrived.

I had my own room until Stu was born, then we shared, but we rarely got in each other's way. Given the choice to do it all again, he probably wouldn't choose the bottom bunk, but he got away lightly compared to how some big brothers treat their younger siblings. I honked on him one New Year's Eve, after a skinful at the local pub. That night, after sorting me out, my mum, Big Rita, went to see the landlord and gave him a mouthful for selling beer to her under-age son.

There was a time, during those bunk-bed years, when I brought a girlfriend back to our room. When I look back now, I wonder if she only wanted me for my GSX-R600. We ended up shagging in the top bunk, with Stu in the bunk below. What was I doing? He never mentioned it. Character-building, I reckon. But I'm getting ahead of myself.

There was very little friction between Stu and me when we were young. Most of the time I'd be in the shed, taking something to bits or reassembling it, while he was more into football, something I've never been bothered about. We didn't have the same friends, and because our hobbies were so different we never did what most brothers do: squabble because we wanted the same thing at the same time. Only years later, when we were both working together for Dad – all the male side of the Martin family working in the same truck yard – did we stop seeing eye to eye for a while. We were all living together and working together and it was too much. Back when we were little, though, as soon as we got the *Transformers* wallpaper we wanted so badly, we were happy.

One of my earliest memories is when Sal and I were given an old but tidy Yamaha TY80 kids dirt bike one Christmas.

After we went to bed on Christmas Eve, Dad would always take the handle off the front room door so we couldn't get in early to see the presents. The year we were given the little TY80 it was literally like every Christmas had come at once. The first time I ever rode it, that Christmas morning, I went straight through the rose bushes in our garden and cut myself to rags on the thorns. My mum was telling anyone who'd listen that I was never going on that motorbike again.

Clearly, I wasn't a natural on the motorcycle. I hear of some racers who got on their first bike, before they could walk, and knew exactly what to do, instinctively; they won their first race and then never lost another until they joined the world championship ranks. Well, that wasn't me. I'm not blessed in the natural talent department when it comes to bikes, but I've loved them since I first sat on that miniature Yamaha and I don't give up.

Sally and I were supposed to share the TY80, but I didn't like the idea of that. I get on a treat with my older sister now, but we didn't then, because of the bike problem: one seat, two backsides wanting to be on it.

Though we were only nippers we had the run of Kirmington. We'd rush home from school to go straight out on the motorbike. We would take it over to Mr Lancaster's farm (where I'd end up living with his daughter, years later) and tear up the fields. He'd chase us in his Land Rover, not happy. It must have driven him mad.

The little Yamaha would do 40 mph or more and we'd never wear helmets. We'd slide off it, but never hurt ourselves too badly. While other Kirmington kids would lose fingers in go-kart chains or slice the backs off their feet in BMX sprockets, we survived countless motorcycle accidents.

For a while, Dad had an old Yamaha trail bike just to muck about on, a field bike really and a full-size thing, three times the size of our TY. He would take me and Sally for rides around the village and surrounding areas on it. One of us would sit in front of him on the petrol tank, the other behind him on the seat. None of us would wear a helmet, obviously. He was a skilful racer, so it was surprising the scrapes he would get in when he was just pootling about, three-up with his two little kids on board. Once, on a pre-Sunday lunch ride-out, we crashed and Sally burned her leg on the red-hot exhaust. Needless to say, Mum wasn't happy and it's hard to blame her. By now you should be getting the picture that the Martins weren't a family that rated the health and safety side of things very highly.

The family is all Lincolnshire born and bred. My dad's a proud Lincolnshire man and I am too. Though I've travelled to Asia, Australia, New Zealand, the Middle East and America, I still think Kirmington is the centre of the universe.

The village has hardly grown since I first moved there in 1984. There can't be many places in the whole of England that have developed less. Only about six houses have been built in Kirmo in all the time I can remember. We let a few in. We don't want to weaken the breed by bringing any outsiders in.

Kirmington is a village of 400 people, and I get the feeling I'll end up living back there. I think we all feel that way. Me, my sister Sally and our friends Sally Harris, Mark Nichols, Simon Thorpe, Andrew Thorpe, Aaron Ash, Kate Lancaster, Craig Nichols – there are only a handful of us born within a few years of each other, but ask any of us and we'd all say Kirmington was the centre of the universe, and I think that's down to one bloke: Mr Acum.

Bert Acum was Kirmington Church of England Primary School's head teacher in the late 1980s and early nineties. He was the man. The younger generation, including my younger brother and sister, aren't as Kirmo-biased as me, because they had a different headmaster. I was the last of the pure Mr Acum breed. His wife, Norma, was also a teacher at the school. Back then, the pair lived in Kirmington too, with their son, and we'd sometimes go to his house to play golf on his own personal putting green. In school time, of course.

When I was attending Kirmington Primary, just a quarter of a mile from home, I could not get to school fast enough. There were only 18 kids in the whole junior school and we all did the same lessons at the same time, but obviously at different levels. Thinking back, we used to have maths and spelling tests on Friday, but that was about it, as far as I can remember, when it came to traditional school-type lessons. The school gave a very different type of education to the one had by most people I know these days.

It was a very hands-on environment. We made loads of stuff, papier mâché Toby jugs being a favourite. Before a sports day we, the pupils, would mark the pitches out with the push-roller. Most schools would rely on a caretaker for jobs like this, and any general maintenance, but at Kirmington there was no need for one. The kids did it all.

In autumn we'd have the thrill of getting the leaf machine out. It was like a lawn-mower, but with spikes instead of blades, that would flick the fallen leaves into a bin on the back. That was another job for the pupils.

I have vivid memories of those early school years. The school building dated from the end of the nineteenth century, but Kirmington was a bomber base in World War II, home to 166 Squadron, and the air raid shelters were still standing. We'd have bonfires in one of them. In school-time!

I feel lucky to have gone to such a quirky school. The stuff we thought of as 100-per-cent normal sounds like I've made it up. It's like we were on a desert island, after a plane crash or a shipwreck, and the only surviving adults took it upon themselves to teach the children whatever they could remember from their own childhoods, with some essential survival techniques thrown in for good measure.

Oncc a week, all the kids would tie rags around their feet and shuffle around to polish the school's varnished wooden floor. I'm not making this up. I even have a scar on my hand from assembling the school Black & Decker Workmate at the age of six or seven.

We thought the school was haunted, by Mr Painter the School Ghost, and our headmaster wouldn't say a word to make the junior and infant children believe anything different. In fact, he'd even tell stories about Mr Painter that would scare us rigid.

A supply teacher would visit the school for a week or two every year to get us prepared for the Christmas play. She was a 50-a-day smoker and would send a pupil to the shop to pick up her Benson & Hedges. Primary school kids! You'd get locked up for that now.

Much as we all loved Mr Acum, he wasn't shy about serving out some corporal punishment. If you were naughty, but not naughty enough to deserve a spanking, you would be sent out to pick up a hundred stones off the grass so they didn't go into the lawn-mower. Yes, the pupils cut the grass that surrounded the school, and Mr Acum's personal putting green, too. If we were naughty enough to deserve a worse punishment, Mr Acum would give us the slipper, after warming it on the old, cast-iron radiator. I don't know if he went through that part of the routine to make the ordeal last longer, so the children would have longer to think about what was coming and then remember the whole ritual more, or if he'd somehow worked out, or been told, that an old slipper hurt more when it was warm, but it definitely became a deterrent.

Every memory of the time is a good one, and school trips were a highlight. A memorable outing was when the whole school cycled five miles through the woods from Kirmington to Brocklesby, all of us on pushbikes. One of the kids' granddads was the master of the local fox-hunt, so we went to visit the kennels where the hounds lived.

We would also have an annual school trip to Skegness, just before we broke up for the summer holidays. On the bus to the coast, Mr Acum would be throwing sweets out at us, like Willy Wonka.

For those of us who knew little more than the Kirmington bubble, Skegness would make us gasp. It was amazing. We'd play on the playground, then go on the donkeys, and finally visit the fairground. Mr Acum would take an old Silver Cross pram that he'd fill with a container, like a miniature water butt with a tap on the bottom, to keep the whole school watered. An essential for a Kirmington pupil going on any school trip was a spare pair of trousers. That was the rule. Mr Acum must have learnt the hard way.

After a round of funding cuts, or a when a hole appeared in the budget, the school's minibus used to get taken off the road, and then my mum would volunteer to help. When it came time for swimming, all the juniors, probably a dozen kids, would pile in the back of the Martin family's VW LT35. It was a large panel van, bigger than a Ford Transit, that Dad would proudly remind us had a Porsche engine, as it had a similar four-cylinder motor to the Porsche 924. Mum would drive, with the pupils rattling around the back. At this time, Sally and I were mad about the TV show called *The A-Team*. Dad would come home from work on a Saturday in time for us to all sit down and watch it together. We all loved it so much that Dad painted our van black with a red stripe on the side to make it look like the one driven by Mr T. That's how it looked when we used it as school transport. Big Rita would go off to do the weekly shop in Immingham while we were swimming and collect us all afterwards.

Looking back, the children of Kirmington Church of England Primary School were an innocent and easily pleased bunch. One of the most exciting and memorable times ever, for both me and Sally, was when one school summer party coincided with the introduction of wheelie bins to the area. Seeing the first wheelie bin in Kirmington was an '*Oooh*' moment. For this summer party the teachers filled the brand-new wheelie bins with water to make two-man plunge pools for the kids to jump in. Later in the day we had wheelie bin races.

School life was mega, up until I was 12 years old, when I left for senior school. The Vale of Ancholme School in Brigg had over 500 kids, so it was a contrast, like black and white. Because Kirmington Primary was such a practical and laidback place, when we went to senior school we were all a bit thick, but we knew how to lift heavy things.

My sister Sally left Kirmington Primary the year before me, along with Wayne Czartowski. Sally now says her first day, walking into the Vale of Ancholme School, felt like she'd arrived in New York City. We were clearly a bit backward.

The following year, Kirmington sent another two victims to the school in Brigg: it was the turn of me and fellow Kirmo resident Rebecca Andrews. I was so nervous going there, and I was right to be. We were under-prepared, like fish out of water. We were green. My dad was still cutting my hair, and I was happily wearing what I soon came to realise were cheap Hi-Tec trainers that few of the other kids would be seen dead in.

I hadn't been bothered about either of those things till I went to senior school. I had been happily living in the Kirmington bubble, insulated from the rest of the UK and all the stuff the country and its sons worried about. At home I lived in my welly boots, with the tops turned over, and blue one-piece overalls. In Kirmo, no one thought anything of it because it was all I'd ever done, but now at school I was different. And not in a good way. I'd get picked on a bit, because of my corduroy school trousers or whatever. I didn't have any school friends until the last couple of years.

Not long after reaching senior school, peer pressure began to play a part in my life. For a while at least. I started trying to toe the line, by wearing the right trainers and clothes, listening to the same music as other people in class, and having my hair cut like the other lads. Two or three years later I realised fitting in wasn't for me, so I stopped trying, and that's how it's been ever since.

Compared to my time at Kirmington Primary, secondary school is far less memorable. I got on with a few teachers, but there was one I had more of a connection with, Mr Frank. He taught a class called Resistant Materials. Metalwork, basically. He had a job on the side putting up marquees. Sometimes he'd wear a T-shirt to school, with the slogan 'Frank's Marquees – The Erection Specialists'. To us he was a legend. He raced 50-cc Kriedler motorbikes, too.

I liked Geography, but I failed the GCSE, which was a bit of a disappointment. Chemistry was all right. Mr Hutchinson, my form teacher through the whole of senior school, took us for it. I learnt some stuff, but most remember blowing down the gas feed to extinguish the flames of the rest of the class's Bunsen burners. I didn't get on particularly well with any other lessons, like English or Maths. I felt that for kids like me who couldn't wait to get out of the door, there wasn't any real direction.

The school just had to keep us off the streets from 9am till 3.15pm.

I was a misfit at school. I don't have any friends from my time at the Vale of Ancholme, except for one, Johnny Ellis, and that's only because we became apprentices together after leaving. I would do enough to get by at school, but I was just waiting to get home and escape into the shed.

Back in Kirmington, things were like they'd always been. There was a gang of us and we'd meet up most nights. If I wasn't working in the shed, I would sit with the rest of them on the corner near our house. This was the meeting spot from where we would go roaming around the area. At the other end of the village was the Kings' House. The Kings were brothers who were older than our group, and they were rebels. There were three of them, Andrew, Nigel and Jason. They had motorbikes and cars we thought were cool, like Ford Fiesta XR2s. They were rum lads. Good people, not wrong 'uns. They were in their late teens when we were 11 or 12, so they obviously didn't hang around with us.

Rum is a description I use a lot, so perhaps I should explain what I mean by it. If you're a rum lad it doesn't mean you're going out robbing grannies. If you did that, you'd be a wrong 'un. A rum lad isn't a wrong 'un, but he is always looking for an angle, a 'better' way of doing something, a way of earning a few extra bob without working too hard for it.

I wouldn't be out on the street as often as Sally. My mates would come and hang around in my shed. Mark 'Shorty' Nichols's family was chucking out an old comfy chair, so we salvaged it for the shed and friends would sit around while I worked on old lawn-mowers with their guts spread all over the work-bench.

Working in the shed would take up a lot of my childhood nights, but our gang would get up to other things. If it was a slow night and we'd seen a car's lights drive up the local lover's lane, Habrough Lane, we'd tip-toe through the woods, creep up on the car and knock on the windows to scare the life out of the humping couple inside.

Around that time we did a bit of experimenting with Ouija boards. Don't ask me how a group of kids from the back end of rural Lincolnshire get hold of a Ouija board, but one turned up and we hid it in our shed. Somehow Mum found it and warned us off it, telling us we were messing with stuff we shouldn't be messing with. We didn't listen, though. In fact, it made us even more determined to try it. Sally Harris was the ring leader. We'd follow her to the football changing rooms on the local playing fields. At the far end of them was an old Portakabin and we'd sit on the bench outside. We did it half a dozen times. The gang would be me, both Sallys, Aaron Ash, Shorty ...

By then Sally Harris and Aaron were smoking – it was the cool thing to do, though I never did. One of them blew smoke in the upturned glass, placed it on the board and we watched as the smoke disappeared. As we placed our fingers on the glass and started the ritual, that someone must have learnt from a horror film or from hearsay, the glass started skating around the board. We all had one finger on the glass, but it didn't feel like anyone was pushing it. Then we tried contacting someone's relation, and it started coming up with some strange answers – to this day I swear we weren't moving the glass – and we panicked, starting screaming like girls and smashed the board to smithereens. We never did it again. I'm getting a shiver down my spine just thinking about it.

We didn't have to make our own entertainment all the time, because for a while a double-decker bus, that had been converted into a youth club on wheels, would come to Kirmington once a week. The driver, Ian, wore a handknitted jumper and a tie.

He was a geek, but a lovely bloke, and he volunteered his time to give kids in villages too small to have their own youth club something else to do.

The bus was kitted out with games, a TV, a Sega Megadrive and a shop that sold sweets. Aaron Ash, who was three years older than me and a rum lad at the time, would keep giving Ian cheek. Word of this got back to my dad, who marched down our drive, got Aaron by the neck and put some manners in him.

As I got older, the draw of the youth club was replaced by booze – but only for a short time. Where a lot of British people seem to live for the pub or weekend drinking, whether it be at a festival, a bike event, a back garden barbecue or whatever, I don't share the enthusiasm. I used to think that one day I would wake up and all I'd want to do would be to go get drunk and shag, but I've never had the urge to go shagging anything that moved – I didn't lose my virginity till I was 19 – and rarely had the desire to get smashed.

I did most of my binge-drinking in my mid-teens, at the tail end of the period of my life when I wanted to fit in and be cool. The place to be was the disco in Broughton – simply called Broughton Disco. It was a bit out of my Kirmington comfort zone. You risked getting in a fight by being a stranger, but there weren't many alternatives in our area. In fact, there weren't any. We would drink out the back of the disco, then go inside to rave all night and try, with little success, to get off with some bird. Even now I can't hear 2 Unlimited's song 'No Limit' and not be taken back to Broughton Disco.

For me serious boozing took place in a very small window of my youth, apart from a few exceptional occasions dotted through the rest of my life. It started at 15 and ended a year or so later. We couldn't get served in Kirmington's pub, The Marrowbone and Cleaver, except on very exceptional days, because we were all known, the landlord had seen us grow up, or knew some of our parents. Big Rita even worked there for a while, but my dad, being quite jealous, didn't like the idea of that. So there'd be a weekly mass exodus from Kirmington to Brigg, where we could get served. Our mates Shorty and Si Thorpe could drive. They both had Nissan Micras. E436 TOH was Si Thorpe's blue Micra. (I don't have a memory any better or much worse than anyone else, except when it comes to vehicle registrations. Ones from decades ago still stick in my mind. In the haulage industry, thc registration is how we refer to the trucks. Now I know that if CV57 EVE is in the diary to come in next week it's not going to be fun, because I saw that the discs would need changing last time I worked on that truck, and they're a right job on that model; but BD57 EBG will be all right because it was only in last month for an MoT and it's mint. Because a haulage firm's fleet are usually painted the same colour and have lots of trucks the same model, knowing their registrations is the only way to tell one from the other, so they all stick in my mind.)

Si was four years older than me. If we'd lived in a town, I reckon it would have been very unusual for someone as old as him to hang around with a lad of my age, but we were all Kirmington lads and because there were so few of us, it's just what we did. We'd go to The White Hart or The Nelson in Brigg and get wankered. I had a spate of drinking cider, but it didn't sit so well and I can't drink it now.

I didn't turn teetotal or anything that extreme, that'll be clear as you read on. In fact, binge-drinking would help shape the rest of my life. It's just that the small town treadmill of work, pay day, then stop at the pub and piss it all up the wall that a lot of British folk find themselves on was never for me. There would always be too many Snap-On tools that needed buying.

CHAPTER 3

THE BOY ON THE BENCH

'The Martin children were bred to work.'

THE OUTBUILDING WHERE I spent so much of my childhood was an old chicken shed my dad had converted to be more of a workshop. The shed was in the garden when we moved to Kirmington, and it's where Dad built and maintained his bikes. There were small panels in the corners, to allow the birds to walk to their outside run, which Dad boarded up. He also fitted an eight-track stereo that hung down from the roof. Next to it on a shelf was a stack of the massive plastic tape cartridges, from the 1960s, before the C90-style cassette was invented. There were tapes of Elvis, the Beatles, the Shadows, Roy Orbison ...

Just by looking at my dad's work-bench in the chicken shed you could see how much he'd used it. There was a vice bolted to it and a small shelf above, with jars of nuts and bolts on it, everything in order. His toolbox, a black Talco, was in the back corner, and a single neon strip light hung from the middle of the ceiling. The whole shed was about a motorbike-and-a-half long, perhaps 12 foot, and six foot wide. You could get one motorbike in there and no more.

Dad only built his current shed in 2003, long after he'd packed in racing, but when he was still riding motorcycles on the road, so I ended up getting much more use out of it than him. This one is massive, 20 foot by 16 foot. I've built, and rebuilt, plenty of my race bikes there, right up until I signed with TAS to race the Relentless Suzukis in 2011. It's a great shed.

When I was a nipper, even before I was old enough to start school, I would sit on the end of the work-bench in the chicken shed and watch my dad work on his race bike engines. He'd normally work in overalls, but if there was anything particularly technical to tackle, like cam timing, he would put on what I'd call a smock – it was like a long blue storeman's jacket, made of fabric. The wearing of the smock didn't alter the way Dad worked, but it was a ritual. Dressing this way signified he meant business. He could've worn his overalls, the same way a judge could deliver a verdict in a vest and jogging bottoms, but it wouldn't be the same. Whenever he wore it I'd think, 'Oh, we're in business tonight.' I was dead keen, and he knew that, so he was happy to have me in there, but I couldn't bring any mates in.

I remember once, when I was seven years old, Dad's race bike had its petrol tank and the top of the airbox removed. The mouths of the carbs were all open, to reveal the inside of the cylinder head. I was told, 'Don't put stones in there.' But, for some reason that is still a mystery, I did, even after being told not to. As a result I was banned from the garage for a while.

My dad wouldn't be in the shed every night, like I am. After work he's always been happy to sit in front of the telly. Now he's got the best shed in the world, and he never goes in it.

Being in the shed didn't feel like it was about spending time with my dad. He'd point to stuff and ask me to tell him what it was called, components like a valve or a camshaft, but he wouldn't explain much to me. For me, it was all about being around engines. I've always been fascinated by mechanical stuff. I want to know how it works and what makes it tick. I'm interested in the history, too. For example, it was the Romans who originally came up with the idea of a piston, con-rod and crank to turn linear motion into rotary movement (or vice versa). You think of Watt and the condensing steam engine, and Stephenson and Brunel and then the birth of the internal combustion engine, but the original idea was from Roman times. For cutting wood, they used waterwheels to spin a crank with a con-rod attached to a saw. And all that fascinates me.

I worked out how a four-stroke internal combustion engine worked when I was about 15 or 16. I'd stripped and reassembled dozens of engines by that time, knowing how they were supposed to go together. They would work when I finished with them, start right up and run properly, but I didn't grasp the real concept of suck-squeeze-bang-blow till about the time I was leaving school.

I started spannering at a very early age. I had spent years watching my dad and working on the scrap he had lying around the chicken shed. He had a few old, good-for-nothing Briggs & Stratton 3.5 lawn-mower engines, but they weren't the best to work on, not for someone still at infant school, anyway. My first proper engineering project was a Suffolk Punch engine. A neighbour, Mr Cassidy, gave it to me. It was an old knackered lawn-mower motor. I wasn't even ten, but he must've known I was into engines.

Mr Cassidy lived opposite some derelict Kirmington farm buildings we'd play in. Our gang would climb up and jump off the ramshackle roof and he would always be coming over to give us a bollocking for making a racket. Then one evening he said, 'I've got something for you.' It was a Suffolk Punch engine and it was mega. The early Suffolk Punches, like this, were cast, side-valve 200-cc engines, but basically this one was scrap.

When word got around that people could off-load their old scrap lawn-mowers without even having to take to them to the tip, folks would give me all sorts of Suffolk Punches and Briggs & Stratton engines. I'd take these engines and literally rev them to death. I wanted to blow them up. The neighbours must have loved it. My dad eventually made me a really trick exhaust for my tenth birthday to help keep me quiet. It was a straight bit of pipe, with holes drilled all around it, then wrapped in wire wool, before another, length of pipe, of a larger diameter, was slid over the top and brazed to collars at either end. The noise of me murdering those engines, running them flat-out till they went bang, must have been horrendous, but I loved it.

Before I was even ten I would strip engines and put them back together. I didn't have specialist tools, like a puller to take the flywheel off, but I could take the cylinder and the piston off and the valves out. The valves didn't have a collet, they had a pin that went through the stem. I couldn't replace this pin. I knew what to do, but my fingers weren't strong enough to compress the spring, so I had to wait for my dad to come home from work to do that.

That Suffolk Punch was the first engine I tuned too. I'd seen pictures of a famous racing bike, like a Manx Norton or something similar, with drilled pistons and con-rods, in one of my dad's classic race bike magazines, so I start drilling the pistons and con-rods of my lawn-mower engine. I've still got the scars from it now. I didn't know anything about centre-punching or drilling a pilot hole. I just tried to drill big holes through the skirt of the piston to lighten it. My dad's Black & Decker drill was bigger than me, so it used to jump off and get me on the back of the hand. Scarred hands are all part of being a mechanic, though. I always wanted hands like my dad's, so I wasn't bothered if I cut them or blackened my fingernails. I wanted my hands to be like shovels. Nowadays I look after them a bit more. I still don't wear gloves to work in, I'm not into them, but I wear barrier cream. I realised my hands are what earn me my money and it's no good for them to look like they've been to Afghanistan and back every minute of every day.

As a boy I used to cut my hands and stuff, but no one died. I'm sure, now, if anyone saw a primary school pupil with a power drill, trying to bore holes through an aluminium piston on the driveway of his house, they'd report it to the social services, but no one seemed bothered in Kirmington – or at least not in our corner of it. Mum didn't stop me. She may have thought it was strange that I would rather be in the shed on my own than out with my mates some days, but her dad was very hands-on, and her husband worked with his hands, so it can't have seemed that unusual that her eldest son wanted to as well.

It wasn't all lawn-mowers. The Yamaha TY80 and my dad's racing bikes had sparked my lifelong obsession with motorcycles.

One day, when I was a few years older, Aaron Ash brought round a Maico 490. This was a huge German air-cooled motocrosser with what I already knew was a very fancy and exotic Öhlins shock absorber. This wasn't the kind of bike to gently ride around the fields and lanes. It was a fire-breathing dirt bike, built to win races. They don't make anything like it any more. What a weapon! I was 12 or 13 at the most, and Aaron was three years older. The Maico had come out of someone's shed, but wasn't running. Aaron knew I'd have a chance of getting it going. It had a big Bing carburettor on it, so I cleaned that out. Then I took the plug out and cleaned that. I drained the dregs of the old fuel out of it and poured some fresh petrol in the tank. We couldn't kickstart it. I was only a pup at the time, so we ended up bumping it off down Gravel Pit Lane. Somehow, we got it going, then took it out on Kirmington playing fields, two kids on this vicious motocross bike. It revved like mad. It shouldn't have been allowed. In fact, thinking about it, it wasn't allowed. That bike had enough power to put some manners in you.

Not long after that, my mum talked my dad into getting me a helmet.

By the time I was 14, I had a paper round. After I'd done that, on Friday nights, my mum would take me to work at my dad's truck yard. During school holidays, I'd cycle the seven miles to his work on my purple Claud Butler mountain bike. On the way I'd sometimes time it just right to be overtaken by a tractor going to the Cherry Valley Ducks factory. I would then pedal like hell to get in the slipstream, where I could stay, going faster but not pedalling so hard, all the way to the truck yard.

At my dad's work I'd fill windscreen washer bottles, check wheel nuts and tyre pressures, sweep up, sort out the scrap heap, clean oily and greasy components in the parts washer – all kinds of odd jobs that an apprentice would do.

Friday nights are always busy, getting trucks ready at the end of the working week, so they were serviced and ready to go back on the road, either the next morning or the following Monday. I'd work there and get a lift home with him in the van at 10 o'clock. We'd be back there at six the next morning. Graft. It's all I've known.

One day we were out on a job. Dad used to do repairs for C & J Haughton, a local firm. We were in their yard on a breakdown and I spotted this bike around the back of the warehouse and thought, 'Bloody hell!' It was a Kawasaki KX125, a 1986 model, the first year the 125 had disc brakes front and rear. It was a full-on motocrosser, a real racer, not a road bike styled to look like one. The bloke we dealt with said it had been there for years, but it ran. I was desperate to have it.

On the way back home in the van I told my dad I thought it was mega and asked him if he thought they'd sell it. He told me he would find out. It turned out they were happy to get rid of it, but it was over a month before my dad picked it up for me. Four weeks, but at that age it felt like a lifetime. Every night he came home and I would ask if he had got it, but he'd tell me he hadn't had a chance. Eventually, my dad did buy it, but I paid for it by working weekends.

I'd ride the KX every chance I could. I'd often go in the gravel pit at the top of the street, but I preferred to ride it through Mr Lancaster's farm. I'd get bollocked for riding on the farmer's field every week. It wasn't that I didn't respect him, I just wanted to ride my bike.

I grew up with parents who were out at work a lot. I remember walking home from primary school and seeing Mum picking potatoes in the fields. That was her job for a while. She is a serious grafter, just like my dad. She has quite old-fashioned views. To her, men having paternity leave is a load of rubbish. The breadwinner should be back at work, earning. The Martin children were bred to work.

After Kate, my youngest sister, started school, my mum studied to become a nurse. Now she's a District Nurse Sister, band seven, the highest you can get. She did it without any wittering or moaning, she just got on with it. Four kids and a career as well.

My mum and dad didn't row. One or the other would just go deathly silent for a week and not talk to their other half. Now I do that a bit myself, but I try not to. There's so much about my parents that I respect, but there's also a few parts of their character and habits I don't like. I've often thought, I don't want to be like that when I'm older. So I fight against it. I worked with my dad for years. Right back to when I was 12 years old. I loved it, most of it anyway. The only things that really began to get on my nerves were to do with Dad being the world's worst for routines.

I worked with him at weekends and during school holidays until I left school. Later, when I was 19, I went back to work with him full-time, after I finished my apprenticeship at Volvo. It was then that I really started noticing he'd eat breakfast the same way, while reading his magazine the same way, always back to front. On the drive to work, me sat next to him, he'd change gear in exactly the same place. Every. Single. Day. It did my head in.

At work every day was different. Yes, I was fixing trucks every day, but each had a different problem, and the drivers were all characters. One of these drivers would inadvertently change the course of my life.

CHAPTER 4

WENT A BOY, CAME BACK A MAN

'The plan was to get their under-age mechanic drinking ten pints of Guinness in one sitting.'

I AM THE son of a motorcycle racer, but I don't see that as the main reason I started racing. My dad's influence obviously rubbed off on me in some ways. I'd see the bikes in the shed every day; I'd sit with Dad as he worked on them; and then I'd be aware of him going away to race them. Still, I think I was too young to be really infected by it all when he was racing. The almost constant contact with bikes – my dad's, my and Sally's little TY80, and the Kawasaki motocrosser I'd own later – all made me want a road bike as soon as I was 16 and legal to ride on the road, but I hadn't made the mental leap to believing I'd ever race motorcycles. It just wasn't on my radar.

I went to some races with my dad when I was young, but not

many. We went to the Isle of Man TT a few times, including the last year he raced there, in 1988, but all I remember about that is losing the rag I used to carry round and suck on. I still had it at seven years old, I don't know why. I lost it on one of the horse-drawn trams that run up and down Douglas seafront. I don't remember any of the bikes or anything of the racing, just losing this bit of comfort blanket. It wouldn't be the last time I lost my rag on the Isle of Man during TT fortnight ...

My dad smashed himself up later in 1988, and didn't race again. The accident happened at Oliver's Mount, Scarborough. He crashed his Yamaha at the top bend of Scarborough, coming past the Memorial, a very tight left-hander. Now I have a lot of experience with that track and I don't see it as a specially tricky or fast corner, compared to some at Scarborough, but you don't think you're going fast until you're sliding along on your arse.

The thing about the corner is, if you get it wrong you go straight into the trees, and that's what he must have done. I was seven at the time, and I remember being in the back of the ambulance with him, Mum and Sally. For some young kids it might have been upsetting to see their dad laid out in an ambulance, but everything was so calm and matter-of-fact that it wasn't shocking in any way.

He had badly smashed his hip. I asked him if he was all right, and he replied, 'Oh yeah, no bother ...' He gave me his trademark big thumbs up. I realise now he was putting on a brave face for his family. He must have been in serious pain, but he is a double-hard bastard. Mum wasn't flipping her lid or anything, just thinking about how she was going to cope with work, four small kids and a husband on crutches for a few weeks. She never gets excited, she just gets on with it.

When I saw Dad in hospital, later that week, surgeons had plated up his femur, with screws and brackets. The injury caused him agony for four years, till they gave him a false hip, a prototype stainless steel thing. I think he was one of the first in the country to have a replacement like this, and he said it was better than the original.

The bike he crashed was a Yamaha FZR750RR, quite a rare machine, and he was offered a good deal when he bought it. This, Dad's last race bike, was Yamaha's version of the Superbike of its day. Four-cylinder, 100-horsepower, if that; aluminium frame, full fairing and trick flatslide carbs. Good for 150 mph. It was a homologation special, built by Yamaha and sold looking like a road bike with lights, but made almost exclusively for racers to buy and convert into a track bike.

This was the start of the era when production bikes, 'proddie' bikes, took over British racing. Proddie bikes have long been part of the racing landscape, but until the 1980s the most important bikes were pure race machinery – designed and built to race, not bikes that were based on converted and tuned road bikes. Machines like Yamaha TZ750s and TZ250s and 350s were made in big numbers, but they were pure race bikes. In the fifties and sixties it was machinery like the Manx Norton and AJS 7R 'Boy Racer', off-the-shelf race bikes. There were also bikes that would use tuned road bike engines in special chassis like Rob North and Seeley frames. That all changed in the 1980s, and except for a couple of classics I've only ever raced proddie bikes.

After the Memorial Corner crash, Dad made the decision to stop racing, or maybe Mum made his mind up for him, but he still wanted an involvement with racing bikes, so he started spannering for a couple of local businessmen who raced classic bikes.

They had a converted bus, a big old Bedford coach, that could carry four bikes in the back and also had home-made bunk beds, enough to sleep six. They were fixed to the sides of the interior, three on either side, and we called them torpedo tubes.

We would travel to the classic race meets as a group. There would be me, my dad, Ian Clark and Rob Cadle. We did that for two or three years, starting when I was about ten. Dad had built a pair of Triumph classic racing bikes for the other two, Cadle and Clark, who were quite well-to-do. Clark ran a double-glazing company and had a Triumph Trident T150 triple (it had a three-cylinder engine) in a Rob North frame, and Cadle had another Rob North Trident, a 'Slippery Sam' replica. The nickname came from the 1970 Bol d'Or race in France when a racing T150 with a knackered oil pump sprayed engine oil all over the rider. Cadle owned a building company.

When Clark bought the brand-new chassis for his racer, my dad bought one from the same company to build a Rob North BSA – the hot bike from the very early 1970s. He'd never race it, but he still owns it now.

Dad built Clark's engine, and as payment for that and for spannering at the race meetings, they'd buy him parts for his own bike.

Even though Clark was minted, he had to justify the price of his bike to his other half. You could buy these race machines second-hand as complete runners, but if you wanted a new one, you ordered the whole rolling chassis without the engine. You'd then buy the rest of the parts you needed to make it a runner. When the three of them bought these Rob Norths I think you paid something like £6,000 for the chassis, bodywork, petrol tank, wheels, brakes and suspension: basically everything but the engine, carbs, exhaust and electrics. When you'd finished paying for everything, the bike would be well over £10,000, especially if you had to pay someone else to assemble it for you. It turns out that when Clark, one of this pair of wealthy businessmen, told his missus that the Rob North kit cost £300, she hit the roof: 'Three hundred pounds! For a motorbike with no engine!' It's one of my dad's favourite stories.

Attending these classic events was quite an eye-opener for me. I would see Dad with these other blokes and how he'd behave when he wasn't just being my dad. I'd be sat in the pub with them and I couldn't believe he swore so much. He still swears a lot. Not in front of my mum, though.

I went to a few of these classic meets, and eventually he started taking my little sister Kate to some. Much later, in 2008, Kate ended up being one of my mechanics. I don't think her interest in bikes came from me in the slightest; it just happened that our paths crossed when she wanted to get into spannering.

When Kate started to go to the races with Dad, I was older and doing my own thing. I was mucking about with mates, or else out on my motocross bike or tinkering in the shed on my own.

Though he had bought me and Sally the Yamaha TY80 for Christmas, all those years ago, Dad had never encouraged me at all to start thinking about racing myself. His reluctance was probably down to the money it cost to go racing and the heartache that came with it. He knew all about that, but he'd still reminisce about his racing days. The older he gets, the faster he was ... Still, in 1983, a year after I was born, Ian Martin was the first privateer home in the Senior TT on his P & M-framed Suzuki GS1000. He wasn't shabby.

By the time I was 15, Mick Hand, the son of my dad's best mate, Jeff Hand, was racing schoolboy motocross, but there was never any mention or even thought of my going racing. It's an expensive game, even at schoolboy motocross level. If I was going to race it would have to wait till I could pay for it myself. And anyway, it hardly mattered, racing wasn't on my mind, because as soon as I turned 16, in 1997, I had my road bike, a 1991 Kawasaki AR50 – registration J121 LVL – and that was everything to me.

My mum let me take a day off school to do my Compulsory Basic Training (CBT) motorcycle test. I bought the bike from a lad who worked in the truck spray shop opposite my dad's work, paying the asking price, £700. I used to see him coming and going from work on it. It was trick. It had an 80-cc engine with a five-speed gearbox in it and a Micron exhaust. It was illegal to have an 80 in a 50, if you were still on L-plates, like I was, but I wasn't bothered. Then I bored it a mil and ended up with a 93-cc kit on it, cut my own ports in the barrel, fitted a KX60 carburettor and a Nikon pipe. I was always tinkering with it.

I used to think up the maddest stuff to make it faster. I'd experiment, like I did with the lawn-mower engines. I would do things like taking the rev counter drive off because I thought it was robbing power by driving the cable.

The little Kawasaki would do over 80 mph, which was crazy for what was supposed to be a road legal 50-cc bike. I'd ride it everywhere, but it kept knocking the main bearings out because the bottom end wasn't designed for the power it was now making. Because it was so highly tuned, I had to buy top quality two-stroke oil to mix with the petrol, to have even half a chance of not blowing up every other time I rode it. The only people to sell decent two-stroke oil in my area were Regent Motocross in Goxhill, but they were in the arse-end of nowhere, so I'd ride a 30-mile round trip just to buy my two-stroke oil – always the most expensive they, or anyone else, had.

At 16, I left school and enrolled at North Lindsay College in Scunthorpe on a motor vehicle engineering course. I don't know what I was thinking, because further education just wasn't for me. I'd been grafting since I was old enough to be able to, but I thought I had to go to college because everyone else was doing it. It was the done thing. It only took a few days before I started thinking, 'What am I doing here? This is a load of shit.' They were either teaching me stuff I thought I would never need or stuff I already knew. And I wasn't being paid to go. I lasted a month, before I left and never looked back.

I had landed an apprenticeship at John Hebb Volvo, a local truck dealer and service centre. It was here that I started working with Johnny Ellis, who would become my best friend. We already knew of each other, because we'd both gone to the Vale of Ancholme School in the same year, but I didn't knock around with Johnny at school. He wasn't part of the Kirmington massive. In fact, when he turned up to school on a motorbike on his 16th birthday, I thought he was a bit flash. It turned out Johnny had been doing the same at this Volvo garage that I'd been doing at my dad's, working on trucks during weekends and holidays while he was still at school.

John Hebb was a top bloke to work for. At Christmas he'd give each of his employees, including the newest of the apprentices, a £100 hamper. I used to take it home and pass it on to my mum and she would knock the equivalent off the money I paid for my lodging. And at Hebb's, if you worked on a Saturday afternoon, you'd get fish and chips bought for you. From the age 16 I was earning over £300 a week and spending the biggest slice of it on my Kawasaki AR50. I would regularly work 8am till 8pm five days a week, and on top of that I'd usually do overtime, 6am till 4pm, on Saturdays. During term time we would attend a local college on day release for classroom-based training.

At that time my dad was self-employed, having set up a truck maintenance business on his own. If there wasn't overtime at Volvo I worked with him some evenings and weekends to earn a few quid extra. One of his regular contracts was a haulage company called A D Jackson, and one of their drivers was called Baz Kirk. He knew my dad had raced at the Isle of Man and got talking to him one evening when I was there. Baz was about 40, not a young lad, and he smoked like a trooper. He was telling my dad he was going to race the Manx Grand Prix that year.

The Manx Grand Prix meeting is a road race, just like the Isle of Man TT, that takes place on the same 37.73-mile Mountain Course as the TT. While the TT is held over the last week in May and the first week in June, the Manx takes place at the end of August. The Manx is run as a time trial, just like the TT, with riders setting off one at a time, or sometimes in pairs, not in a mass-start like a MotoGP or British Superbike race. The difference is that the Manx Grand Prix is aimed at amateur racers on modern bikes and keen classic racers. The Manx GP was always used as the stepping stone to the TT. For years, if you hadn't raced the Manx, or didn't have an FIM (Federation of International Motorcycling) international race licence, you couldn't enter the TT, but that's all changed now, and although I have raced the Manx on a classic, I made my Mountain Course debut at the TT before I raced the Manx. But I'm getting ahead of myself again.

Many racers just want to compete at the Manx and never progress to race the TT. They prefer the atmosphere and level of the Manx. It's like a big club race, but held on the most famous motorcycle race circuit in the world. The Manx also meant that riders who were disillusioned with the commercialism of the TT could still race the Mountain Course, with less of the glitz and bullshit that had developed around the TT.

On the classic side, the Manx GP is the cream of road races. It always attracted very serious and seriously fast classic racers like Bill Swallow and Chris McGahan, but eventually some of the top current TT men were offered rides, like Ryan Farquhar, Michael Dunlop and me. But the Manx wasn't bringing in enough cash to justify the effort needed to put the race on. It was only attracting something like 9,000 spectators, compared to the 40,000 that were visiting the TT.

For 2013, the Isle of Man Department of Tourism and Economic Development, the government department that promotes the races to bring more money and investment to the island, changed the Manx GP, incorporating a newly packaged event, the Classic TT, into the middle of it. The idea was to try to give it more of a festival feel and bring in more spectators and sponsorship by using the island's race heritage and the TT name. For the 2013 Classic TT, the Isle of Man organisers brought in a load of a current TT top names like John McGuinness, William and Michael Dunlop, Cameron Donald, Bruce Anstey, Conor Cummins, Gary Johnson and James Hillier to compete against classic specialists like Ollie Linsdell and Chris Swallow.

But that was all in the future. Back in 1997, Baz Kirk was telling my dad he had rented a house on the island and that he was going to do this and that at the Manx. I was listening away, while doing a poor job of sweeping up, and he must've noticed me cocking an ear, because he turned to me and said, 'If you want to come and get mucked in, then get yourself over.' As soon as I heard those words, that was all I wanted to do.

I booked the days I could get off work, and a few weeks later I jumped in the van with Baz Kirk to head off to the Manx. It would be my first time back on the Isle of Man since I was seven years old. We drove to the ferry, stopping in Settle, Yorkshire to pick up another racer called Adam Knowles and his bike.

Baz Kirk's bike was a scruffy 1993 Honda CBR600 'bitsa' (made from bitsa this and bitsa that). It seemed to be held together with jubilee clips and cable ties. My role as mechanic was to make sure everything was tight after each outing, change the oil and clean the carburettors out, and give it a wipe down. Then, on the morning of each practice session, I'd queue up and take it through scrutineering for Baz. The scrutineers are set up in a garage under the grandstand, right at the top of the pit-lane and in the thick of things. The scrutineers give each and every bike a thorough check over before every practice or race, ensuring everything is tight and safe. I wasn't trained for the job, but I was helping where I could.

I'd do most of the preparation back at the house Baz and Adam had rented, but during the time I was in the pits, either in the queue for scrutineering or while Baz was out on the track, I noticed another rider who would stick in my mind for years. Keith Townsend was a dead confident Southerner, who owned a motorcycle shop, and his race bikes were absolutely mint. I think his mechanic used to work for Rumi Honda, the Italian-based World Superbike team. I remember looking at Townsend's race bikes and thinking, 'When I get a race bike, that's what mine is going to be like.' His bikes did it for me. It was the way the cables were routed and the cable ties were trimmed. You could tell that whoever had built it had a real pride in their work. If a bike looks right, it normally is right. It sounds obvious but there are loads of racers, Baz Kirk included, who turn up with a shoddy bike and waste their money when it doesn't perform or sometimes even finish the race. Looking at Keith Townsend's bike was the first time I seriously thought about having my own race bike.

The Manx Grand Prix meeting lasts a fortnight, and I could only be out at the Isle of Man with Baz for the first half, practice week, so I missed his race, but it was still a hell of an experience.

During that practice week, Baz and Adam had to get their eye in for their races, but they also had another target. The plan was to get their under-age mechanic drinking ten pints of Guinness in one sitting. That was the goal for my last night before travelling back home. And I did it.

My mum said later that I went to that Manx GP a boy and came back a man. And it was nothing to do with the Guinness. After I'd been involved with motorcycle racing, really in the guts of it, not just as a spectator, all I wanted to do was race. From then on, I couldn't stop thinking about racing.

I had only been back from the Manx a couple of weeks when I was in the local pub, The Marrowbone and Cleaver, for my sister's 18th birthday. I was 16, but I ended up showing everyone I was the man, by demonstrating my new party piece, drinking ten pints of stout. It hardly needs saying, I was absolutely wankered. I can't even imagine being able to drink that much now.

Somehow I got up the next morning in time for my day release at college. I must've still been trolleyed. I'm not proud of it, but this is just what happened. I was riding my Kawasaki to Scunthorpe when I went straight through a junction where I was supposed to be turning right, and smashed head-on into a car at Barnetby Top Services.

I was so loose, totally not on the ball in any way, that I flew over the top of the car, flailed down the road like a rag doll and got up without a mark on me. I was still so, how would you say it, *relaxed*, that I didn't even think to tense up before hitting the ground – and, ironically, I reckon that's what saved me from breaking anything.

The Kawasaki, my pride and joy, didn't fare as well. It was completely smashed up. It's never been the same since, but I never sold it. I still have it now, in the vague belief I'm going to restore it one day. The car, a Fiat Punto, was wrecked too. It was so bent out of shape the back doors couldn't be forced open. Luckily the young lass driving didn't have a scratch on her.

The police turned up, but I wasn't breathalysed. I'd had a major let-off in a load of different ways and even then, though I clearly was not the sharpest knife in the drawer, I started to realise that things had started to get a bit dangerous. I was riding flat-out, taking crazy chances on every journey. Lots of people have had similar thoughts when they've had near misses in life and changed what they're doing. But my idea of making things a little less risky for myself was not to start saving up for a nice little car – no, I was going racing.

Everything seemed to come together: the accident; spannering in the Isle of Man with Baz and experiencing all that; being mad about bikes, but loving working on them as much as, if not more than, riding them. I wanted to make stuff go faster all the time. Previous to that month, I hadn't dreamed of being a racer. As a kid I had my motocrosser, the 1986 Kawasaki KX125, a bike that was built for competition, yet I wasn't that bothered about racing it. But now the switch had been flicked and I was on the hunt for a motorcycle to go racing.

CHAPTER 5

CLUB RACER

'But it wasn't all motorcycle racing and picking up vomit. About this time I was invited to an orgy ...'

HAVING DECIDED I was about to start racing, I needed a suitable bike. Even if it hadn't been stoved into the front of a Fiat Punto, my Kawasaki AR50 wouldn't have cut the mustard. Because I was so fired up, it didn't take me long to find what I reckoned was the perfect machine. And it was through yet another connection in the local haulage industry.

It was 1999, and Dave Johnson, from just up the road in Killingholme on the Humber, was being tipped as the next big thing. Dave was the same age as me, 17, and dead confident, but not in an annoying way. He was selling a 1997 Honda CBR600 F-V, a popular road bike that had been converted to race. This Honda had survived two hard years of competition, and was a bit rough, but it had all the right bits fitted to it, like Spondon front brake discs, and it came with a spare pair of wheels for wet tyres. Crucially, for a race bike, it was fast.

I did a quick test ride out of the back of his house, but it was a bit pointless. I wouldn't know a good CBR600 from a bad one. Coming straight from a bored-out 50-cc two-stroke, I felt like I had been strapped to a rocket. And, anyway, I had already made up my mind. I paid the £3,000 asking price, with £2,000 coming from my savings and my dad loaning me the rest.

Dave was selling the bike because he had been signed for the Honda Young Guns team. He'd already made the step from paying for everything himself to having 'a ride'. By that I mean he would turn up to race a bike he didn't even have to buy. In other sports, he would be at semi-professional level.

Dave's dad, Keith, had plenty of money, but he was as rough as arseholes. Keith ran a haulage company called Old Goat Trucking, serving the docks and transporting imports and exports to and from the Humber ports. Fifty per cent of the time, the guys who run these companies are rum buggers, and Keith was the definition of rum. His son Dave was rum, too, but not in the same league as Keith, but both were right blokes, a hundred per cent.

Keith's nickname was Animal. He was skin and bone and looked like he'd have a bath once a year, whether he needed it or not. He would always call his wife the Old Crow in front of everyone.

A lot of people who run haulage firms, or, perhaps I should say – so I don't offend too many people I still deal with – a lot of people who *were* running haulage firms back then, were turning over massive amounts of money, but they weren't clever enough to handle these sums. I would see it all the time. Anyway, Keith wasn't one of them. He was doing all right for himself and was happy to spend some of his earnings on his lad's motorcycle racing.

We quickly did the deal, and I took the bike away that night. I kept in touch with the Johnson family, and Keith helped me out for a couple of years. He gave me bits of advice and, later in that first season, he paid the hundred-odd quid for a track day so I could have some practice away from an actual race weekend.

Even if Keith did help get his lad get into racing, it wouldn't have made any difference if Dave didn't know what he was doing, and he was obviously talented. Dave would progress to race for the Red Bull Ducati team in the Supersport class on the 748. If you do well at that level, the next step is usually racing in either British Superbikes or going into the World Championship in the Supersport class, where it's all becoming a serious career.

Supersport, Superstock and Superbike are descriptions that are used a lot in the race sections of this book, so it's worth explaining them here.

Supersport is a class for 600-cc motorcycles. It has long been thought of as a stepping stone to the bigger bikes of the Superbike class, but because 600-cc bikes became so important to the Japanese manufacturers' sales figures, the Supersport bikes got more and more advanced, until the top teams were spending hundreds of thousands on them. Of course, a very basic bike, like my first Honda CBR600, could also race in Supersport. This class of bikes run on road legal tyres, though now they've developed to the point where they look like slicks with a few slash marks cut into them.

Superstock is a class where the budgets have been kept tightly under control. There are Superstock 600 and 1000 classes run in various championships around the world, but at the current Isle of Man TT races the Superstock class is for 1000-cc machines only. A Superstocker is very close to the specification of a road bike. Like all race bikes, the original brittle bodywork is swapped for a fairing that is lighter, tougher and less expensive to replace. Lights and mirrors are removed, too. Tuning is forbidden, but a relatively cheap ECU (Engine Control Unit – an electronic gizmo that helps give you optimal engine performance) is installed to change how the fuel injection works. The exhaust is swapped, and so are the rear shock absorber and the front fork internals. The Superstock 1000 has less power than a Superbike – although still over 180 bhp – less vicious power delivery, and the suspension, wheels and brakes are not as high specification and nowhere near as expensive. The Brembo brake calipers that we run on the Superbike cost over £4,000 a pair. The Superstock 1000 uses the brakes the £11,000 road bike comes out of the showroom with. The Superstock can't have any of the electronic 'rider aids', like traction control, that the Superbike has, unless it comes as standard on the showroom bike.

The modifications we make when prepping the Superstock bike are regularly made by thousands of keen road riders to the bikes they ride to the races. Superstockers run on the same kind of road legal tyres as the Supersport class.

The Superbikes are referred to as a 'silhouette' class. It means they must look like the road bike they're based on, but that leaves a massive amount of room for interpretation. The Superbikes raced at the TT and other road races are currently a higher specification than those raced in the British Superbike Championship (BSB) races. Superbikes have seriously tuned engines; advanced, bespoke electronic systems; completely different suspension units, brakes and wheels; and petrol tanks are altered to hold more fuel and even position it differently to its road bike brother for improved weight distribution. Hundreds of parts differ. Superbikes also run racing slicks, in the dry, or specialist racing tyres in the wet. Some teams spend up to £200,000 building a competitive TT Superbike, where a Superstocker could be built for less than a tenth of that. Superbikes also need a team of mechanics, including suspension and electronic experts, to really squeeze the most out of them. In the road race world Superbikes are often just called the big bikes.

A while after buying my first race bike I remember going to Cadwell to one of the British Superbike meetings. I went with mates and camped there to watch a couple of days of racing. The first thing I saw was the Australian Troy Bayliss come over the Mountain on the orange INS Ducati. It blew my mind. Bayliss was obviously something special. He wouldn't be in England long before he moved into World Superbikes and became champion, but it wasn't just him who was impressive. They were all incredibly fast and, on top of that, I was amazed how professional everything looked. I tracked down where Dave was pitted and went to see the lad whose bike I'd bought. By then he was part of this really professional-looking team. I struggled to take it all in. I was in awe of it.

Dave was team-mates with James Ellison in the Young Guns Honda squad (and James and I would be team-mates for a season, years later, when we were both racing for Shaun Muir). James subsequently had two spells racing for privateer teams in MotoGP, and for very good teams in both the British and American Superbike series and World Endurance. He was still winning races in 2013. Back in 1999, when they were starting out, James and Dave were at the same level, but sadly few people remember Dave Johnson's name now.

This wasn't the be-all and end-all, but I don't think having a dad as blunt as Keith helped Dave when he began to get involved with those bigger teams. His dad would call everyone a See You Next Tuesday, whoever they were. I liked Keith – you knew where you stood with him – but I can see why some people might not want a person who had earned the nickname Animal around their swanky Superbike pits.

Another thing that derailed Dave's motorcycle career was finding out there was more to life than racing bikes. It had been all he'd known, and he was mega talented, but then his eyes were opened to other things. He discovered he liked beer and women, too. Finally, a family tragedy finished him as a racer, or seemed to from the outside. Dave's younger brother, Ally, died in an accident with a bonfire. Ally was 14 or 15 at the time and it really affected all our family too. I haven't seen Dave for years and years, but I do know he's a truck driver now.

My own effort was a little different from the team set-ups I'd seen at the Cadwell Park British Superbikes round, but I was still trying to look as professional as I possibly could. Even though I'd never raced a bike in my life I still managed to get some backing. My first sponsor, besides my dad, was Bill Banks of local company BB Haulage, who gave me £1,000 to go towards my first racing season. It didn't take long to spend that. I was earning decent money too, and my bike was mint. A mate of my dad's had painted it. It was blue (paint code RAL 5017, if you're interested) with lime green wheels. A truck signwriter stickered it up for me. It said Guy Martin on the tank, which was a bit much, I thought.

I had the sense to do a track day before my first race. It was at Mallory Park, Leicestershire, on a Wednesday afternoon. There were dozens of track days going on every month, when road riders could get out on track and wring the neck of their bike without fear of the law or a car pulling out on them, but this Mallory date was the regular weekly track session exclusively for race bikes and riders with ACU competition licences. Back then, to get a race licence you just had to send off your application form with a cheque and proof of a recent eye test, but now you have to sit a test before they'll give you one.

I was so nervous I couldn't sleep the night before the track day. I went out with the experienced 125s and the handful of other novices and got through the day without crashing, but I didn't have a clue what the racing line was. Looking back, I didn't have a clue what *a* racing line was. I can't imagine how slow I must have looked. And no, I didn't scuff my pristine kneesliders. I didn't get my knee down for a year. Still, a few days after the track day I was set to make my racing debut.

My very first race meeting was run by the Grantham and Pegasus Club and held at my local track, Cadwell Park, near Louth, Lincolnshire, just 20 miles from Kirmington.

I had ridden the track just once before. I had been round it on my dad's Rob North BSA classic race bike, his pride and joy, at an owner's club rally the previous year. I stalled it over the Mountain, and because his hand-built British bike was bigger than me he had to run out on to the track and rescue me. That, and a few times spectating, was the sum of my experience of this very challenging track.

Cadwell Park, as the name suggests, is what the British call a park circuit. It is in the same family of circuits as Oulton Park, Donington Park, Mallory Park and Brands Hatch. You can pretty much split Britain's race circuits into two camps: the park circuits and the airfield tracks, which were developed from disused World War II runways. Where the airfields, like Silverstone and Snetterton, are as flat as a pancake, the park circuits have big changes of elevation, as the layout was designed to make the use of the surrounding landscape. Cadwell does this in a more extreme way than any UK circuit, with the Mountain now acting as a short runway launch pad for powerful Superbikes. If you've never seen it, don't expect Mont Blanc – Cadwell's Mountain is a short, sharp hill.

In the run-up to my debut Dad hadn't given me any advice

at all. And I hadn't asked. I don't resent that. I had to work it out for myself. Perhaps he thought I'd picked up more than I had done from going to races with him. If so, he was wrong. I could not have been more green going into my first actual race. And I knew I'd be racing. There was no need to qualify. Paying your entry fee guaranteed you a place on the starting grid as long as you made it through the short practice session in one piece.

Dad drove me to the race, but I turned up not knowing a thing. I was going from riding an AR50 – a hot one, mind – commuting to work and back, to racing a tuned Honda CBR600 – a 140 mph Supersport bike – for my very first race. I know now that I should have started off with a smaller 125, a lighter machine with not much power that I could use to get into the rhythm of racing while I was learning the precise lines needed to have half a chance of survival. But that's only with hindsight. Instead, I was in at the deep end, racing a bike that was so fast and intimidating that it took all my concentration just to stay on the track.

I scraped through the short untimed morning practice and then was told I had to blindly pick a peg with a number on it out of a bag. This was the way the club decided places on the starting grid. When my race was called, I pulled on my helmet and rolled down to sit in the holding area, under the trees, next to the café. The bikes all around me were being revved to warm up and I waited, in a fog of fumes, not knowing what to expect. I was buzzing with nerves and excitement as the previous race finished and the riders funnelled off the track, a marshal in orange overalls directing them up the narrow return road, through the trees and into the paddock high above the start line. My exact position on the grid hasn't stuck in my mind, but I was somewhere in the middle, surrounded by blokes who had been racing for years.

I took my place, one foot on the floor, arms bent, eyes staring at the flag. As the rules demanded, I wore an orange bib over my leathers, to show everyone I was a novice rider.

Although I don't remember which row of the busy grid I was on, but I won't forget what happened as soon as the flag dropped. I got a surprisingly good start and was determined to make an impression. I truly was young, dumb and full of cum. I was in the mix through Coppice, the first corner that sweeps uphill to the looping right-hander, Charlies. Soon I was flying down Park Straight, knees and elbows tucked in to be as aerodynamic as possible, managing to pass a load of bikes, thinking, 'Check me out!'

What I didn't realise was that everyone else was hard on the brakes for Park, the sharp right-hander that was approaching at 100 mph plus. It was the third corner of my very first race and I crashed, taking three other lads out. Less than 60 seconds had passed since the flag signalled the start of my racing life and I had barely covered a third of the 2.2-mile circuit. My introduction to bike racing looked like a bomb scene. It was absolute carnage. My bike, the Honda CBR600 I'd spent weeks preparing, and all my money, went end over end. The impact ripped the petrol tank off and bent the forks. Luckily I didn't injure anyone in the crash, and they were all standing when I went round the pits apologising without making eye contact.

Still, the thought that I might not be cut out for motorcycle racing never entered my head. I was never a natural. I realised that early, and have never kidded myself into believing anything different. I've had to work at it. My brother, Stuart, is the one with the racing talent. He started racing in 2003, when he was 18, after seeing the craic I was having. He raced Supermoto, then Honda Hornets and Superstock 600s. He crashed a lot, but he was fast straight away, and they say it's easier to stop a fast racer crashing than make a steady, but safe rider into a race-winner. I was both slow and dangerous, but I wasn't going to give up. What I didn't have in talent, I made up for in knuckle-headed determination.

I made my racing comeback a month or so later after saving up to mend my Honda. Mum took me to the race in M303 GRH, my dad's works van, a really nicely sign-written Ford Transit. Even though I had a racing licence, I still hadn't passed my car driving test at the time, so Big Rita drove and sat reading *Woman's Own* while I raced. She supported me like this even though she didn't even want me to start racing in the first place. This was the first of many years during which she would have the dilemma of supporting me in something she'd much rather I would just pack up. She would be on edge, biting her nails, while I was doing what I loved.

My second competitive outing was at Mallory Park, Leicestershire. It was a circuit I knew like the back of my hand after that highly successful half-day ACU track day. Despite that, I crashed again, but this time it was just a stupid one coming out of the Hairpin and I didn't torpedo anyone else. I did finish the day's other race, well down the field, but anything was an improvement at that stage.

I crashed 13 times in my first year, sometimes twice in a meeting, because I definitely didn't do 13 different race meetings that season. It was costing me a fortune.

For the last meeting of the 1999 season, back at Cadwell, I bought a cheap tyre from a bike shop in Grimsby. The Michelin Pilot Sport had been sat there for a while, which is never good for a high performance tyre, but I didn't know then that tyres went off.

Even after I'd done practice and a couple of races on the tyre, it still looked like brand-new, not a mark on it. This tyre was so old, it was obviously rock hard, but back then tyres were just black and round as far as I was concerned. I must have been half pleased that it was lasting so long, so I wasn't having to cough up yet more money to replace it. This early in my racing life, I wasn't listening to the messages tyres were giving me and couldn't tell if one tyre was better than the other.

I learnt the hard way that this wasn't a good one. I highsided out of the Gooseneck and badly twisted my ankle. I had seen and read plenty about highsides. It was something Grand Prix riders had to deal with. For those who've never heard the term or seen a highside, they begin when a bike is leant over, going through a corner and the rear tyre loses grip and starts to slide sideways. If it just continued to slide, the bike would fall onto its side and the rider would suffer a comparatively gentle lowside crash. When I say, 'I lost the front end,' it means exactly the same but with the front tyre. I lost the front end in 2010 TT at Ballagarey, the crash that ended with the fireball ...

During cornering both tyres are being asked to grip while the bike is leant over and the weight of the bike and rider is pushing the tyres across the surface of the track, not down into it. When the front tyre loses grip, the bike slides off line. If a bicycle rider slides off going around a wet corner, as you see in the Tour de France, they always have what a motorcycle racer would call a lowside. If you're ever going to crash a motorcycle, a lowside is usually the lesser of all the evils on the menu.

Sometimes, though, halfway through its sideways slide, the rear tyre starts to grip again, the sliding comes to a sudden stop, and the sideways energy combines with the spinning of the rear tyre to cause a vicious and dynamic change. The pairing of bike and rider goes from leaning on its side to being stood upright and the rider is flung up into the air. A really powerful bike highsiding in a fast corner can chuck a ten-stone rider well over a couple of metres out of their seat and fling a 140 kg bike a similar distance off the floor, before they both come crashing to the deck. You're very lucky to survive a highside without an injury. And I wasn't lucky.

I landed heavily and thought I'd broken my ankle. The next day I went to work as usual, but I was as white as a sheet and couldn't do anything, so my Granddad Martin took me to the hospital. It turned out I hadn't broken anything, so they strapped me up, gave me some crutches and sent me on my way. Those became the family crutches. Since then my brother has used them, and I had to have them back off him when, in 2011, I had a blood infection that caused my knee to swell up and I couldn't walk, meaning I missed the Scarborough Gold Cup that year.

Clearly, these crashes weren't putting me off. In fact, I was determined to go even quicker. I would read any magazine I could get my hands on that covered bike racing. I had read in one of them that the highly respected Dutch team, Ten Kate Racing, changed the cam timing of their World Supersport bike from circuit to circuit. They had 600-cc Hondas, and so did I, so I thought I would try this in-depth and very high-level tuning method too, but I didn't know a thing about it. It was only years later I learnt why they did it. In that first season I genuinely wasn't bothered where I finished. I was racing and that was it.

I got the odd top-ten finish that year, competing in the bottom rungs of the British motorcycle racing ladder. This was hobby racing, for fun and a plastic trophy if you were lucky. When I raced with the New Era, a bigger club than Pegasus and District, I might get in the top 15. I had not bothered the podium in the slightest, but I didn't care one bit. The next year, 2000, I had the same attitude. I had passed my driving test by then, so I could drive myself to meetings and friends would come with me.

One time, I took a bunch of mates to a race at Mallory Park. We were nearly at the track, having just gone through some traffic lights, when we were overtaken by a nutter in a Yugo, a Yugoslavian jalopy, one or two steps down the quality ladder from a Lada.

He'd gone the wrong side of the traffic island through the lights – obviously a man in a hurry. A couple of miles later, we went round a corner and there's a bloke stood in the middle of the road with a blank expression on his face, holding a car door that was no longer attached to a car. Up the road, buried in a hedge, was the Yugo. The bloke holding the door must have had his car sideswiped just as he was climbing in. His car was absolutely battered, all leant over to one side where the suspension had collapsed from the impact, but the windscreen wipers were still going. We didn't want to hang around for the police to arrive, because I had so many lads in the back of the van, but as we drove past, my good mate Johnny Ellis wound down his window and said, to the dazed fella with the car door, 'You want to turn your wipers off, mate. You'll flatten your battery.' That was it – we were in tears for the rest of the day.

Memories like that sum up the time. I was racing for the craic. There was no pressure, just pure fun.

I didn't crash as much in that second season, but I still didn't know where the line was. I'm not talking about the racing line now. I was picking that up, slowly. I mean the line you can ride up to and if you pass it you might crash. This isn't a line on the track, it's not something you can see or touch – it's 'the edge', I suppose, and where it was depended on the conditions, the bike and my skill at the time.

Now I know where my line is, I can sense when I'm right up to it, and if I have to go over the line to get past someone I know I've taken a risk. Crossing the line doesn't necessarily mean I'm going to crash, but it means I'm pushing my luck, something you've got to do in races from time to time.

Back in the club racing days I just went as fast as I dared, and if I crashed it came out of the blue. I often knew why and how I crashed – I'd lost the front end by being too hard on the brakes leaning into a corner or whatever – but I didn't really know what to do to stop crashing. People I was racing against were still riding miles faster than me on the same bikes and the same tyres. We both had two arms and two legs, so I had a lot to learn.

I wasn't being methodical or thinking deeply about racing. I didn't have any mentors pointing things out to me. Racing was just something to do. I didn't care where I finished until about two-thirds of the way through that 2000 season, when I won the Yellow Belly. This was a race at Cadwell Park exclusively for riders who live in Lincolnshire. It used to be annual and it's a race a lot of very good riders have won: Steve Plater, Roger Marshal, Roger Burnett ... From that win onwards a switch was flicked and I was hungry to do well. At the end of the year I went to a meeting at a miserable Snetterton held on a grim October day, with the rain coming in sideways, and won a couple of races. Keeping up my impressive record of crashing, I still managed to slide off at some point that day.

By the end of 2000, I had done two full seasons of club racing, the highlight being the Yellow Belly win, but there wasn't much else to write home about. Club racing is different to the racing you see on TV. It's hobby racing, purely amateur. You still get club racers who spend a squillion quid on their bikes and equipment, but their ability doesn't allow them to move up to the National classes – the championships for the best riders in Britain. The comparatively big budget club racers are happier finishing near the front of a club race and going home with a plastic trophy than going up a league, racing a much better calibre of riders and finishing nowhere.

After my two seasons of club racing I was thinking differently. Now I seriously wanted to improve. It had gone beyond having a bit of fun with my mates, so I decided to make the step up to National level for 2001 and enter the Junior Superstock class I'd read about in *Motorcycle News*. Club racers want to win, but it's for fun; it's regional, often lower-budget racing. It's the equivalent of Sunday League football. National level racing is like the football league structure, with the British Superbike class being the Premier League, Superport being Championship, Superstock being League One and Junior Superstock being League Two or even the Conference League, but still a team that could hammer a Sunday pub team. In club racing, I'd usually turn up early on the morning of the race and leave for home in the evening. For National racing I was away from Thursday night or, if the race was local, Friday morning until Sunday night. I would also be racing at a lot of unfamiliar tracks in the National championship. I'd only raced at three or four different tracks during my club racing years.

Junior Superstock was a new class that was part of the British Superbike race weekend. It was for Superstock 600s, with the Superstock rules enforced to keep the budgets down. You could change the exhaust end can, and Micron sponsored the series so you got them dead cheap. Pirelli supplied the control tyres at a good price, and everyone had to use the same tyres, but riders could choose to buy and race the suitable bike from Suzuki, Honda, Kawasaki, Yamaha, Triumph or anyone else who made an eligible 600-cc Supersport bike. A much cheaper race fairing replaces the standard plastic bodywork. Racers always sell 'on the road' bike components, like bodywork, lights and mirrors, to people who have crashed on the road, to help fund the bits the racers needed to convert their bikes to a racing spec. And to be classed as a Junior, for this new series, you had to be 16 or over and 23 or under.

It seemed, from reports in magazines, that the Suzuki was the bike to be on that year, so I sold both the Honda CBR600, that would be out-gunned in this new series, and my Vauxhall Astravan to buy my own brand-new 2001 Suzuki GSX-R600K1for £5,700 cash. From now on I would be racing in classes where only the current bike would really cut it, so I was back to borrowing Dad's work van for race weekends and cycling if I needed to get anywhere else.

Even though I was making a big step up, Dad still wasn't offering me any direction with my racing. He was helping in lots of other ways, buying me the odd set of tyres, and he helped when I needed it, often coming to races with me, but he wasn't saying, 'You need to do this ... You need to race here to get on.' I'm sure he would have if I'd asked, but I never wanted to. I was happy all the drive was still coming from me.

Eventually, he'd sell his own road bike, a Honda VFR800, to help me buy a race bike, and that caused a lot of grief in our house. Mum didn't think he should be encouraging me, so she gave him the silent treatment for weeks. It wasn't a case of her being upset that Dad was spending money on me that should have been spent elsewhere. It wasn't stealing food off the table. If he'd sold his Honda to buy me a car or van to get to work and back, it wouldn't have caused the same trouble, but Mum didn't want him encouraging me to race. Sally and I remember it as a very awkward time.

The first race of the 2001 season, and the new Junior Superstock series, was at Donington Park – then the home of the British Grand Prix and so, arguably, the most prestigious track in the country. The pit and paddock were full of race transporters.

Artics for all the British Superbike teams and some of the leading Supersport teams were parked in perfectly neat rows. Steve Hislop was on the Monstermob Ducati, John Reynolds and Sean Emmett on the Red Bull Ducatis; James Haydon and Jamie Robinson were riding for Virgin Mobile Yamahas ... The riders were well-known on the British scene and most of the big names were back in the UK after racing on the world stage. These riders were on the covers of the magazines I lapped up, and now, while I wasn't racing against them, I was in the same meeting as them. That would never happen in club racing. I was a bit starry-eyed. I'd turned up in M303 GRH with the wobble-box behind it, a caravan. When I opened a Biffa dustbin to put an empty carton of milk in it, there was a Virgin Mobile Yamaha R1 Kevlar fairing that had been dumped in it after one crash. I took it and cut up the fairing to make lightweight brackets for my bike.

Some of the established Superbike and Supersport teams had entered young lads into the Junior Superstock class, so right from the off I was up against riders who were racing as part of the famous teams, and while the Junior Superstock riders were down the pecking order of these squads, they were being kept an eye on and had the back-up of some very knowledgeable blokes – both on the riding and set-up side. Crescent Suzuki were sponsored by Q8 and Clarion. They had John Crawford and John Crockford, and James Hutchins was on the Junior Superstock bike that looked identical to the Superbikes. They looked proper.

If you look back at the riders who lined up in Junior Superstock that year, it was quite a group of riders: Tom Sykes, Tommy Hill, the late Craig Jones ... They all turned out to be class acts, British or world champions or at least in the hunt for titles. It seemed lots of the top lads, who were still unknowns then, were riding for teams, even at that stage. It was obviously a massive leg-up to their careers. There weren't many other lads doing it like me, without much support and out of the back of a Transit van. One who was doing it that way, out of his own van, was a bit older than me, a rider I'm still mates with called Matt Layt. Ross Conley was another.

To register to race in Junior Superstock meant committing to the whole season. It wasn't like club racing, where you simply entered two or three weeks before the next race and if you didn't have any money you missed the race. The company running the British Superbike series wanted £1,800 up front from anyone running in Junior Superstock. On top of that was the expense of the bike, tyres, oil, fuel, brake pads, travel, food, leathers, helmets, boots, crash damage …

That first Junior Superstock race was daunting. I'd never had to qualify before, but now I had to ride in a timed session to determine my place on the grid for the race. In club racing it was either a case of pulling a peg from a bag or the grid was determined by championship standings. Now I was racing against hungry young lads with one-track minds. They might have been the same age as me, but they were different. They all had a career progression in mind. They were already behaving like professional racers, some not even working for a living. A few had personal trainers and were under the wing of the biggest teams in Britain, being nurtured. They knew where they wanted to be. I didn't even dream about progressing, I was just thinking about that weekend.

Very rapidly, the series turned out to be a crash-fest. It was a popular class, with up to 40 riders trying to qualify and race. There were bikes everywhere and there was regular mechanical carnage. It wasn't too long before the class was given the grim nickname, Junior Suicide.

I was up into sixth in that first Junior Superstock race before I binned it. But riding that close to the front made me think, 'I can do this.'

Actually doing it was still a way off, though. For the rest of that 2001 season I never got that near the sharp end again. I was in the points at the second round, Silverstone, finishing14th (points were given down to 15th). I only had two non-point-scoring rides (meaning either a DNF – Did Not Finish – or outside the top 15) in the 13-round season, so at least I was consistent. My best result was a seventh, at Mallory Park, and I finished 12th overall in the season-long championship. I might have only scored a couple of top ten finishes, but I never gave in. The champion that year was Ben Wilson, another Lincolnshire lad, from Boston, who would become a British Superbike and Supersport regular.

During the season Johnny Ellis, my mate from John Hebb Volvo, started coming to every race with me to be my mechanic, something he would do on and off for my whole racing career to date. My dad would come to a lot of the races too, but not all of them.

Racing at National level was a massive learning curve. Now I had to turn up on Thursday night, for official practice on Friday. There'd be two qualifying sessions on Saturday and the race on Sunday. Even though I'd been there from Thursday night, the Junior Superstock was always the last race on Sunday. There was so much carnage they couldn't risk putting it on between the two Superbike races. If there was a massive Junior Superstock pile-up, as there often was, there could be oil, petrol and wreckage all over the track and they didn't want that delaying the main event, the star race most spectators had paid to watch. So, race day was always a long one.

Many of the lads I was now having to race had already been on the National scene. They'd raced in the Superteen series, on 125s, when I was club racing. Superteen was the launching class for up-and-coming riders. Racing those fellas really made me progress. I watched what they were doing and realised I had to copy some of it. I could watch their lines, their tactics, their body position, everything. I was a sponge, taking it all in.

I learnt so much in that first year of British championship, because everyone else was so much faster than me. I had to learn, and fast. Sink or swim. I couldn't believe how much of a gap there was between club racing and this. I had an idea National racing would be quicker, but not by such a massive percentage.

I still crashed regularly enough, but less often in the races. I'd got an idea of what I could do with the bike. I realised that just because I was getting my knee down it didn't mean I was going fast. I could be leaning less, putting less stress on the tyres and still lapping quicker.

The level of the competition and the ambition I was beginning to develop, a fairly simple desire to run at the front, meant I was spending a fortune. I had worked all winter, between the end of one racing season and the start of the next, doing several jobs just to save up enough to be able to race through the summer.

I was still doing my day job, which was fixing trucks obviously, but that alone wasn't enough to pay for this level of racing, even though I was living for cheap at home. So I had to work three jobs for nearly six months, throughout the winter, before the season started.

One of the drivers whose trucks we fixed also worked on Immingham docks driving coal lorries. Down on those docks is a two-mile private road. The ships would arrive from South Africa or Poland, full of coal. A big crane would go into the belly of the ship and fill a hopper, and trucks would drive under the hopper and be filled up. From there the articulated trucks would be driven to the grading plant, at the other end of the dock road, and tip the load. Between every load, the driver had to climb up on the back of the trailer, yank a heavy cover over the top of it, and tie it down, so the coal dust didn't billow out and cover the hundreds of brand-new cars that had also been unloaded and parked on the dockside. It meant there was a physical side to the work too – it wasn't just sitting in the cab listening to Zane Lowe.

Because it was a dock road, not a public highway, drivers didn't require the Class 1 licence they would need to drive an articulated truck on the road, so I ended up being one of the drivers there, doing a 12-hour shift for £80, two nights a week. I'd transport 35 loads on a shift. I was living on Pro Plus caffeine tablets and two or three hours' sleep a day. But, heck, I was earning. For a time a fella who worked there would hand out tablets he said were EPO – the drug that Lance Armstrong and loads of other athletes have been banned for using – which he said he'd mixed with caffeine and aspirin. I don't know if that's really what the stuff was, but it would keep me going all night and there was no comedown.

At weekends, I was also working at the Chicago Rock Café in Grimsby. My big sister Sally worked there. She had been away travelling, to Australia, Malaysia and Thailand, and got a job at the bar when she landed back in Lincolnshire. She loved the place and quickly worked her way up to deputy manager. She also got me a job glass-collecting on Thursday, Friday and Saturday nights. Thursday was £1-a-drink night. In Grimsby. I'll let you chew that prospect over for a minute ...

I would keep busy, wiping tables, collecting glasses, then I'd climb in the Biffa bins and crush everything down so they could pack them even more full. A memorable evening was when someone ralphed against a window where people queued up to get in and it was my job to pick up all the half digested chicken.

It was always kicking off in the bar, too, but just among the customers. The staff didn't get dragged into it.

The Chicago Rock Café didn't just rely on £1 drinks. It also had a gimmick. When certain songs came on, the staff would have to climb on the bar and start dancing. 'Build Me Up Buttercup',

'YMCA', 'Greased Lightnin'', 'Hand Jive' … I was a bit reluctant to dance on the bar, so I would make sure I looked busy when the trigger songs came on. I couldn't always escape, but I never learnt the right moves.

All this was just so I could afford to race my bike. I needed to do it. Club racing was an expensive pastime; National level racing was something else again.

In club racing, I'd use whatever brand name tyres I could get on the cheap. In Junior Superstock, I had started using four brand-new rear tyres and three fronts in a weekend, just to be in the hunt. That's over £500 on tyres every race weekend, plus fuel for the bike and £100 on diesel to the track and back.

In the second year of Junior Superstock, the control tyre changed to Dunlop and I soon noticed a massive difference in the way the bike behaved and the feedback I could feel from the tyres. I could predict if they were about to slide, and even started controlling slides, whereas before, at the first hint of a slide, I'd close the throttle. 2001 was when it really clicked what a difference tyres could make. By this stage I'd learnt a lot and the tyre suited me.

But it wasn't all motorcycle racing and picking up vomit. About this time I was invited to an orgy …

A bunch of us were hanging around at a friend's house, when another mate of ours – let's call him Dave for reasons that will become clear – turned up with a new girlfriend. It turns out she was very open-minded and was as keen to experiment as Louis Pasteur. She wasn't hard to look at and basically invited the five of us to get to know her better. A lot better. None of us had a house or flat of our own, so it was decided that my works van, W173 JDO, would be the ideal passion wagon. We'd meet the next day and go do the business. I thought, 'Mint, I'll have a go at this.'

The next day I turned up with the van and was the only one there until 'Dave' arrived with a mattress under one arm and his other round his girlfriend, a tube of lube stuffed in his pocket. That there were only three of us didn't seem to put a dampener on proceedings, so we drove off to find a suitable spot.

As I explained earlier, I've never been that bothered about shagging, and being in the back of a works breakdown truck that stank of gear oil wasn't doing it for me, so there was this weird scene of me sat in the buff, except for my socks, on the wheel arch in the back of a Transit van eating a Mars Bar, watching Dave rattle into his new girlfriend. I was never more than a spectator, but they seemed to be enjoying themselves and it all ended well because the two of them were still together years later.

Back in the world of racing, I signed up for the 2002 Junior Superstock series. My Suzuki GSX-R600 was still the current model, so it just needed a thorough going over before the season started.

At the first round, I was ninth, not much better than the previous year, but at the next race meeting, Brands Hatch, I was running second when I slid off. I came away with no points and a scuffed bike, but proud that I had put in the fastest lap of the race. Next up was Donington, and I was fourth when an oil spill meant the red flag came out to end the race early. Then followed a pair of ninths, another fourth and a fifth.

The racing was so close, the bikes being very evenly matched, that you had to be aggressive to get a decent result. I don't mean you had to ride dirty, but if you didn't attack at every opportunity, someone would do it to you and you'd be nowhere. It wasn't the kind of racing where you could make a break or plan a move for a lap in advance, but I was beginning to get in sight of the podium. Then, at the very next race, an incident occurred that would change the course of my life.

CHAPTER 6

I'M A ROAD RACER

'It was enough to push me over the edge and I dived at him, slamming the laptop he was working on down onto his hands.'

AFTER TWO SEASONS of club racing and a full year competing in National level racing, I had signed back up for another season of the very competitive Junior Superstock series for 2002.

So far, the results had been right enough. Except for a DNF, when I was in second before sliding out, I'd been in the top ten for every round and had three top five finishes, two of them coming back to back before I went to Rockingham for round eight.

This circuit, near Corby in Northamptonshire, is nothing like a traditional British circuit. Then it was still virtually brand-new. All the other tracks that the British Superbike series visit date back to the war or before. Rockingham has huge stands, a big block of corporate suites and offices, and a track that, like some other British circuits, has a few different configurations depending on who or what was racing there.

What Rockingham has, that other UK tracks don't, is a banked section, like Daytona and American NASCAR tracks. I think they hoped to attract NASCAR races to Britain, but the idea never caught on. The British motorsport fan is spoilt for events and tracks. There can't be anywhere in the world that has as many motorsport venues packed into such a small area as the UK. When I see the massive stands full of flipdown seats at Rockingham, I always wonder how many of those plastic chairs have actually had a pair of arse cheeks land on them.

2002 was only the second year the British Superbike series had raced at Rockingham and I liked the place. I got on with it a lot better than some of the other racers did.

The meeting was going like any other. Arrive Thursday night; unload; sign on; get my bike, leathers, boots, gloves and helmet checked by the scrutineers; then prepare to ride. As practice and qualifying got under way, through Friday and Saturday, some riders, in all classes, not just Junior Superstock, were out-braking themselves and cutting through the chicane, bouncing over the dirt, rather than sticking to the tarmac. We had to go through a left-right chicane after coming off the relatively high-speed section of banking.

Out-braking yourself happens at lots of tracks and in every type of racing, from novices in their first club race up to the so-called aliens in MotoGP. Every racer is trying to ride at their limit, and there are times when we all think we can squeeze up the inside of the rider in front and block them through the chicane to make a pass. To do this you leave your braking a second later than you did on every previous lap so you can edge in front and take the other rider's line, meaning they have to back off and you've made the pass. But it's easier said than done. It's a race. Pride is at stake and everyone is braking as late as they possibly can, and getting on the power as early as they dare. If you're racing with someone who is at a very similar level – whether you're racing for first or 15th place – you have to hang your balls out once in a while to get past.

Sometimes, at the last minute, a rider realises they've gone in too hot, they begin to doubt themselves and, not wanting to take out the guy in front, they head straight over the chicane to avoid a collision. Of course, there are times they can't avoid an accident and wipe each other out. I've done both.

Racers must have been getting their braking wrong and running over this chicane more regularly at Rockingham, because the Clerk of the Course, the man in charge of the meeting, noticed and sent out a message to all the racers explaining that if anyone cut through the chicane and made up a place they would be docked time after the race. This kind of official stance isn't that unusual either.

I qualified well and finished the race in second behind Cal Crutchlow, who would go on to be probably the best British Grand Prix rider of his generation. I was well chuffed. I went up on the podium, collected my trophy and was back at the van, packing up with my dad, when one of the marshals came up and told me I was going to be given a ten-second penalty for running through the chicane. I knew I'd done it once in the race, but I had lost time and a place by making the mistake, not gained it. I'd braked too deeply, gone off line, stood the bike up, run over the dirt and grass, still braking as hard as I dared so I didn't crash straight into the side of anyone when I rejoined the track. After my mistake I was still riding well and got back into the rhythm, trying, and managing, to make up places. I made the mistake early enough to be able to take back the place I lost.

The racing in Junior Superstock was so close that adding ten seconds to my time would put me back to fifth place or something. I was told I could have the decision reviewed, if I paid £100 to lodge an official appeal. The racing authorities always make riders and teams pay to appeal. If you think another team or rider is cheating, you have to put your money where your mouth is. It's done this way to make people think hard before they start slinging mud. If the accused team or rider is found to be guilty of cheating, the person who makes the complaint gets their money back. If they are not found to have broken the rules, the person who accused them loses money. Because I wanted to disagree with the officials, it was me who had to put the money up.

Coughing it up was the obvious thing to do, because I was right (I'm always right ...). So I wrote a cheque and went to see the Clerk of the Course in one of the track offices. I was annoyed, but I knew they'd see my side of things. There had been a simple mix-up, it just need ironing out. No problem.

I waited a while until I was told I could see the official. He asked me, 'What would you have done if there was a brick wall there?' Obviously I wouldn't have ridden through it, I replied. I explained I'd lost time by running off the track, but I got the feeling he wasn't listening. He was ancient, and I was just a young nobody racer in the Support Class of the big-name British Superbike series. Right from the moment he opened his mouth it was clear I was wasting my time. I was fuming when my so-called appeal was over. When I left the Clerk's office, one of the race officials, Stuart Higgs, who would go on to be the top man – Series Director of the British Superbike series – said, in a way I thought was very sarcastic, 'Did you get sorted?'

It was enough to push me over the edge and I dived at him, slamming the laptop he was working on down onto his hands while shouting a few obscenities and telling him, 'You can shove your series up your arse!'

Pretty diplomatic, I thought. Dad was waiting for me, so he saw it all happen. He quickly put an arm around my shoulder and told me it was time to go. While I was packing up the van I knew the job was buggered. The next day I cancelled the cheque for the appeal I'd made at the track. I didn't think I'd had a fair hearing, so I didn't see why I should pay.

I'm one of those people who truly believe that everything happens for a reason. Perhaps this post-rationalising just makes it easier to deal with difficult situations. Whatever it is, this time of my life is a perfect example.

The week after Rockingham, I was entered to race in the Cock o' the North meeting, at Oliver's Mount, Scarborough. I'd also been sent a letter telling me I had to attend a hearing at the headquarters of the ACU, the governing body of UK motorcycle racing.

Oliver's Mount is mainland Britain's last remaining real road racing circuit (I'm counting Aberdare Park as a park circuit, not a public road). It's a road, but a road to nowhere really, on a big hill outside Scarborough. For a few weekends a year it's a race circuit; the rest of the time it's open to the public to drive or ride around. You don't need special permission, a ticket or time slot to ride it, just turn off the main road into Scarborough and loop round it, obeying the speed limits and the laws of the land.

They've been racing bikes there for 50 years. Once it was a track the world's elite grand prix racers competed on – thought of in much the same way as the Isle of Man or Monza, but as the top riders became more concerned with the safety of tracks, the Isle of Man and Scarborough began to struggle to attract the international names. The main men really were dropping like flies back then, so Oliver's Mount, the Ulster GP and Isle of Man tracks were left to British and Irish riders who were either road specialists, had grown up in the era in which being a good TT man was key to being signed by a team or, a bit later, were riders like future four-time World Superbike champion Carl Fogarty, who raced the roads on their way to World Championship racing.

In the 1970s, Barry Sheene used to arrive at Scarborough by Rolls-Royce for a day's British Championship racing at Oliver's Mount. At the time, he was at a similar level to Valentino Rossi – world-famous, two-time world 500-cc champion; a guest on primetime TV shows like *Parkinson*; a playboy recognised by everyone in the UK; the face of Brut 33 aftershave in TV adverts when Britain only had three TV channels. He was bigger than motorcycle racing alone; yet, back then, Sheene, like fellow former world champions Phil Read and Giacomo Agostini, would turn up to one-off non-World Championship races at Mallory or Scarborough for start and prize money. Contracts in MotoGP and World Superbike are so tight now that modern racers could never do that even if they wanted the money, and I'm sure plenty would like it.

When Sheene and real road racing are spoken about together, people often mention that he helped to ensure the Isle of Man TT lost its grand prix status. That might be true, but it was the right thing to do. Whatever people say about the dangers of road racing, at least no one is having their arm twisted to race at the TT nowadays. It's not part of a bigger championship, like it was from the end of the war up till 1977, when the British Grand Prix moved to Silverstone. Even back in the 1970s, however, only the best six results of a ten-race season counted towards the championship total, so in theory riders could choose to miss it anyway.

The Isle of Man was out of step with the way mainstream racing was developing, and it took the Isle of Man until the early 2000s to realise this and do something about it. In his autobiography, the former TT and World Championship racer

Mick Grant put the blame on the ACU for not moving with the times, and it wasn't until the Isle of Man authorities themselves started having a big hand in the organisation that things really changed.

The TT is still out of step with every other kind of racing, but now that's seen by fans and the motorcycle industry as a strength, not a weakness.

Still, while Sheene might have hated the Isle of Man TT, he had a soft spot for Scarborough, and he clearly wasn't short of balls when it came to racing unforgiving circuits. Sheene still holds the record for the fastest ever average speed for a motorcycle lap of a race track, at 137.15 mph at the old nine-mile Spa-Francorchamps, and that was virtually a real road race circuit for most of the lap, because the track left the Spa short circuit for the Belgian roads of the surrounding Ardennes region.

It was my dad's idea for me to race at Oliver's Mount. It was one of his favourite tracks, even though he'd been badly hurt crashing there. I'd sent off my entry weeks before the Rockingham laptop incident.

After finishing my apprenticeship, in 2000, I had been working full-time for my dad. As long as I got the work done he was flexible with my hours, so I could go racing. We were quiet during the week on the run-up to the race, and Dad suggested we knock off work early and drive the 50-odd miles up to Scarborough in the van so he could show me round. This was my fourth season of racing, and though he'd been a great help and had come to races with me, this was the first time I remember he'd really tried to share some of his racing knowledge.

Now I realise Oliver's Mount isn't the kind of track I enjoy the most, because it's quite tight and nadgery, but I liked it from the very first lap. About 200 metres from the Oliver's Mount start line the track funnels into the uphill, left-hand Mere Hairpin, one of the tightest on any track in the world. It is also one of the few places anywhere on the circuit with run-off – somewhere to go if you make a mistake, or someone else makes a mistake for you. Get it wrong anywhere else at Oliver's Mount and you're into a fence, a tree or a six-foot grass banking. Just ask my dad.

After the Hairpin there's the climb up Sheene Rise. It's nearly as steep as the Mountain at Cadwell Park, and three times longer, and you go under a footbridge and through a tunnel of trees. There are blue and white kerbs on the apex of each corner.

Then it's through the Esses with a raised banking and hedge on the left. The left-hander leading on to the straight has loads of positive camber, which allows you to exit fast. It's 180 mph down the not-very-straight straight. Hedges are on one side, oak and cedar trees on the other. The road is smooth by road race standards, but not wide enough for a white line.

I've seen this track described as claustrophobic, because the grass banks and trees shadow the track. To me it never feels like anything but home.

Next up is a tight left-hander in front of the café. From flat-out in sixth, it's back four gears for this corner, then get on the throttle gently past the café and into a slight right before the first-gear left. The right is what I'd call Memorial. Dad's race career was ended at the tight left directly after it.

The circuit passes right in front of the hilltop café, with its great view of the track one way and Scarborough and the North Sea the other.

Next is a third-gear straight, a right-hand hairpin and a hill down to the left-hand Mountside hairpin.

Two bumps make the bikes wheelie viciously, then there is the new chicane. It's more of a loop than a chicane and has a tricky off-camber section where it rejoins the straight just before the grid markings and the end of the lap.

The race meeting I'd entered was the Cock o' the North, a major club event and the middle meeting of the three big ones held annually at Oliver's Mount. It's not seen as an International meeting, like the end-of-season Gold Cup, but all the top Irish lads would come over for it. I entered the 1300 cc Open and 600 Supersport classes on the same Suzuki 600 I had been racing for the majority of two seasons, a bike I knew inside out.

I was entered with Jason Griffiths, who was on a Kawasaki, and the massively experienced Ian Lougher was racing for TAS Suzuki. These two, both 15 years or more older than me, were the top roads men at the time. Lougher had won TTs, and Griffiths, after he retired, was regarded as the fastest rider never to win a TT. They were riding for well-known teams and were used to winning. By the end of the two-day meeting, my very first competitive visit to Oliver's Mount, I had beaten the pair of them.

I was on my Suzuki 600, in very basic Junior Superstock specification, even though I was competing against trick Supersport bikes built using much bigger budgets and more freedom. The only person I didn't beat in the 600 class that day was Gary Jess, a shit-hot Northern Irish racer. Unfortunately, he was killed later that year, at Deer's Leap on the Dundrod circuit, competing in the Ulster GP Superbike race.

I finished the day thinking, 'This is it! This is what racing is about.' I'd done over a year and a half of National racing, a support class to the British Superbike – probably the most important domestic racing championship in the world at that time. I wasn't at the pinnacle of racing by a long shot, but I was on a rung of the ladder, and believing that BSB was what motorbike racing was all about. I was even beginning to have the odd thought along the lines of right, the next step is British Supersport – on a higher spec and more expensive 600-cc bike –

then after that British Superbike, then maybe into a World series.

I didn't know there was an alternative. I was developing a mind-set like most British racers, following, or at least trying to follow, the well-worn route of club, National support class, main National class, World Championship. Then I did this Cock o' the North meeting, a real roads race, and realised there was more to motorbike racing than competing in the British Championship. I wasn't at the stage where I was thinking I was going to be the next Mick Doohan, but if I'd have stayed on that British National route much longer who knows what daft stuff I'd have started believing. After all, Cal Crutchlow, the lad I finished second to in my last ever Junior Superstock race, has done all right for himself, having signed a multi-million pound deal to race Ducati's MotoGP bike in the same year another ex-Junior Superstock racer, Tom Sykes, became World Superbike champion.

One of the main things I liked about Scarborough was that everyone was working out of the back of a van or a seven-and-a-half tonner, not big articulated lorries. The BSB paddock was full of fancy motorhomes. There was even more money in that series back then than there is now.

At Scarborough, half the grid will have been on the piss the night before. It was laidback, but the racing was hard. Bloody hard. The racing at the front was as committed as that in Junior Supersport, but on this very different kind of track. When I turned up at Oliver's Mount I was dead cocky, I thought I'd smoke them all, but I didn't.

A few key things, those things that happen for a reason, occurred at that Cock o' the North race meeting. The first was finding this thriving scene of professional racing away from the BSB series. Another was discovering I could cut it racing on this kind of track. The last was a being approached by an Irish journalist who pointed me towards another door I could barge through.

After one of the races, Leslie Moore, the editor of *Road Racing Ireland*, came and found me in the pits and suggested I should think about going over to Ireland to race. It was an idea that had never occurred to me.

Muir told me about a meeting called Kells that was coming up just the following weekend. Even though I'd never heard of it, I didn't think to ask him any questions about Kells – the track, the other competitors or anything. I just assumed it would be like Oliver's Mount. I went home, checked the ferry times and booked a crossing from Holyhead to Dun Loaghaire. Me, my brother Stu and a mate and fellow racer, James Andrews, from nearby Bardney, went over in the Transit, W173 JDO. We docked on the outskirts of Dublin and headed straight for the town of Navan, in southern Ireland.

When we turned up it was a case of right then, where's the track? The answer was, you're on it. There was cowshit everywhere. The race paddock was a farmer's field and people were getting towed *into* the pits because it had been raining so heavily for a few days before. You know you're there for the duration when they're using tractors to pull the racers' vans into the pits before the meeting even starts.

My mate James was the same age as me, and racing a Suzuki in Junior Superstock at the time, the same class as me, so we took his spare wheels as well as mine, meaning I had tyres ready for every eventuality – rain, shine or anything in between.

I was 20, it was the first time I had ever been to the Republic and it was an eye-opener. Even coming from Lincolnshire the place seemed backward. Though it's called the Kells Road Races, the race track is actually based around the village of Crossakiel, six miles away.

On our first evening, the night before the meeting started, we went for a curry and waited a lifetime for a meal that cost a fortune. Not a good start, but then we went to the pub and the trip started looking up. Crossakiel, in County Meath, is half the size of Kirmington, but it had three pubs, proper dingy places with sticky floors, but dead friendly.

The circuit itself, I would learn, was typical of a lot of the smaller Irish tracks. Many Irish road circuits are in the shape of a triangle, formed out of three country lanes that intersect with each other. The Crossakiel circuit that hosts the Kells Road Races is one of these. The sections you'd call the straights have bends and jumps on them, bloody big jumps at Kells, but the main corners are the road ends, where one road makes a T-junction with another.

Arriving at Kells, after my success at the Cock o' the North races the week before, I thought I'd just use my short circuit experience to brake harder than everyone else into these road-end corners and show everyone how it was done. I'd been on the podium in the British Championship and Scarborough, and I knew how hard I could push a bike.

I sat on the grid, bike revving to 6,000 rpm, ready to launch at the first corner. I had it all planned in my head and was determined to brake later than everyone into the first corner of the first lap, but hadn't accounted for just how bumpy the road was. I was braking hard on these rough country lanes, not much wider than a suburban semi's driveway, and my back wheel was off the floor. We were approaching Magee's Crossroads, and I felt if I braked any harder I'd flip the bike and fly over the handlebars, so I released a bit of pressure on the front brake lever and ran on, taking out Richard 'Milky' Quayle. We both hit a wall that lined the corner. Milky (so nicknamed because his blond hair and glasses made him look like the Milky Bar Kid) was screaming in his helmet. I genuinely thought, 'Shit, I've killed him!' It turned out he'd only twisted his ankle, the girl!

Back in the pits, Milky's sponsor let rip at me, calling me every name under the sun as I apologised. Strangely, he nearly ended up sponsoring me down the line, but we certainly got off on the wrong foot. Milky is now one of the key men in the running of the Isle of Man TT races, so we still bump into each other quite a bit.

After the coming together with Milky I had hell getting the bike back to the pits, because any bikes that crash or break down get pushed into a field and collected later. There are so many races within an Irish meeting like Kells that the next grid is waiting to get out on the road to line up as soon as the previous race finishes. And these road circuits are not like Silverstone, where there are service roads that the recovery trucks can use to bring bikes back to the pits. Eventually, though, we got the Suzuki back and taped the fairing up for another race.

I didn't know a lot about Irish road racing. I was in the British National series and blinkered to what was going on in Ireland. The road-race scene was hardly reported in the UK at the time. Even the TT was on the wane. Everyone was interested in World Superbikes, BSB and MotoGP, but I'd seen pictures of the Northern Irish race star Adrian Archibald, in his Red Bull-sponsored helmet, and now I was sat next to him, thinking, 'Bloody hell ...' Archibald was the man in Ireland at the time, a TT contender, who, the following year, would win the 2003 Isle of Man Senior TT. And I actually passed Archibald in my very first race. Unfortunately it was on the way to taking out Milky ...

The jumps at Kells were something else, too. I was hitting them flat-out and flying for 50 metres or more. I didn't have any particular skill, I just wasn't scared. And that seemed to work in Irish road racing. At least for me.

After the raced where I tangled with Milky, I was out in the support races, for the lower level of racers – where I should've been from the start – and won three of them, including the Senior B and the Grand Final B races. After the prize-giving I ended up with a pocket full of prize money and a new outlook on life. We went out on the Guinness that night, got hammered, and drove home the next day, me realising, for the second time in two weeks, that I'd seen the future. I didn't have to work 100-hour weeks to pay for my racing. I didn't have to dance on the bar of Chicago Rock Café to the bloody 'Hand Jive' all winter, putting money away for tyres that were chewed up and spat out in 20 minutes. I could win a few quid and pay for it that way.

It wasn't the money that was attracting me to the roads, though. I enjoyed it all. Everyone involved with the race were the friendliest people I'd ever met. They couldn't do enough for me. That's why I've always had a soft spot for Kells, even though the track's a bit nadgery compared to the ones I now enjoy the most, the Mountain Course and Dundrod. And the Irish race community lived by a saying I learnt and loved – We're not here for a long time, we're here for a good time.

A couple of weeks after the Scarborough meeting, and a few days after the life-changing race at Kells, I travelled down to the Auto Cycle Union's headquarters in Rugby for a hearing on the whole Rockingham incident. I went with Dave Johnson, who I'd bought my very first race bike from. He came to give moral support, but it didn't make any difference. I went in front of the board, a spray of Lynx deodorant covering any whiff of nervous sweat. I think I even wore shoes to make an effort, but I was made to feel my crime was worse than Fred West's. They sent me out of the room while they deliberated and decided to suspend my ACU racing licence for the rest of the season. Weirdly, they gave me the impression the punishment was for cancelling the cheque, not for slamming the laptop on Stuart Higgs's hands, but I'm sure that didn't do anything to help my cause.

By this time, I realised that if I did go to race in Ireland it meant I could apply for an Irish race licence, through the MCUI, the Motorcycle Union of Ireland, and not have to deal with the ACU.

Once I had decided I was going to be a real road racer, things moved fast. And again, it was weird twists of fate and chance meetings that brought it about.

James Andrews, who'd helped me out by spannering at Kells, was racing his Supermoto bike at Anglesey in North Wales. I went and spannered for him, to return the favour. During the weekend I bumped into Sam Finley, an Irish fella who ran a small road racing team. We'd had a yarn between the races at Kells. He had someone riding for him at Kells and at Anglesey too.

When we bumped into each other in Wales, we got talking and he asked what I was planning to do in 2003. I told him I was going to buy a bike and do some Irish road races. Sam said perhaps I could race for him. I can't have taken it seriously, because I never asked for his phone number and he didn't take mine.

Then, some weeks later, I went with a bunch of mates to watch a big Supermoto race at Mettet in Belgium. We were in a pub at the first corner having a few drinks and there was Sam again. This time we did swap phone numbers. He said he definitely wanted me to ride for his outfit, Team Racing, and asked did I want to go and live over in Ireland.

These random meetings, the last one in a pub in Belgium, led me down a completely different path. I wouldn't be paid to ride for Sam; it wasn't that kind of deal. It never entered my head that I would be paid, but I was being supplied a 750 to race, a van to turn up in and the chance to win a few quid in prize money. It meant I didn't have to buy my own 750. I could race the 600 I'd been racing in Junior Superstock, at Scarborough and at Kells, and also Team Racing's Suzuki 750.

Sam had a job for me too, so I starting planning for 2003. It meant packing in working for my dad and moving out. I was 22 and leaving home to go to race motorbikes.

So, in the spring of 2003, I moved to Northern Ireland. I originally lived in Sam's spare room, sharing the house with him, his wife and his kids. He owned a few bits of property, so I eventually ended up moving into the bare shell of a bungalow at the back of a filling station, once we'd got the electricity and water plumbed in. The kitchen and toilet were fitted, but that's all. The place was renamed the Fungalow.

During the week I worked as a labourer for a building firm that dealt with the maintenance of a casting factory in the west side of Belfast. At weekends I'd race both on the short circuits and the roads.

The 'shorts' are what the road racing community call purpose-built tracks, however long they are. Donington, Silverstone, Laguna Seca, Misano, Valencia ... they are all short circuits. The racing that goes on in series like MotoGP and British Superbikes is often called road racing, to differentiate it from motocross or any other kind of motorcycle sport that happens on dirt. That's why the TT and Irish road racing is also known as real road racing. It's racing on a *real* road.

Riders in their first year of racing on the Irish roads, are restricted to what was called the Support Class and to bikes no bigger than a 750. They call it the B race at most places now. Somehow, probably because of my good showing at my first Cock o' the North, I was allowed to race in the main class at Kells, the race where I took out Milky, but the authorities saw the error of their ways and I was in the Support Class for the 2003 season.

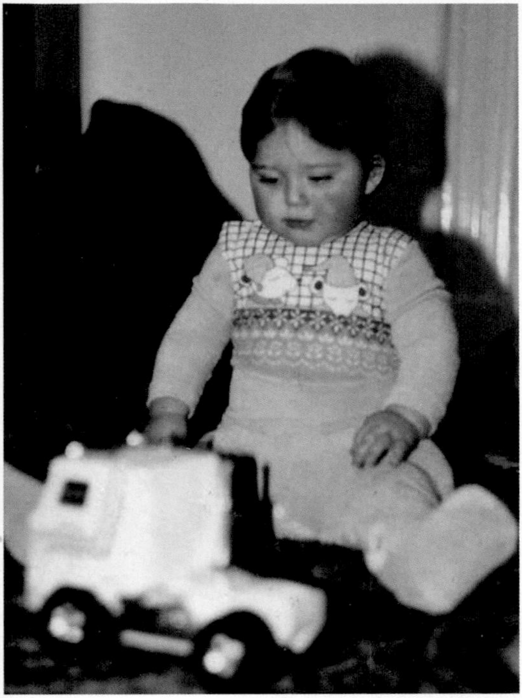

Left: My love of trucks started here. I'm thirteen months old and it's my second Christmas. The truck was a present from Mum and Dad.

Below: Me and my grandma, Double-Decker Lil.

Right: My mum tells me this is Silverstone. We'd go on a Thursday and come back on a Sunday night when my dad was racing. We had an old ambulance converted into a camper that the four of us, Mum, Dad, me and Sal, would sleep in.

Above: Me and Big Rita. The best mum I could hope for. A proper grafter who didn't take any nonsense. Looking back, she did everything the right way as far as I was concerned.

Right: The four Martin kids and my dad. He still looks the same now, over 20 years later. That's Sally at the back, with Kate in front of her, Stu next to her and then me.

Above: On my Raleigh Chopper with my dad's bike workshop, a converted chicken shed, in the background. I spent many a night after school watching him build his race bikes.

Above: The Martins. Me, eight; Kate, two; Sally, nine; and Stuart, three.

Above: My first-ever motorbike, a Yamaha TY80. I still have it now. The little trial bike started the motorcycle obsession. It also started a lot of arguments with my older sister Sal, who I was supposed to share it with. That's my dad's works van in the background.

Left: On the KX125 at Barnetby quarry, just up the road from where I lived. My first motocross bike, paid for by working with my dad. I rode it every chance I got, more often than not in one of Mr Lancaster's farm fields. That got him revving.

Left: The VW LT35 that my dad painted to look like the A-Team van because we were all so mad about the TV programme.

Above: The Transit van, M303 GRH and my Suzuki GSX-R600 Junior Superstock bike.

SHOEI
74
BSA
Rocket3
74

Sally, my brother Stu and Shorty, an old mate from Kirmington, came over from Lincolnshire to support me, driving the five hours up to Stranraer for the ferry over to Belfast in my sister's Vauxhall Corsa. I remember I was up till after midnight preparing the bikes for what would be my first outing for Team Racing, the next day's race at Aghadowey, a short, airfield circuit that had a bend called Shithouse Corner.

I did well in the Support Class. I was fairly confident, because I had won at Kells, my very first Irish meeting in 2002 – when I'd travelled over with my own bike. Then I won quite regularly through 2003 for Team Racing. The race at Aghadowey didn't go without incident, though. I crashed three times in a day on my debut for Team Racing. I actually crashed getting from the truck to the pits. Quite impressive.

I also raced at the short circuits of Bishopscourt and Kirkistown. Then the road racing started with Cookstown and Tandragee. Sally would come over to Ireland regularly and do the pit board for us – hold out the bath towel sized board with numbers that would show me where I was in the race and how many seconds the riders in front and behind were away from me. Even then she knew I might not have a long future with this team. They'd bought a few sets of Fandango headsets, with big headphones and microphones so they could talk to each other. They never worked properly and looked right out of place in Irish road racing, more suited to a Formula One pit-lane.

That year I didn't race at the North West 200, the season's biggest race in Northern Ireland. My Team Racing team-mate, Liam Quinn, another businessman who owned a company that sold industrial air compressors, raced at the meeting, and I ended up spannering for him. Liam was a good 20 years older than me.

My job was to prepare my Suzuki GSX-R600, that was in the orange, white and black Team Racing colours, for him to borrow and race. Once we were at the track, I was to get the bike through scrutineering, making sure it was safe and ready to race. I understood all that, no problem, but in the week before the race, Liam said to me, 'Why don't you try and get the Suzuki 750 engine out of your bike into the 600?'

I was surprised he was willing to cheat so blatantly in a class that was supposed to have standard engines, but Liam explained that plenty of people were already cheating by porting the head of their 600s or changing the cams to gain an advantage, but why mess around like that? The class at that time was notorious, with 600s going faster than 750s. Loads of people were pulling a fast one. Liam's thinking, he said, was that if he was going to rob the sweet shop he wasn't just going to just take the penny sweets, he'd have the whole till.

It made some weird kind of logic and he was the boss, so I did what I could. The 750 engine was 10 mm higher, so I made some engine mounting brackets and got it in. It didn't do him much good, though; he still didn't come anywhere near the podium.

I never felt guilty about helping him break the rules, Liam's plan wasn't keeping me awake at night. Cheating was rife, right up to the top level, in the generation before I got involved, but it's much harder to get away with things now, at the top level at least. There's too much scrutiny.

I even rode that bike in a 600 race at Nutts Corner, a short circuit in Northern Ireland. The bike was so much faster than anything else, that I ended up waiting for everyone so it didn't look too obvious. I planned to win on a dash for the line, but, what I hadn't worked out was, the finish line was past the braking marker. That meant, every other time I'd crossed the line, I was already braking to slow down for the first corner. This time I accelerated over the line to pip whoever I was racing. By the time it clicked it was too late. and I ended up crashing in a field. That was the first, and last, time I cheated in a bike race.

I made a few good friends early in that 2003 season. One was Martin Finnegan, who would become probably my best mate among the other racers.

I first met him in 2001. He was one of a bunch of lads racing in England under the name Team Ireland. He was with other Irish riders including Woolsey Coulter.

I raced Martin in British Junior Superstock. We knew each other enough to say hello, but not much more until I went to race at Kells in 2002. I saw him there, and he gave me some petrol to allow me to keep racing, because I couldn't get out of the pits to buy more when I was close to running out.

He was racing the big class in my support class season and we got talking. He was a year older, but he seemed more mature, and was running his own show himself.

Martin came from Lusk, right near the famous Skerries circuit. He was a man mountain, compared to other bike racers. He was built like a house side. He'd grown up racing motocross and he was spectacular on a Superbike. He always looked great in photos, jumping the furthest, right out of the seat, and often with the front wheel crossed up like a motocrosser. He rode the bike – the bike didn't boss him, that's for sure. He was a top TT man, on the podium, but never won one. He was also the top road racer from the Republic of Ireland so he always did all right for sponsorship.

I saw Martin the following year, 2003, at the Cookstown 100, the first road race of the year of my first full season in Ireland. I think he told Sam Finley he needed a mechanic for the upcoming Isle of Man fortnight, and Sam said I'd be good for the job.

Martin then asked me to work for him at the 2003 TT, which would be his second time racing there, and I was happy to. I drove down to his place in Lusk, not far from Dublin. I had tea with his mum and dad, then he gave me an envelope full of £1,000 cash to spanner for him for the fortnight. This was before I'd even done anything, and it was more than I wanted or expected, but he wouldn't take it back. He just said, I want you to do the job right. The friendship grew from that TT.

I'd prep the bikes, which was work I loved doing and took pride in. There was no pressure from that side of things, because I had confidence in my own ability. I would also be one of the three blokes doing Martin's pit-stops. I did the wheel change for him in the Senior and it was probably the most pressure I've ever felt at a TT. I'd rather race the bike than be responsible for changing the wheel. I did it, no problem, but I didn't like being in that position.

A light goes on, on the top of the historic old scoreboard opposite the grandstand, when each rider goes past Hillberry. The pit crew then know the bike is less than two miles away from the pits. Once I saw the light go on, I got an instant shot of adrenalin. An Arai man, one of the fellas who spend the fortnight servicing helmets for the racers, did Martin's visors; Martin's brother-in-law, Alan, did the fuel, and I changed the rear wheel.

As Martin came in, I jumped behind the bike, put it on the rear paddock stand. I took off the nut with a pneumatic 'windy' gun; took the spindle out; pushed the wheel forward; unhooked the chain; pulled the wheel out, and placed it down so it didn't roll away in front of the other bikes all coming in and out of the pit-lane. When the new wheel and tyre go in, you have to be careful to guide the brake disc into the caliper; then you push the spindle through; hook the chain on; roll the wheel backwards; pull the wheel back; put the nut on with the gun; crack it with a torque wrench to be sure it's tight; check the back brake; take the bike off the stand and then wait for the fuel to finish. The TT fuel systems are different to those used in motorcycle endurance racing. They're slower at the Isle of Man, taking about 35 seconds to fill up the tank, rather than about five, but that's a good thing, because it gives the wheel-changers more time to make sure everything is right. You're still expected to change a back wheel in 20 seconds, though.

Once the fuel was finished I'd give him a push off down the pit-lane, then the three crew would stand there in silence, letting out a big breath of air, before one would ask, 'What do you reckon then?' and we'd talk about how the pit-stop had gone.

Martin was dead professional, and when he came in after the race he'd give a list of changes he wanted to make. It was a massive buzz and an education to be involved with a rider who was doing well at the TT. I think it also helped me, in the future, that I'd been both sides of the fence – riding and spannering.

That July I travelled back to the Isle of Man, this time to race at the Southern 100 meeting. It's a mid-week race, held on the outskirts of Castletown. It would become my favourite race meeting of the year, but the first visit was a disaster.

CHAPTER 7

IT'LL CATCH UP WITH YOU

'Rather than bide my time and weigh up the options, I let my "inner chimp" get the better of me.'

AFTER WORKING AS a mechanic for Finnegan at the 2003 TT, I was back in action racing myself and, only a few weeks later, on the ferry to Isle of Man to race at the Southern 100 meeting. It would be the first time I raced on the Isle of Man.

The Southern is another real road race held on the same small island as the TT, but it's a very different event. For one thing, it's on a completely different circuit. The Southern 100 takes place on the historic 4.25-mile Billown Circuit that runs through Castletown and the surrounding countryside. It's also a lot more low-key, and happens mid-week, with the big race on the Thursday. And, crucially, it's a mass-start race, not a time trial like the Tourist Trophy. The bikes line up in rows on a grid and fight for position into the first corners. First across the line wins. It attracted the top road racers then and still does now.

I made a good start on my first visit to the track. After Wednesday night's Senior race I was on the podium,third behind Ryan Farquhar and Jason Griffiths on the 2001 Suzuki Superbike my dad had sold his road bike to buy me. Because this was the Isle of Man, not Ireland, and the race was run by a different governing body, I could take part in the big feature races and on a 1000-cc bike, where, in Ireland, I was still limited to a 750-cc. Because I wasn't limited to the Support Class I was going into the final race, the big one on Thursday, thinking to myself, 'I can win this.'

Looking back, I was riding wild. I might have been getting good results, but I was pushing my luck. More experienced road racers, men I respected, like Finnegan and Richard Britton, had noticed the way I was riding in the Support Class races in Ireland and took the time to tell me I had to calm down. Keep riding like that and it'll catch up with you, I was told. They were saying it in a jokey way, with smiles on their faces, but they were serious. I know they cared or they'd have kept their mouths shut, but they said it in a way that showed they weren't telling me what to do, just giving me something to think about. I might have nodded to say I heard them, but I wasn't listening.

I was riding by the seat of my pants, loving the buzz and winning the support races, but I was taking too many chances.

I lined up for the Championship race, as they call it, which that year was sponsored by the Ronaldsway Shoe Company. I looked across and saw Ryan Farquhar next to me in the purple and turquoise colours of McAdoo Racing. Farquhar was already a big name in road racing, and the Northern Irishman would go on to win more Irish road races than anyone in history. Being cocky and over-confident, though, I reckoned I had the beating of him ...

Farquhar got a characteristically good start, but I was in second place behind him. Rather than bide my time and weigh up the options, I let my 'inner chimp' get the better of me. I have a handle on the chimp now, and a better understanding thanks to having read the book *The Chimp Paradox* by Dr Steve Peters. The inner chimp is this primal, prehistoric part of our brain, which makes rash, heat-of-the-moment decisions. I don't make those kind of decisions during races now, but I still did then.

I was following Farquhar going into Iron Gate, a sort of downhill kink, one of the quickest bits of the course, where you are in top gear, then braking and shifting down to third for a right-left, a section lined with stone walls. Jason Griffiths, Martin Finnegan, Ian Lougher and a dozen more were nose-to-tail behind me.

But it was to be one of those moments when my enthusiasm outweighed my skill. I was looking to pass Farquhar for the lead, but I was nowhere near close enough and I braked way too late. I was trying to make up too much ground on him. I was coming from so far back I didn't even get alongside him before I ran out of tarmac, lost the front end and slid feet first straight into the wall. I was lying on the edge of the road, with a newly broken tibia and fibula, bikes everywhere, because it was still the first lap of the race when everyone is bunched together, not having had time to spread out. It could've been carnage. I nearly, so nearly, took Ryan out.

I was taken to Noble's Hospital, where I was operated on and kept in for a week. Dad drove out to pick me up and take me back to Kirmington. Breaking my leg obviously threw a spanner in the works for much of the rest of the season.

I was supposed to race at the Manx Grand Prix in late August, but although I could walk, no doctor I visited would pass me fit to race a motorcycle and I missed out. So my focus changed and my next target became being fit for the Scarborough Gold Cup meeting, the big one, in September.

Still, the two English-based doctors I visited wouldn't pass me fit to race at that meeting either. They could see I could walk, just about – I made sure I hobbled in without the help of crutches – but because my leg had been pinned and still had the metal freshly fitted, they weren't keen on signing me fit to race a Superbike. They had quite valid reasons and my leg was still very sore, but I was dead keen not to miss any more races. It wasn't like I was involved in a season-long battle and needed to get back in action to try and clinch a championship. I just loved racing, and even having a broken leg wasn't enough to put me off.

While I worked out what to do, I was rebuilding and developing my Suzuki GSX-R1000. I'd ported the cylinder head, carefully grinding away metal to change the shape of where the air and fuel mixture enters the engine and the exhaust gases leave it, so it made more power. I put different camshafts in and prepared to build it all up ready for the Scarborough Gold Cup. The bike would be ready, even if I wasn't.

It was during these weeks that I met one of the people who had a big influence on me. I needed a cylinder head skimming and couldn't find anyone locally who I trusted to do it. My dad remembered someone he half knew through racing and it turned out to be Chris Mehew – one of the best motorcycle engine tuners in Europe.

I rang him and arranged to visit his workshop in the nearby village of Ulceby, North Lincolnshire, riding over on my brother's Peugeot Speedfight 2 moped. Walking through the door of Chris Mehew Engineering nearly knocked me off my feet. From the outside his workshop was a weird-looking place, like a bunch of Portakabins all bolted together. It felt like a 1970s primary school, but the machinery he had there included lathes, valve seat cutters, milling machines and all kind of grinders – some of the stuff I'd never seen before, but I was immediately fascinated by it. There was a £30,000 Reve Red Bull Ducati Superbike engine sat on a bench, from the team that won that year's BSB title with John Reynolds, and Mehew wasn't making anything of it. He was busy when I visited, but the politest man I have ever met. He'd turn around to do something, and as he did, he'd say, 'Excuse my back.'

Mehew had raced when he was younger, but then become a race mechanic, before working on the wildly ambitious Elf Grand Prix project. As I got to know him better he'd tell me stories of the incredible lengths they went to for that project. He was working so hard on it, he lost stones in weight. He would work on the Elf till he fell asleep at the bench, then lie down in the corner of the workshop for a few hours, get up again and get straight back to work.

I eventually ended up doing the odd day's work with Mehew for a couple of months, three days here, two days there – five days if he was stacked out. I was still working at my dad's too, in a pot, or cast, with a rocker on the bottom, so I could walk about. I'd be under a truck trying to get a gearbox back in. A Scania gearbox weighs more than a ton. It's raised up to the truck on a gearbox lift, but you have to wrestle it into position. I was on my back with my foot, encased in its plaster cast, jammed under the gearbox as I tried to get the shafts lined up, with oil running down my leg, covering the pot. Not clever.

During the six weeks I was out of action with my broken leg, I was itching to see what difference all the tweaking had made to my Superbike, but I still hadn't been signed off to race.

I spoke to a few lads and was told there was a doctor in Northern Ireland who understood bike racers and might sign me off. Fred MacSorley worked at many of the Irish road races as a travelling doctor, riding around the circuit on a bike in his orange helmet, ready to be on the spot if a crash occurred. He would have seen some sights in that role, there's no doubt about that. MacSorley was a normal doctor too, so I arranged an appointment and booked the ferry for Ireland. The plan was to visit the doctor, get signed off and go surfing, up on the north coast, with my mate from Lincolnshire, Jonty Moore. I was also going to race my dad's Rob North BSA at the Killalane road races, just to get some time on a bike without too much pressure. I hadn't raced for something like six weeks and the Scarborough Gold Cup was the following weekend.

We found Dr MacSorley's surgery in Portadown, just near the Tandragee road race circuit. I walked into the doctor's office and told him I was here to be signed fit to race. Dead nonchalantly, he said, 'No problem, just climb onto the bed, and jump off landing only on your bad leg.'

The bed was the doctor's examination table, and seemed much higher than a bed you'd sleep in at home. We both knew this was going to end in one of two ways: either the leg had mended and was strong enough to take my 11-stone weight, landing from three and a bit feet, or it would break again. If it was the latter, at least I was already in the doctor's surgery.

I didn't know if it was strong enough, but I hadn't come all that way to bottle out, so I climbed on the table, bent my good leg up behind me and held it with my hand, took a breath and hopped.

It hurt. It hurt like hell, but it held in one piece and I got the all clear to compete. A few days later, I raced at Killalane on my dad's BSA Rocket 3, only the second time I'd ever ridden it.

I'd broken my right leg and the old Brit bike had a right-side gear-shift, not left-side like a Japanese bike. Normally I prefer right-side one, but not this time – my injured leg was getting some stick. At times I was sure I could still feel things moving around, like a bag of wet gravel. I managed to win the classic race, and that was the last time that bike has ever been raced.

After my crash at the Southern 100, when I was laid up in Noble's Hospital for a week, Sam Finlay had taken one of my bikes and all my tools back with him to Ireland. It was when I was back in England that my Suzuki GSX-R600 race bike and my Snap-On tool-chest, full of thousands of pounds' worth of tools, were nicked from Sam's place.

He'd bought a brand-new Suzuki GSX-R1000, and he gave me that as a replacement for the tool-box. It was worth less than the tools that went, but I didn't have much choice. We had sold the Suzuki I'd raced at the Southern 100, so Dad had his money back. Then the 600 that had been stolen was recovered, so I had two Suzukis: the new 2003 GSX-R1000 from Sam and my faithful old 600, but with no tools I felt as though my hands had been cut off. At the time they were just about everything I owned in the world.

At least now I was officially fit for the big Scarborough meeting, even if, in reality, I was still way off 100 per cent.

Like I said, I clicked with Scarborough straight away and I've always had a soft spot for the place. I'd already won the Cock o' the North on the GSX-R1000 earlier that season, but this was the big one, the Gold Cup.

The Team Racing crew came over and Dad and my little sister, Kate, were there too. Every time I got off the bike, after every practice or race, someone would have to pull my boot and sock off and yank up the leg of my leathers so I could dunk my ankle in a bucket of freezing cold water, just to try and ease the pain.

In 2003, Prince Philip handed out the trophies at the Gold Cup, and he gave the biggest one to me after I beat a field including Ian Lougher, Jason Griffiths and Ryan Farquhar. The last time they'd seen me I was skidding along on my arse towards a drystone wall on the Southern 100 course. This was the biggest win of my racing career to that point, and it was also the end of the road for me and Team Racing.

I only stayed with Sam Finley for one year. We didn't see eye to eye. His management style could be summed up like this: we either did things his way or no way. I had too many of my own ideas of how things should be done, from my time racing self-supported in England, to agree with everything. Sam also kept wanting to take me to the barbers to get my hair cut! But we get on a treat now. Both Sam and I know that if it wasn't for him things probably would have still worked out for me, but it would have taken a lot more effort on my part to get things to move along, so I'll always be grateful to him.

By this point I'd totally turned my back on the British National racing scene. I was racing and living in Ireland and loving it. Racers have to re-apply to their governing body for a licence every season, and I've had an Irish licence ever since. I won't go back to having a British ACU licence while there's a choice.

The atmosphere at races in the south, in the Republic, was slightly more laidback, though events in the north were hardly full-on. And in the south we'd race on a Sunday, where in the north the races were, and still are, always either mid-week evenings and Saturdays. No races are held in Northern Ireland on a Sunday for religious reasons.

I was once asked to tune an engine by Paul Cranston, a well-to-do Irishman who would always run around in a scruffy old van. He must have been 50-odd the last time I saw him, but was still racing all the Irish National meetings. When I collected the engine I was tuning for him, we discussed what he wanted doing and when he needed it finishing for. Then, just as I was strapping the motorbike engine in the back of my van, he took me by the elbow, led me to one side and just whispered, 'Do us a favour, don't work on that engine on a Sunday.' He looked me in the eye till I nodded that I understood. It was almost like he was half embarrassed to say it, but he had to. Some people take their Sundays very seriously in the north. Winston McAdoo, a well-known name to Irish and TT fans, ran race teams, with riders like Ryan Farquhar, Ian Hutchinson and Conor Cummins, and supported Michael Dunlop too, but he'd never let his bikes be raced on a Sunday, so anyone who wanted to race at Scarborough, or in the Republic, would need to do deals with two teams to have any kind of meaningful season. While I'm not religious in any way, I can admire commitment to principles like that.

For the 2004 season, I joined Uel Duncan's team. Uel was a fixture on the Irish roads scene. He had been paralysed, and was in a wheelchair, after a crash in 2000 during practice for the Ulster Grand Prix. Up until then he'd be a regular top six man on the roads, knocking on the door of the podium places, but often edged out by Archibald and the other top Irish racers of the time – Richard Britton and Darran Lindsay. I had never seen him race, but I had heard he was fast but a bit wild. He had loads of experience, which helped me. Specifics about gearing, lines on the road, how to take the jumps …

He always had a well-run team and was good at spotting talent. Cameron Donald raced for him, and so did Keith Amor and Les Shand.

The deal with Uel came about through Paul Phillips. Now Paul is one of the top men at the TT. He's employed by the Isle of Man government and has helped make it the financial success it's become in the last few years. He realised it wasn't living up to its potential and knew what to do about it. He made some decisions the old hands and the hardcore didn't always like, but no one can argue with the success he's brought.

Under Paul's direction the TT has also done a lot to try and make the race safer for riders and spectators. He made the organisation concentrate more on making sure riders coming to the TT are up to speed and know where they're going before the first night of practice. He's also worked more closely with the marshals. The TT can never be as safe as a track like Silverstone, but Paul and his team have done a lot, no doubt about it. Back, in 2003, he was a mad-keen race fan and ran a website called realroadsracing.com. I used have one of the website's stickers on my helmets. We were good mates, and he advised me to go to Uel Duncan's team, so I did and it was the right move.

Me and Martin Finnegan were the only racers at Paul Phillips's wedding, but more recently my relationship with Paul has gone pear-shaped. I still think the man is spot-on, and I've never had a bad word for him. I've had success outside the racing world, since the 2009 TT, off the back of North One Television and their coverage of the TT, so I don't know if Paul or his department think I owe the TT more than I think I do. They want me to turn up at all the press gatherings, but I don't want to because I don't enjoy them. I do press stuff that I think promotes the races I'm in, but I'm not a performing monkey, that's going to every TT press event. Simple as that.

A turning point for me, regarding the TT, was in the spring of 2011 when I was over in the Isle of Man for the press launch of that year's race. I was told to get up to the top of the Mountain for seven o' clock in the morning for a group photo with some other riders as the sun was rising. I got up early and cycled to the meeting point, but only the photographer, Stephen Davison, was there. All the other riders had been on the piss the night before and didn't bother getting out of bed. I waited for everyone to eventually turn up, did the photos, and then we were supposed to be at the bottom of the island to do another thing, but I thought, 'Fuck that. You kept me hanging about here, I've got other things to be doing.' That was the beginning of the end for me and the TT lot.

Then, in 2012, the TT press office said I was racing at the Classic TT, in August of the following year, when, as far as I was concerned, it hadn't yet been agreed that I could compete on the bike I wanted to race – we were still talking about it. Once something has been announced like that, if I decide I don't want to do it for any reason, it looks like me letting everyone down and turning my back on the TT and its fans, but this situation all came about because someone jumped the gun with a press release.

I didn't think they'd been straight with me, so instead of doing an hour on the TT stand at the Motorcycle Live show in 2012 at the NEC, I told them I'd do half an hour, on principle. Then it all got very personal. I felt people from the Isle of Man were claiming I'd said stuff that I hadn't. It's a shame it's gone like this. But they have more to worry about than me, and I have more going on than the TT.

None of that was an issue when I signed for Uel. No one knew who I was and I hadn't raced a TT.

Uel's team was sponsored by Robinson's Concrete, and when I joined the team, Johnny Ellis, who I had done my apprenticeship with at John Hebb's Volvo truck yard, moved over with me for the race season to be my mechanic. Johnny and I lived in a few different places, but for weeks, on and off, our home was the race truck, a big old Mercedes, parked at the concrete yard. Gareth Robinson's dog, Blade the Spaniel, came to live with us.

We'd knock off at six or seven o' clock and then we'd go out on Johnny's motocross bike that he brought over from home.

I'd have a go, but I always get the sound of ambulances ringing in my ears when I ride a motocrosser. We never went to the pub, but one of the team's sponsors enrolled us in a gym and we even went a couple of times. We'd potter about getting the bikes ready. Johnny is as anal as me when it comes to getting bikes right, so we'd spend nights just getting things as right as they could be.

From time to time we'd stay in a flat owned by one of the sponsors, if it wasn't being rented out. We thought we'd made it. When we were living in the truck I'd sleep on the bench seat in the van's kitchen, with the dog on top of me, and Johnny would be up on the bed in the Luton bit above the cab.

Johnny and I would maintain the fleet of concrete mixing lorries. All the money I earned I would give to Johnny to be my mechanic at the races. I raced my 1000-cc Suzuki, in Robinson's colours, Uel's 600 and Gareth Robinson's Superstock 1000, basically his road bike. All painted in red and blue.

My GSX-R1000 had been updated over the close season. It had a Spondon swinging arm in it, and my Uncle Rodders, who isn't really my uncle but is my dad's cousin, cast me a subframe to hold the seat and move my body position more over the handlebars.

The other big change for 2004 was the fact that I was out of the Support Class and into the main feature races with the cream of the world's road racers.

I'd obviously watched the likes of Farquhar, Lindsay, Archibald, Finnegan and Britton race. I'd even beaten a few of them the odd time at Scarborough and the Southern 100, but to be racing them on tracks they'd grown up on was another massive eye-opener. I'd been around them and racing on the roads for a year, but I didn't realise just how hard those boys were riding. It was an education.

I hear it all the time, from people who think they know what they're on about, but don't have the first clue, that road racers aren't pushing as hard as short circuit racers. They say stuff like they're only riding at 90 per cent, but they really don't know what they're talking about. The lads that are winning the big races in Ireland are pressing on, riding as hard as is humanly possible without crashing. They might not be leaning over as far as a MotoGP rider, but that's because a road covered in cowshit with a huge dip in the middle of it doesn't have the same level of grip as a GP circuit. Those boys were, and still are, hanging their balls out to win. If they don't, some other hungry young bastard who thinks he is invincible will cut them up and leave them in the dust. And those fellas were racing to feed their families. Especially a rider like Farquhar – this was his job. For much of his career, Ryan didn't have a plan B or a big sponsor to cover costs if he had a few bad meetings. He was racing for prize money, as his family's breadwinner. He wasn't handing wins to any bugger.

After winning a lot of races in the Support Class, I struggled for much of 2005, my second season with Uel. It was tough going in the National Class. Farquhar, Archibald and Britton were doing the winning. I was a top six man, if that. I was loving it, but I was out of my comfort zone. It was a hell of a step up from the Support Class. I knew it was going to be tough, and I never imagined I was going to be at the front, but by the end of the season I surprised myself by how much I'd come on. I had learnt a lot from the other riders. I learnt just how hard I had to push to stay in touch. I thought I was pushing hard before, but no. I was always strong on the brakes, but the top men would be berming kerbs and hedgerows, dust flying off their elbows and knees, and they would be hitting jumps much faster than I was before. It was bareknuckle stuff.

The bikes would be getting so out of shape, but you couldn't back off if you wanted to have a hope of winning. We would race every bit as hard as the British Superbike racers would at Brands Hatch or Donington, but the bike didn't know where it was going because the roads were so rough.

The other thing that meant a lot to me was the Irish fans. They would appreciate that I was over from England, committed to racing in Ireland and trying to make a go of it. Joe Coleman and Will and Rosemary Graham, racing enthusiasts from up near Cookstown in Northern Ireland, used to give me sixty or eighty quid every other meeting just to help lighten the load. And they weren't squillionaires, but any stretch, just good folk who loved their racing. Me and Johnny were living on breakfast cereal or, if we were flush, the odd microwave meal we could cook in the truck, and we would go to the Grahams for a feed. We couldn't wait to get round there. We were fed and watered like kings. Joe Coleman was their next-door neighbour and we'd go there too.

When it came time to race, our truck, that was our home for much of the time between the races, would be loaded up with bikes. Then we'd leave on a series of little road trips. We had no insurance, no MoT and no tax. We'd been given red diesel and did not give a damn about any of it. We would drive this dodgy truck all the way to Scarborough and back like that, never worrying about what might happen if we got pulled over, and surviving because we never did.

It was like the student life Johnny and I never had, because we'd become apprentices straight from school and stayed living at home. But it was better than being a student, because we didn't have to go to university, we were getting paid and racing bikes. It was the whole carefree feel of being between adolescence and proper adulthood – with all the bills and worries that come with that – that made it so special. And we were doing what we loved.

Johnny has said he looks back on those days as the time of his life, because it was just so simple. We had nothing to worry about and we were on this adventure.

I managed to get an entry into the 2004 Isle of Man TT without having to miss another year and cut my teeth at the Manx Grand Prix. Back then, the TT used to want riders to race at a Manx Grand Prix first, but that wasn't a hard and fast rule, just a recommendation. And I was ready for the TT.

Me and Johnny drove to the Isle of Man straight from racing at the North West 200. Since then there has nearly always been a week of work between leaving the North West and travelling to the TT for the first evening of practice, but that year the Jurby roads meeting was being held in the North of the Isle of Man and I had an entry.

There was drama before we even got to the ferry. We were driving to Belfast from Londonderry in the race truck that was fully loaded with everything except a tax disc, when we came to Glenshane Hill. This hill was so steep, and the truck so heavy, I had to brake going down it or the revs got too high for the diesel engine. For some reason I thought it would be clever to knock it out of gear and coast down, ticking over in neutral. The next thing, Boom! A tyre has blown out and ripped part of the bottom of the truck out. Luckily the only two people on board were both truck fitters, so we got stuck in. Uel sent a spare tyre and we got it fixed, slept on the docks and arrived at the Isle of Man a day later than expected, but still in time for the start of practice.

The Jurby meeting is a race that's hardly known even among road racing fans, but I remember it as being a big breakthrough for me. The track, near the village of Jurby in the north of the island, is wide, but it's probably the roughest racetrack any racer of my generation will ever compete on.

During practice I couldn't hold on to the bike as the handlebars were trying to jump out of my hands, and I was thinking, 'If I can't cope with this, how will I manage in the TT?'

Luckily the practice sessions were long enough for me to try a few things with the bike. I worked out that the bumps were coming so fast that the suspension hadn't recovered from one pounding before it had to deal with another. This meant the forks and rear shock were getting backed up.

When you're working for a high-level team, like TAS Suzuki, you'll have a suspension man from one of the suppliers – Öhlins, Showa or K-Tech – working with you, and it's they who change the front or rear springs, the shims that let the oil flow past or the oil level. There are a thousand different variables. Some alterations require the forks or shock to be stripped to change them. I tell them what the bike is doing, then stand back and the mechanics are on it, changing the forks and rear shock in minutes. But there are smaller, but still very significant changes, that can be made with a spanner and a screwdriver. And this is what I set about doing between the practice sessions at Jurby.

Not having a crew of experts, I had to work it out for myself that backing off the rebound damping might help. In very basic terms the front and rear suspension of a racing motorcycle is provided by springs that have their rate of compression and rebound damped by pistons moving through oil. If you didn't have the piston and oil, the bike would bounce along like a pogo stick. When the bike wheel hits a bump the springs compress. By adjusting the compression damping you can set how quickly it compresses. With loads of compression damping the spring compresses very slow and therefore feels firm. A lot less compression damping and the suspension feels softer and spongier.

Rebound damping controls how quickly the spring returns to the length it was before it hit the bump. If you push down on the seat or tank of a bike set up for a smooth short circuit (or a standard road bike) and compress its suspension, when you let go the bike comes up in a slow and controlled way. You do it on my TT bike and it rebounds a lot faster, almost at the rate of the spring, with next to no damping.

The problem I had at Jurby was the frequency of the bumps, and the amount of rebound damping I had was causing the suspension to bottom out. There was no more movement to be had and the bike became close to unrideable. The suspension was no longer moving to keep the tyres tracking the road. Instead, it was just bouncing off it. Do that when you're leant over going through a 100 mph plus corner and you can imagine what might happen next.

When I wound the rebound completely off, so that after dealing with a bump the springs were as close as they were ever going to be to a pogo stick, the bike was transformed. The suspension would hit a bump and the damping would control the speed at which the spring would compress, but it would return to full length extremely quickly, with very little control, to be ready to deal with the next impact. Then the bike handled OK and I won the big race of the meeting and started thinking about the TT.

One of the Uel Duncan team sponsors that year had a house on the Isle of Man and he wanted it painting. He paid me a tenner an hour and it took me two weeks. It's on Bray Hill and I regularly look at it when I pass. I still try to line up a job like this when I'm over for the TT now. It stops me getting bored, and I can paint a wall while thinking through the race or a problem with the bike. Or I can just let my mind wander.

For that 2004 TT, John McGuinness was the main man. He'd taken over that position from his good mate, David Jefferies, who had died after crashing in practice the previous year. McGuinness would become the leading TT racer of my generation. He was the man to beat, on the Superbikes at least – the races I always thought were the big prizes – that year and every other year I turned up to the TT. Of course, there were other great TT riders through all those years, the New Zealander Bruce Anstey for one, but it was always the big fella from Morecambe who I knew I had to beat to win a TT on the big bikes.

McGuinness has the ability to always look like he's riding to the shops, even when he's on lap record pace. He also looks, especially now, like he could do with a couple of passes through the bacon slicer, but he proves you don't have to be someone's idea of a stereotypical gym-addicted motorbike racer to be fast. I think I wind him up, without even trying, but I don't mean to. I have massive respect for the man.

People have asked me if the death of the leading man and lap record holder, David Jefferies, affected the way I approached the TT. They wonder if I had thoughts like, 'Well, if the very best around here can get it wrong and be killed, what chance do I have?' But thoughts like that never entered my head. I don't know if anyone was killed in my first year there. If they were it can't have affected me, because I don't remember it. I'm not being heartless, it's just the way I approach it. I'm not trying to deal with the death or crashes in any particular way, it's just how I naturally react. I can't pretty it up.

I was nervous of the task ahead, but not scared. I'd done massive amounts of preparation. In a weird way I think I knew the track better then than I do now. I knew the place inside out, from watching Duke videos of other racers' onboard laps religiously to see what lines they took.

I was doing five laps of practice every night and that helped me go so fast, so soon. Because the way they've changed things at the TT, no one gets five laps of practice in a single session now.

My main mechanic was Johnny, and my dad was there too. Mates from Lincolnshire, Benny and Dean came over as well. I'd sleep in the back of the truck while the other lads would be out on the beer and then top and tail in the beds in the front of the truck, like sardines in a tin.

One of them lost their key to get in the side door, so they were trampling over me in the back, sometimes with a bird in tow, pissed as handcarts at silly o' clock in the morning. I wouldn't be annoyed. It made me laugh. I miss that kind of thing, to be honest.

My sister, Sally, also came over to watch. As soon as she got off the ferry she went up to Signpost Corner, on the outskirts of Douglas, and her first sight of me was braking like mad and overshooting the corner right in front of her. The friends who had come with her used to tease Sally, because she'd sit for the whole race with fingers on both her hands crossed.

Despite that, I started the week well, coming 12th in the Superbike race from 24th on the grid. My first TT.

I wasn't like some of the newcomers who race now. Lads are racing at the TT who have never raced on the roads; they've done all their racing on short circuits. They might have done the North West 200 a couple of weeks before, but that doesn't prepare you for the TT. I was nervous, but not over-awed by any of it.

I had a couple of DNFs. I broke down in the Production 1000 – that is now the Superstock – because we didn't put enough petrol in the bike. That year there were two 600 races, like there are now, but one was the Production 600, while the other was called the Junior (though there were no age restrictions – the name was a hangover from history). The Junior had the same rules as the current Supersport 600, so we had to change the engine between the two races. In one of the races the tilt switch, that stops the engine when the bike falls over, was faulty and kept cutting out every time I braked into a corner. We had a faulty switch in practice and changed it for a brand-new one – which turned out to have exactly the same internal fault.

In the Senior I started in position 29 and finished seventh after doing a massive amount of overtaking, compared to what the front runners have to do. Setting off at ten-second intervals, if you're faster than those in front you're catching them and overtaking them. Dealing with that is a skill in itself. If you don't overtake them soon, your pace drops to theirs and it's a struggle to raise it again. That's happened to me. You have to be ruthless, but you don't want to cause a problem.

I was racing a 600, a Superstock and a 1000-cc Superbike. Road racers are different to World or British Superbike riders or modern grand prix racers. Those fellas ride one bike all year, spending their practice sessions tweaking it in the tiniest ways to make it the least compromised it can possibly be. Real roads guys are racing three or more different bikes in a single day.

At many race meetings now I'll race a Superbike, with over 210 bhp, running on slick tyres. I'll also race a Superstock 1000 on treaded tyres and the Supersport 600, a really trick bit of kit, with fancy ignition, but much less power and weight than the 1000-cc Superbike, meaning it needs a very different riding style. The Supersport 600 – that all of us in the team refer to as 'the little bike' – runs on treaded, road legal tyres, not slicks.

Some of the other real roads riders will also compete on a Supertwin – the 650-cc, two-cylinder racers, like Suzuki SV650s or Kawasaki ER-6s – or 125s, little two-strokes.

During that first TT, I had a big moment. I was on the straight before Glentramman, one that doesn't really have a name, and hit the kerb. It's a straight, but the bike got into a bit of a tankslapper. This is where the motorcycle is going more or less in a straight line, but the front wheel is shaking violently from one side to the other. It's called a tankslapper because when the wheel goes from side to side, so are the handlebars you're hanging on to, and they whack your arms against the petrol tank. Sometimes a tankslapper is so vicious it won't straighten out before the next corner and you've had it. The bike obviously won't steer when the front wheel is going mental. Other times you can loosen your grip on the handlebars and the gyroscopic forces of the spinning front wheel will bring it back in line. Little tankslappers are nothing unusual at the TT.

Where this one happened was a section taken flat-out in sixth gear, as fast as the bike will go. Normally, I'd be right in the middle of the road, but because the bike had got a bit lively, and out of my hands, it had sent me off line and I was in the gutter, tyre hard against the kerb – but the next thing I know I'm back on line, going in the right direction, full on the throttle, wondering how I'd got away with it.

I just thought, 'Hell, that was amazing!' I thought it was ace. From that moment I went even harder. It was the buzz of that near miss, of being so, so close to disaster, to be risking the whole lot, but getting away with it, that I've been chasing ever since.

CHAPTER 8

GETTING NOTICED

'Perhaps I needed to be called a See You Next Tuesday and told to get my finger out of my arse and get on with it.'

AFTER THE SENIOR, the main race and the last of the TT fortnight, I finished seventh and sat in the holding area, next to my bike – and it was *my* bike. Johnny and my dad had pitted for me all week and mates had given me a hand, but I'd done the engine, and it never missed a beat for the whole fortnight. I can't remember who won the race, it was all about who finished seventh as far as I was concerned. It was a massive point in my life.

I think about that TT a lot. I was fastest newcomer, even though I hadn't gained experience by racing at the Manx. I was on a bike I'd tuned and developed with the help of my dad and Uncle Rodders. The feeling of satisfaction I got from that TT has hardly ever been equalled in my road racing career.

I had done a 123-mph lap at a time when McGuinness upped the outright lap record to 127.68 mph – and I remember coming back and thinking, for a whole year, 'Hell, I can't go any harder. I can perhaps brake a little bit later here or there.'

It took me a while to realise I was still thinking with a short circuit mentality. I'd used that on the Irish National circuits and it worked, because you're in a mass start race and braking so hard for the road-end corners on a short lap. It was all about getting into these first and second gear corners hard and getting out of them fast for the high-speed straight between them. The TT is not about how late you can brake and how quickly you can get back on the throttle after a corner's apex. The technique for the TT, and the Dundrod circuit, the home of the Ulster GP, is all about getting on the brake a bit earlier, letting go of it sooner and carrying the momentum. It's a different way of racing a motorbike.

During those two years with Uel and Robinson's Concrete, from the middle of May to the end of the season, I was racing almost every weekend and I was loving it.

I had started to win in the big class too. I won at Dundalk and Killalane. I did well at the 2005 Southern 100, but came in second behind Lougher.

That Southern 100 is my favourite race meeting of any year, and that particular one was probably my favourite meeting ever. Johnny and Ivan Linton, who is now a road racer, but wasn't back then, came with me. We got over there really early on a Monday morning and drove straight to the Sound, right at the bottom of the Isle of Man, where the Calf of Man is, and had a kip on some benches. I was woken up by an old grannie prodding me with her walking stick because she wanted to sit down.

In that week's feature race, I was racing my GSX-R1000 K5

that wasn't quite as fast as Lougher's Fireblade. I'd lead for a couple of laps, but then he'd come by and I'd be scratching my nuts off to keep with him. I've always liked Lougher. The Welshman was a veteran when I first started racing on the roads and was still going ten years later. He showed me, at my first TT, just how quick the top lads were. It was Lougher who I said was going so fast he was sucking rabbits out of the hedges, a description that became a slogan printed on Red Torpedo T-shirts.

It still felt like a carefree time, and my second TT is the one I look back on as my best ever, all things taken into account. My results were better in 2007, when I was on the podium four times, but balancing the resources and experience against the results, the race two years earlier felt more satisfying.

It didn't start well. My Superbike had blown up at the North West. Uncle Rodders had made a fancy tank breather for it, and everyone else in the paddock probably thought it was my preparation and tuning, but it was a common fault with the Suzuki that year, the piston to bore clearance was too tight, and two hours after mine went, Darran Lindsay's did too.

The week between the North West and the start of TT practice was a panic. I ordered the parts from Crescent Suzuki and had the crank sent to Mehew's for him to balance. There's nothing wrong with how the crank comes from Suzuki if you're only putting it in the road bike, but for racing you want to get them balanced, so they run smoother. We were so tight on time we had to leave for the Isle of Man and have Mehew send it by courier to follow us over.

My dad was out with me helping for the fortnight, and we were building the engine and bolting it in the frame, late in the night before the first practice. We were filing con-rods, making sure everything fitted just right, but it meant we had no time to run the bike in.

I must have got away fairly early in the first session, because Archibald, one of the favourites, came past me. He had seen my bike leaking some oil and pulled up at a marshal post for them to put the message out on the radio to black flag me and make me stop. He ruined his lap to make sure everyone kept safe – I don't think many racers would do that.

I stopped at Ballaugh, and it turned out to be just a sprocket oil seal, another common problem for that model Suzuki.

Archibald had helped me before, lending me a helmet when mine failed scrutineering because of a stone chip, before a race at Kells, in Ireland.

The rest of practice week went all right, and that half-decent form led into the races. I started 2005's TT race week with a sixth in the Superbike, then followed up with fifth in the Superstock 1000. I scored another fifth in the first Junior 600 race, then bettered it by one place in the second 600 race. I'd been in the top six all week. I was starting from 15th position on the road, a fair measure of where I was in the pecking order before the week had started. The top men were Britton, Finnegan, Farquhar, Lougher, Archibald, Anstey, McGuinness … Hutchinson was racing, too.

In the final race of the TT, the Senior, I came third from a starting position of 15. McGuinness won, Lougher was second. It was my first TT podium, and my mates Finnegan and Britton, riders with more TT experience, came just behind me.

I must have gone to the press conference, but I can't remember anything about it. I remember plenty about the race, but not much after it. It's not so much a blur as a black hole.

It wasn't my intention, but I was doing enough to be noticed by other teams. Still, the TT didn't have the level of interest it has now. Back then race meetings had a different, more relaxed feel for me. Only road race fans had heard of more than one or two TT riders, and a lot of people in mainstream motorcycling thought that the Isle of Man TT should celebrate its centenary, that would come round in 2007, then stop. The ones who were writing and saying stuff like this would describe the TT as dangerously out of date, adding that it couldn't consider itself to be a sport when so many people had died while competing there. They viewed the TT as an event that was decades from its golden era and they couldn't see it ever recapturing any of its former glory. I didn't give a damn about these opinions. I loved racing there and couldn't really see it stopping any time soon.

AIM Racing approached me at the end of 2005, through a race mechanic called Dwayne McCracken. He told me they were dead interested in me joining the team. AIM was funded by the businessman Alastair Flanagan. His company, Elec-Track Installations, put the electrical systems in the Eurotunnel, worked with Network Rail and was worth squillions when Flanagan sold it.

Flanagan was in his early fifties and had a broad Scottish accent. There must have been a bit of Glaswegian in him, because he always sounded to me like he wanted a fight. He was very into his motorbikes without knowing too much about them, but he didn't need to know a lot, because that's what he paid experts for. He financed race teams for a few years, but doesn't now.

Before AIM, Flanagan had bankrolled the ETI Ducati team in British Superbikes, but this was a different set-up with different mechanics and managers. The team was run by Steve Mellor, who had been one half of V&M, a very successful, Rochdale-based tuning and race team firm started by Steve Mellor and Jack Valentine. They'd had TT wins with David Jefferies and John McGuinness, but the pair had split to run their own projects. It was Mellor's involvement that attracted me to the team. He was a clever bloke when it came to engines. The work he did on the inside of an engine wasn't as tidy-looking as Mehew's, but his bikes always went like shit off a shovel. AIM didn't have direct factory support, but being the main Yamaha team on the roads meant they might have got their bikes a bit earlier to start building them.

I met Alastair at a BSB round. Once I'd agreed that I'd race for them they put a contract in front of me. At that time I didn't really know riders got paid for racing, not at the level I was competing at anyway – I was still an up-and-comer on the roads – so I was confused when I saw the numbers for a while. I was trying to count the noughts. I didn't know if it was £15,000 or £150,000. In the end, I saw it was £15,000 and I still couldn't believe it.

Everything was geared up to make a good showing at the TT that year, but it didn't happen. AIM's Yamaha R1 Superbike had an oil leak that the team just couldn't get to the bottom of. It caused me to pull out of the Superbike race. They thought they'd cured it, so I would go out, and it would do it again. In the end, too late to salvage that TT, they discovered it was something to do with the engine breather. Pressurised oil was being blown into this fancy collector thing, and it was the collector that was leaking. It dripped oil down a gasket line on the engine, so it looked like a failing gasket. The oil mist would then blow back onto one of my feet.

I would notice oil on the boot, because my foot would start slipping off the footpeg. Once that happens you might as well put the bike back in the van. If you've got oil on your boot, it could be leaking onto the tyre too. With that to contend with, I was just making up the numbers. I was sleeping in the race truck that year, and at the end of the Senior, the last race, I parked the bike, got off without saying a word and just climbed in the back of the truck. My back had gone, because I wasn't able to take the load on my legs, so I was straining my back just to finish the race.

During the TT fortnight, a week of practice followed by a week of racing, I can wear through the soles of a pair of race boots, just with the pressure of pressing down on the knurled alloy footpegs to help control and steer the bike. I'll wear out a pair of handlebar grips on each bike too. After the end of this race I could hardly walk. I had a DNF in the first Superbike race, was fourth in the Superstock and finished fifth in the Senior. Which, in my ambitious mind, was shit.

I was disappointed because this was a team that had won TTs. They had bloody Steve Mellor in charge, an absolute legend, but they couldn't get to the bottom of an oil leak.

The rest of the year went better. I won the 600 race at the Southern 100 and then won four out of five races at the Ulster – a very high point of my racing life. When you're lining up for five races in a day, you have five minutes between each race. I wasn't clued up on the eating and drinking back then, the whole nutrition side of things, like I am now. I'd have a quick cup of tea and a burger from a van or something.

The Ulster was the icing on a shit cake. As a stand-alone race, it didn't matter what went on before or after. I was very happy with it and still am.

I also won the Scarborough Gold Cup, the fourth back-to-back at that event. I did a few British Supersport rounds for the AIM team, too, because the lad who was riding for them, Chris Burns, had crocked himself. It meant I rode Cadwell the weekend after the Ulster.

I nearly stayed with AIM Yamaha for another season. They were making a big push to go with Pirelli tyres. In the autumn of 2006 Flanagan, the team owner, invited me, Steve Mellor and Jason Griffiths, who had by then retired from road racing and was Pirelli's man on the road racing side of things, up to his mansion to try work out a deal for the following season. They were saying all the right things, but I was struggling to forget all the shit we'd been through at the TT and the failure to find what was just a daft oil leak.

By this time Shaun Muir had been on to me. Back then his Hydrex-sponsored Shaun Muir Racing (SMR) team didn't have much of a reputation. They were a small outfit and had never raced on the roads. Apparently, what got him thinking about signing me was seeing me turn up to Cadwell in the Porsche GT3 RS I had at the time. If I saw myself do that, I'd think, 'What a cocky arsehole.' But seeing a 23-year-old driving a £70,000 car got Shaun wondering, 'How the hell has he got that? He must be good at riding a bike to be able to afford a new GT3.'

I like fast cars and I had sunk all my money into it. I was still living at home, or at the Lancasters' farm, with my girlfriend, Kate, so I didn't have a mortgage. The money came from a lot of overtime and race winnings. Whatever, the car got Shaun's gears turning.

I raced for AIM in Macau at the end of 2006, where Shaun's team would make their road racing debut. They didn't paint a very good picture of themselves. SMR didn't work out, till the morning of the race, that their petrol tanks couldn't hold enough fuel to complete the race. Shaun had Martin Finnegan and James McBride racing for him and they set off with nowhere near enough petrol on board. It's a long race, and a lot of it is flat-out, so you burn plenty of petrol. The SMR team had only been doing BSB races, where you could get away with a 20-litre tank. At Macau only 24 litres would do it.

And I still ended up riding for them!

Shaun Muir is a former British Superbikes level racer. He's a straight-talking bloke, and I like that. He was a really good motocrosser who went short circuit racing. I'm sure he would admit that he got as far as his skill allowed, and that wasn't to the top in Britain. He was clever enough not to flog it to death, and moved into owning and running a team, not riding for one, and his results speak for themselves – he runs one of the best teams in the country now. He half understood what makes me tick too, which is a lot more than most people. He was fit for his age, because he did a lot of cycling, and was probably in his mid-forties when I started racing for him.

When he was younger, he worked on the North Sea oil rigs as an engineer, and earned a decent wage, because he was a grafter. He'd then invest the money in houses and rent them out.

Shaun's dad was one of the bosses of a big company of steel erectors in the north-east, called Booth & Partners. When his dad was ready to retire he gave his shares to Shaun's brother. Shaun explained to his dad he would've liked to be involved, but was told that because he was doing so well on the rigs he could look after himself. The way I heard it, Shaun then raised the money to buy out all the co-owners and became the sole boss of Booth & Partners. Shaun also set up a corporate hospitality business that works in British Superbikes and provides the official hospitality at the TT. He owns a pub too, and still runs his race team.

I liked Shaun's enthusiasm. He'd just been joined by Mick Shanley as chief mechanic, the man who would oversee all the technical side of things for SMR. Shanley had just come from spannering for a grand prix team, and that impressed me. I liked his enthusiasm and knowledge too. I had struggled to forgive the AIM Yamaha team for the TT failure, and I didn't have many other options, so I signed for Shaun to ride his Hydrex Hondas. He was offering me the same money, but it was the commitment they said they were going to give that hooked me.

The first year with Shaun was mega. I was on the white Hondas which had on the side the big red logo of Hydrex, a company in the railway engineering industry. We went to the North West 200 and found the Supersport bike wasn't quick enough, but I was on the new model of Honda CBR600, that had just been launched, and it sometimes takes time to develop a brand-new bike to get the most out of it. I qualified on pole in the 600 race, but I got smoked by Anstey on the Suzuki, Hutchinson on the Kawasaki and more besides. The race was televised, and it was plain to see, from the helicopter footage, that they were pulling away from me on the straight run down to University Corner, a section where I should have easily been able to stay in the slipstream of the other bikes. That section is nothing to do with skill, or how well you get out of the previous corner, not that either of those riders are lacking in skill or balls. In that part of the track it's purely down to horsepower. And the Hydrex Honda 600 was down on it. I knew we couldn't go to the TT with it like that, so I talked the team into allowing me to tune the cylinder head.

When it came to the TT the 600 felt better, and though I didn't win, coming third in the 600 race behind Hutchie and McGuinness, six seconds covering all three of us, I broke the Supersport 600 lap record. And with an engine I'd tuned and built myself.

The Superstock bike ran out of fuel near Ramsey, a long way back from the finish line. Something had shorted out, or a fault had come up on the electronics side of things, so the ECU – the Engine Control Unit, the bike's electronic brain – had put the engine into a safe mode, feeding more fuel, making it run stupidly rich, to try and protect it from a problem it wasn't even having. The fuel light came on at Ginger Hall, meaning I had five miles of petrol to cover 17 miles of track.

That year, 2007, Ian Hutchinson was on the factory-supported HM Plant Honda. He was setting off sixth, I was eighth. I caught him on the road in both the Superbike and the Senior, and he put out his leg for me to pass him. You can hear a bike coming behind you, or sometimes you get a glimpse of shadow depending on where the sun is.

I didn't have a very high opinion of him back then. He'd been going out with my younger sister Kate, and he was much older than her. I wasn't being protective towards her, but I didn't think it was right. He was very fair on the track in those Superbike races, though, and he's proved to be a great TT racer.

I came second in the big races, both times to McGuinness. I didn't have the beating of him, but felt I was still learning, and I wasn't far off. That season would be the last year I would be using Dunlop tyres, for good or ill. The next year I was riding on Pirelli, and mainly because of their man, Jason Griffiths.

All season Buckle and Wozza were my main mechanics, with Shanley over them. Wozza is a good old boy. In his forties, he's been about the racing scene for ages and still is. He has loads of experience and is a really nice bloke. Perhaps he was a bit too nice. At times, if I was struggling with set-up, I'd be saying we could try this and try that, and he'd agree with me, when perhaps I needed to be called a See You Next Tuesday and told to just live with the bike misbehaving a bit, get my finger out of my arse and get on with it. But it's a fine line, because when chief mechanics do that and I know I'm right it causes friction and we get nowhere fast.

Buckle was the spanner man below Wozza. Another Lincolnshire man, a good mechanic, a keen cyclocross rider and the brother of a very good 250-cc bike racer. Buckle lived in a caravan in his parents' yard and loved microlights. He'd shag the world if it let him. But it never did. A nice lad, but perhaps not the most reliable, I'd discover.

Towards the end of the year, I raced at Brands Hatch for Russell Benney's Phase One Endurance team. This wasn't an endurance race, just a British Superbike round that Phase One had entered because Russell was courting some sponsors.

Russell had built up his endurance team and ran it with highly skilled volunteers, not full-time paid mechanics. Still, they'd been world champions. I liked him a lot. He worked in a nuclear power station and once explained to me why tea tastes better if you put the milk in before the water. It's a theory that would help change my life a few years later.

At Brands Hatch, just before I went out to race, Russell told me to go steady because the bike had an important race coming up, in the World Endurance Championship that was their main focus. He added they didn't have the time, money or inclination to rebuild it if I slid off. That's not what any racer wants to hear before they go out. Racing is pretty pointless if you're told to go steady. Anyway, I brought the bike back in one piece and Russell must have been happy enough with what I did, because he offered me the chance to do some World Endurance rounds with him the next year, something I was dead keen to try.

Shaun knew I'd ridden for Phase One. I wasn't hiding the fact – I couldn't have, even if I'd tried. I told him about the offer Russell had made and he said, 'Fine, get cracking if that's what you want, but you won't have a bike to race at the TT.' He wasn't interested in the kind of loose arrangement that I was toying with: a bit of Endurance, a good go at the roads. Instead, Shaun made an alternative offer that was for another proper go at the International road races plus a full season in British Superbikes on the Fireblade Superbike. It sounded like a great opportunity.

After that had all been aired, it was just a matter of the last race of the 2007 season, a trip out to the Macau Grand Prix, the exotic and often incident-filled race off the coast of China. I just wish the incident it was filled with didn't involve me so often.

CHAPTER 9

MAC-OW

'When I woke up in hospital I thought I'd be like a dog trying to explain to a vet that it needed its appendix out.'

THE MACAU RACE calls itself a Grand Prix, but it's never had Formula One or FIM motorcycle world title status. It's a big deal for some of the Formula classes that feed into F1 – like Formula Three – and some of the great F1 drivers have won at Macau on their way up. It is a World Championship round for World Touring Cars as well.

From the motorcycle side of things, Macau is regularly referred to as a 'holiday race'. And the motorcycles definitely play second fiddle to the cars. They are there to pad out the race programme and give the few spectators who do go something to watch.

Teams are given a budget to take out bikes, mechanics and riders, and there is the opportunity for a cheap holiday in Thailand at the end of it. The majority of the teams are those involved with British real road racing, but there are also competitors from Germany, Portugal and the USA, and locals from China, Macau and Hong Kong. I'd first read about the place when Gus Scott and Ronnie Smith, two racers who were also test riders and writers for *Performance Bikes* magazine, used to go out and get up to all sorts.

Macau is to Portugal what Hong Kong is to the UK. They're both islands off the coast of China and were colonies before being handed over at the end of the last millennium. Macau is also the Las Vegas of Asia. The Chinese are well known for their love of gambling, and casinos on Macau take much more than those in the USA's gambling capital.

Macau was my first race outside the UK, but my trips there tend to be memorable for all the wrong reasons.

The Macau Grand Prix always takes place in November, and my first visit was at the end of 2005. I raced Billy Baron's Superstock 1000, a bike I'd been using in the Robinson's Concrete colours. Billy was a lovely older fella who was in the haulage business in Northern Ireland and one of Uel's sponsors.

I soon discovered the timetable at Macau is very relaxed. There's lots of time to kill and not a lot to do, so that first year I decided to have a massage. I chose the spa on the second floor of the hotel where the race organisers were putting me up. I'd seen lots of racers and mechanics going into the spa. It must have been popular, because the button in the lift for that floor was worn out, the number two completely rubbed off.

The receptionist pointed at a menu of what the spa offered, but the English translations were terrible, so I didn't bother reading it and just went for one that wasn't the cheapest or the most expensive. Then I was given a gold dressing gown to change into. I went and did that, then came back and sat down, with my pile of clothes and trainers on my lap, until a lady masseuse appeared and took me to a room.

When I race now, there is often an independent sports physio in the paddock, who goes around with a fold-out table, giving riders massages between practice and the race. At an endurance race, like the Le Mans 24-Hour, teams employ their own masseurs to give mega rubdowns between the 50-minute sessions of racing. I like these massages. They make a difference, but back then I was just killing time. It was going to be the first massage I'd ever had.

I did what I was told, in pidgin English. I put a towel around myself, hung up the bath robe and lay, face down, on the table. Even though this was my first massage it was all going as I imagined. I then rolled over onto my back, careful not to lose my towel, when – Woah, woah, woah, Nelly!

It seems I had chosen a rub-down with extras. Looking back now, and thinking about the worn-out button in the lift, perhaps everything on the menu had extras. I was so naïve, it hadn't occurred to me. I might have been the only westerner on the island who genuinely thought he was going for just a massage.

Macau is a track of two halves. One half of the lap, after Lisboa, is mainly first to third gear stuff, tight and twisty. The rest is as wide as the M1.

The first corner, Reservoir, is not far off flat-out. It's a shallow left-hander and a big balls corner. You go from sixth gear to fifth for the next corner, Mandarin, another man's corner, the fastest bend on the track. Then it's back up to sixth and wringing the bike's neck all the way to the bottom gear, 90-degree right at Lisboa. That's the corner you do a lot of your passing going into, out-braking the rider in front. Shift up into third gear, before going into a right and climbing San Francisco Hill. There are a few little kinks, while you're accelerating and shifting up to fourth gear before the Hospital Bridge and Maternity Bend. You shift back to third and hold it. I just roll the throttle on and off, not really braking hard, and remaining in third all through this back section, including the Solitude Esses.

Next, the track goes down Faraway Hill, then climbs again up Moorish Hill. The famous photos by Irish photographer Stephen Davison of riders scuffing their shoulders were taken through this back section. I've rubbed my shoulder on the concrete and steel Armco barriers a couple of times, but never purposely. All it would take is a little screw sticking out of the wall or the Armco to catch you and pull you off the bike.

It's back to second gear for the right at the top of Moorish, then it's into Donna Maria Bend, a really steeply cambered left-hander, that comes back on itself. A quick blip of the throttle and then round the Melco Hairpin. The hairpins are tight at Oliver's Mount, Scarborough, but not as tight as this. If you don't get the line right you can't get around, because the handlebars of a race bike don't turn enough, there just isn't enough steering lock to make it around. If you try to dive up the inside of someone here, you can't make it around the corner.

From the Melco Hairpin you're driving really hard downhill to sea level. There's a little right kink and the bike is unsettled as it's accelerating down the slope, the back wheel fighting for grip.

This is where the track turns from tight and twisty in among the buildings to very wide and flat-out by the harbour. You take the second gear Fisherman's Bend, and then you're onto a straight that's as wide as a motorway. You don't get a good impression of speed here, because the fences and walls at the side are so far away. Up to fifth for the straight run before clicking back to second for the R bends, then you're back to the start–finish line.

After the massage with the unexpected ending, the 2005 race

that followed a day later was also memorable for a strange reason. I couldn't get on with the bike. I thought it was me, struggling to read the track, but that was odd, because I had become good at learning tracks quickly. I can go to a new circuit, get to grips with it and often be competitive in the races on my very first visit, but I just couldn't get on the pace at Macau.

The lad who rode the Billy Baron bike the following season was Les Shand, a Scottish road racer who knows what he's doing. He struggled with the Suzuki and decided to investigate what was up with it. It turned out that the bike's frame was bent, and it had been bent when I raced it at Macau. When I was told that, I remembered that before the bike had been shipped out to the Far East I had come off it at the end of Park Straight at Cadwell in a British Superstock race. This was the site of the bomb scene crash in my first race, back in 1999, and like then, the bike I'd just lost control of went end over end. Johnny and I patched it up and I raced later in the same day at Cadwell, but came nowhere. After the race we had to quickly mend it, then delivered it to be shipped out to Macau. In the rush to have it ready we can't have had a very close look at the bike.

The next year I raced at Macau for AIM in 2006, but I wasn't in the best physical shape. And this time it was due to a self-inflicted wound suffered before I arrived.

My mate Jonty Moore would always have a Guy Fawkes Night bonfire on his farm not far from Kirmington. Towards the end of the night, when the kids had gone home, more boxes of fireworks would appear and people would start playing with them. It was at the time when *Jackass* was really popular, and we'd come up with daft stuff to do.

Jonty also had these huge tyres, called flotation tyres, for the digger he'd been using for his family's building business. These tyres are three feet wide to spread the load, so they don't damage farmer's fields when they're out putting fence poles up. One of these tyres had split, so when it was replaced Jonty ended up with a tyre. He reckoned a person could climb in, like a human inner tube, and roll down the big hill near his house. Because of the weight distribution of one body, the tyre would speed up and slow down on each rotation, as the main weight of the body went over the top. My thinking was, if you got two bodies in there, it would even out the weight distribution, so me and our mate Mathieu would climb in it together. It went well. Then Jonty built a ramp for us to jump ... It didn't go so well. But that was earlier in the summer. We had another plan for Bonfire Night.

In the farmyard was a corn drier. It's like a large hopper, 40 ft in diameter and 60 ft tall. It's enclosed, with a welded-on lid. To get in it, you climb through an oval hole in the side; it's a tight squeeze until you're in.

I crawled into it, wearing Jonty's BMX helmet, and someone would fire a rocket in through the hatch. The rocket would fly round and round the perimeter of the corn drier before exploding.

After that, Jonty was trying to talk me into gripping a rocket between arse cheeks, instead of using the more normal launch pad consisting of a tube of cardboard stuck in the lawn or, the old school method, a milk bottle. I wasn't having any of it, so he grabbed a rocket from the Black Cat box, but as he tried it the rocket's stick snapped and he backed out. For reasons that I still can't put my finger on to this day, I said, 'Give it here,' having decided to show everyone how it was done. With the same broken-stick rocket.

I dropped my jeans and gripped the, by now, very short stick between my bum crack. I reached round and lit the fuse and could feel the intense heat when the rocket started shooting explosive sparks out as it tried to launch into the sky. The mixture of pain, heat, nerves, fear and whatever was going through my head meant the signal from my backside that was screaming, 'Release your arse muscles!' wasn't getting to my brain – or else the orders weren't getting back. I was still bent over, trousers and undies round my ankles, hands on my knees, when the bloody thing exploded.

I've never seen so many grown men in tears of laughter. One person who wasn't laughing was my girlfriend at the time, Kate. I'd never seen her so revved up and angry before. She was on the rev limiter.

My backside looked like it had a six-inch diameter red circle burned onto it. The next morning it was dripping pus and plasma. Two days later I was sat on a plane to Macau – a 14-hour flight with my undies stuck to my wounded bum.

Looking back at the list these experiences, it's clear that something about being around Jonty made me do the stupidest stuff without thinking of what might come next. We'd go to Rossington in South Yorkshire where there was a foam pit, a huge open container full of off-cuts of thick upholstery foam. The foam pit gives a soft landing for BMX and motorcycle riders wanting to learn and practise dangerous new tricks, like backflips. I couldn't do a backflip on a BMX, so – and I realise this is becoming some kind of theme – I have no clue why I thought it would be a good idea to attempt a two-person back flip, again with my equally daft mate Mathieu.

We set off, Mathieu pedalling like hell, and me sat on the handlebars. It wasn't until our front wheel was hitting the ramp that I thought, 'This is going to hurt.' It hadn't occurred to me all the time we were planning and preparing. I nearly broke my nose with my own knee, there was blood pouring everywhere, while Mathieu had a massive graze on his arm.

I didn't always need encouragement to do things that were plain daft. During a slack few minutes at work, I was riding round Dad's truck yard on my Whyte 46 mountain bike. I got it into my head that I could, and should, jump into the pit that the trucks straddle and we, the mechanics, climb into to work on the underneath of them. This is very different to a foam pit. It's concrete, soaked in decades of old oil and 8 ft deep and about 15 ft long with a steel ladder, fixed to the wall, at the end. Add together all the time I'd spent in the pit under a lorry and it would come to solid months at least, but, again, there was a lack of planning and consideration when it came to potential consequences, and I just went for it.

At no point, until I was lying on the floor of the pit, having properly spannered myself – tearing my AC joint in my shoulder, the acromiclavicular joint that allows you to move you arm above your head – had it occurred to me that the handlebars of the mountain bike could possibly be wider than the pit ... What a wanker.

But back in Macau, in spite of a badly burnt backside, at least I finished the race, in fifth place.

The next year, my first visit with Shaun Muir, I crashed in qualifying. It was while entering the downhill right-hander, where you have to work the front hard, before the climb up Moorish Hill.

The crash was down to me not being aware how much difference a qualifying tyre would make to the lap. All my previous laps had been on regular race tyres. Qualifiers offer more grip but aren't designed to last race distance, just help riders set a good time to put them closer to pole position. But I wasn't used to them, and it caught me out. For this particular downhill right, rather than use a braking marker on the track, I was braking just as the shift lights came on. Because of the increased grip of the qualifier, though, I'd got much better drive out of the previous corner, was travelling faster and, when I got the signal to brake,

I was closer to the corner. I grabbed too much brake, hit the ground hard and smashed into the side of the bridge.

I was out cold, and apparently shaking at the side of the track – looking like I was having some kind of fit, one of the other riders said, though I remember nothing of it. I was told some of the marshals thought it was just my final nerve movements and I was dead. I was out for an hour. When I woke up in hospital I thought I'd be like a dog trying to explain to a vet that it needed its appendix taking out, but the local medics were spot-on.

I'd actually only broken my thumb on one hand and wrist on the other, but both hands were in plaster. I couldn't even wipe my own arse, so I had one of SMR's mechanics cut off one of the casts with a steak knife.

There are different emotions for every crash. When I return to the pits after a big crash, broken and bruised, I never think other racers are judging me, and when it happens to other people I don't judge them. I sometimes wonder why they were pushing so hard in particular conditions, but this is motorcycle racing and shit happens. It was much worse that I was trapped out there in Macau, that I couldn't just get a lift home and try to forget about it.

When I finally got back to Kirmington I was contacted by a faith-healer nicknamed Johnny Hot-Hands. He told me he thought he could speed up the healing process of my broken bones. He also said I had nothing to lose, except a bit of time, because he wasn't going to charge me.

I was lined up to present some trophies at the Aintree Racing Club's end-of-year presentation. I'd just taken delivery of a new car, too, FV57 NBA, a brand-new BMW M3 V8. I couldn't wait to get out in it, but my wrists hurt so much I couldn't even drive, so Kate drove and I decided we'd call in at Johnny Hot-Hands on the way home. He was right, what did I have to lose? I was clinging on to anything that offered hope of getting better. Even though there wasn't any racing or even testing for another three months at least, I'm not someone who is happy just sitting and waiting, or seeing it as a time to take things easy.

The faith-healer was based just south of the M62, in Yorkshire, so it wasn't even out of my way. Before we knocked on his door – not that I was in a fit state to do any knocking – I was aware that Johnny had worked with the late Steve Hislop. A brilliant racer, from Hawick in the Scottish borders, Hislop had won one of the most memorable TTs ever, the 1992 battle with Carl Fogarty. He'd also been the British Superbike champion, but died in a helicopter crash in July 2003.

Walking into the house I could see that magazine articles mentioning Johnny and Hislop together had been framed and put up on the walls.

We sat in his front room and Johnny put his hot hands on my wrist. I felt a slightly unusual sensation, like more heat than I expected, and at the time I thought it had done something, but now I reckon it was just wishful thinking. I don't think any magic happened and I don't believe in miracle cures. I was so desperate for it to work, but now I'm more cynical.

Johnny wanted to meet me at a few race meetings the following year, 2008, and because he was a nice bloke I had no problem with it, but I wasn't asking him for any treatment and instead Johnny started doing stuff with my team-mate of the time, James Ellison. James must have been more impressed than I was, because they saw each other for ages.

My last visit to Macau, in November 2008, was the biggest disaster of the lot, because I crashed at the top of Moorish Hill on the very first lap of practice. I don't even know what happened. I genuinely don't know what went wrong. I must have had a bad earth or something. I was so beaten up I couldn't race. It was a long way to go for bugger-all.

Macau never really flicked my switch. I was never chomping at the bit to get back there, but most teams would want to go, because it didn't cost them anything and for the mechanics going out it was an opportunity to tack on a free holiday.

There was plenty of talk about Macau being a holiday race, even from some of the riders, because there are no championship points and very little prize money, but the lads pushing to win aren't having a holiday. They're hanging their balls out like they would at any race back in Britain or Ireland. And racers still get killed at Macau. Does that sound like a holiday?

I'm not bothered about going back to the place unless I can line up something special to race, like a turbo bike. I love racing my bike, but I was happier concentrating on the British and Irish races.

CHAPTER 10

TWO STEPS FORWARDS, ONE STEP BACKWARDS

'Race fans at the roadside poured beer and bottles of water over it to put out the flames. I wouldn't have been bothered if they'd let it burn.'

I SIGNED TO stay with Shaun's SMR team for 2008. I would race Hondas again, but this year would be sponsored by a new and short-lived website, Bike Animal.

All the Honda teams would be racing the brand-new Fireblade Superbike. As often happened with new models, the standard road bikes that needed to be converted into race bikes were delivered to the teams later than anyone expected, so plans for pre-season testing were scuppered. I had ridden the bike before many other people in the world, though, because I attended the launch for *Performance Bikes* magazine, out at the Doha track in Qatar.

I still had a broken wrist, but I could ride on track and it gave me the chance to quiz the lead designer to death.

Shaun and I both suspected that racing on the short circuits would make me sharper for the roads, the races I really wanted to win. So we committed to do a full season of British Superbikes, or at least all the races that didn't clash with the big road races I was already committed to.

My team-mate was James Ellison. He had raced MotoGP and won a World Endurance Championship. Lovely lad. Clean. Very clean. Shaved his armpits. I think he shaved everything. Not a skerrick of hair on him from what I could see. He would concentrate solely on BSB, not competing in any road races, though he would come to the TT as a spectator to support the team.

A complication with the 2008 Fireblade, as far as I was concerned, was a new design of Showa 'Big Piston' forks (BPFs) that we ran, that I just couldn't get on with. I've never claimed to be the fastest short circuit rider, but I know what I know. If I know the bike isn't right, then it's not right. With these forks fitted, in fast corners where you'd go through on a closed throttle, neither braking nor accelerating, the bike would chatter like hell, a big vibration running through the whole bike, a resonation coming from the wheels up. It's something a lot of riders complain about and it plagues some bikes in MotoGP.

I struggled in testing at Thruxton, the first BSB round, qualifying something like twenty-fifth, and told Shaun we were wasting our time. I wanted to try the previous year's forks. My 2007 TT bike was still in the team's hospitality unit as a showpiece, but Shaun had previously told me I had to persevere with the BPFs, because they'd be better when we got them right. At tests earlier in the year I had pleaded with the team to let me try the old ones just as a comparison, because I couldn't get on with the feel of them. When I was so far back on the grid, and had made a right dick of myself, I told them I might as well bugger off home, because I was wasting everyone's time, petrol and tyres for eff-all. Shaun eventually backed down, told the mechanics to get the bike out of the hospitality unit and fit the previous year's forks, and I ended up coming ninth in the second BSB race. No one said anything after that. I didn't need anyone to say anything.

For 2008, the mechanics were my younger sister, Kate, and 'GP' James, with Wozza over them and Shanley overseeing both my and Ellison's team of mechanics. GP James had worked for Kenny Roberts's team in MotoGP, hence his nickname. He was shit-hot, but he had a very particular way of doing things. After every meeting he wanted to strip the bike right down to the nuts and bolts, with the engine out, like they did in GPs. My thinking was, if the bike was running well and not in need of a scheduled rebuild, you'd clean the flies off it, change the oil and filter, give it a once-over and that would be it. GP James thought differently, because of his experience, so I just let him get on with it.

At the second race of 2008, a British Superbike round at Oulton Park, the throttle twistgrip came loose, and nearly slid off the end of the handlebar, going into Island Bends. That was enough for me to have doubts about GP James, or more accurately, his method of working, for the rest of the season. We never argued, you couldn't get angry with GP James, he's such a nice fella, but it was in the back of my mind. Looking back, I should have just realised shit happens and put it out of my head, but so much of racing is in the mind that it became a distraction. He was a good mechanic and perhaps I was harsh on him.

I was getting loads of time on the bike that season. It's the thing that reminds me I've contradicted myself in later years, when I've been only racing the roads and saying that I've had enough time on the bike. In 2008 I was doing a full season of BSB and I feel I was riding at my best then, when I was on the bike nearly every week.

I went to the North West 200 and led both big races. In the first I ran out of brakes, because there was no more adjustment in the lever, and I came second to Michael Rutter.

I like the front brake lever set fairly near to the bar, but sometimes, as the brakes get hot, the lever moves more and then it's reaching the handlebar grip before the brakes are fully on. So I always wanted a big adjuster that made it easy to move the lever out at 190 mph on the straight, the only chance you get to do it. My dad made one that worked perfectly, but because it looked a bit old-fashioned and agricultural, the team wouldn't fit it. Shanley overruled GP James and my sister and wouldn't let them fit it. Would I have won if I could've adjusted my brake? I don't know, but it certainly didn't help me.

They let me put the big brake adjuster on for the second Superbike race, but another part – one that I'd asked to have changed, unsuccessfully – failed when I was leading by a fair bit. During the race, that I was comfortably leading, the temperature gauge went up and up and a red warning light came on. Dodgy sensor, I thought – ignore it, we'll be fine, keep on trucking. Then the engine went off song and it was cooked. I was leading by five or six seconds, fit for winning, and one of the hose clips I'd asked them to change had broken and a radiator hose came off halfway through the race.

Later that day I had a massive crash in the 600 race. I was pissed off about the breakdown robbing me of a good win, something I thought was avoidable because I'd always asked for my bike to be fitted with the kind of hose clips we used on trucks, but Shanley wouldn't have it. He didn't want anything as simple as that on the bike, so we had these fancy hoses and hose clips, and one of them failed.

That year the Honda 600 was slow compared to the opposition, but I was trying like hell to make the best of a bad job, trying to win, or at least salvage a decent result, even though our CBR600 wasn't really good enough. I was trying my nuts off, and it all ended in tears.

I was going into Black Bridge, an over-the-crest left-hander, taken at over 100 mph. I tipped in and caught the kerb on the inside with either my leg or a footpeg. That was enough to take the weight off the front tyre, causing it to lose all its grip. We slid across the road, me and the bike, and hit the kerb on the other side of the road. The bike flew 20 feet in the air and I belted the kerb with the bottom of my back, really battering myself. I was so sore I couldn't drive, so my friend Paddy drove me home. I was living with Kate on the farm and she told me she'd hidden the door key on the wheel of a car and to let myself in. Paddy dropped me off at 4am on the Sunday morning, the pair of us having driven and caught the ferry back straight after the Saturday race. It took me all the effort in the world to bend down and get the keys off the top of the car wheel. I was cursing, knowing the TT was only a week or so later. I hadn't broken anything. I just had to grit my teeth and go back to work.

That North West Supersport race was one of the rare times I was trying to make things happen, trying to get a result when everything wasn't quite right. Still, I walked away from it.

That was the weekend Robert Dunlop died after his bike seized during practice for the same meeting. I knew Robert a bit and got on well with him, but I'd seen plenty of racers get killed and he was another one on the list. Shit happens. It was that weekend that a lot of people really noticed Robert's youngest son, Michael, for the first time. He was on track when his dad died on the Thursday evening. We never used to ride on the Friday at the North West, so the very next time Michael rode a bike in anger was the Saturday morning, in the 250-cc race.

I wasn't entered in that race, but while I was waiting to go out in the next one I looked up at the big screen as it showed Michael sat on the grid. I knew, as soon as I saw him, that he was either going to win that race or bin it trying. He won, and that race was the making of him. Up until then he wasn't really a go-er. He was still on his way up, but this was a turning point for him. From that moment on he was fast. He chucked his balls to the wall on that 250 and realised how hard he could ride and get away with it. Ever since then he's been doing the business.

I left Northern Ireland injured, but knowing I had the speed to do well at the TT. The BSB had been doing me some good. I would've won at the North West if it wasn't for the hose clip. So I went to the TT full of confidence, but still sore. The big crash at the North West was only a week before.

During practice week, I visited the hyperbaric chamber, near Quarterbridge. It's a pressure chamber that is pumped full of 100 per cent oxygen. These can be used to cure and relieve all sorts of ailments, but racers use them to try to speed up healing after accidents. More oxygen is in the bloodstream and delivered to the injured area, which is what the break needs. There were certainly other racers in there. I don't know if it works, but it didn't do any harm. I'd go in and sit for an hour, reading a bike magazine or something, while my ears popped with the change in pressure.

Other than that, practice week on the Isle of Man went without any bother. The first race of the TT couldn't have started better. I was leading the six-lap Superbike race by 20 seconds from Cameron Donald on the TAS Suzuki. McGuinness seemed to be struggling with the Showa BPF forks, then he broke down. After that my Fireblade's crank snapped. That was no one's fault, except Honda's.

I got a third in the Superstock, then suffered an engine failure in the Junior Supersport 600. The next race was the second

Supersport 600, but I wasn't confident. Our 600 couldn't pull your foreskin back that year, and I came in sixth.

Before I knew it, it was Friday, Senior day, and the last TT for another year. I'd rebuilt the bottom end of the engine, then handed it over to the team to finish off and fit back into the bike. When the crank broke, the detached end had rattled about in the generator cover and damaged the generator, so the team replaced it.

I went for the one lap of practice, on the Wednesday before Friday's Senior race, but I took it easy because I was running in the new engine. It was slow through the speed traps, but I wasn't worried. Friday's race started and I was nowhere from the very beginning, even though I'd led the first Superbike race by 20 seconds. The bike got slower and slower over the first two laps of the six-lap race. When I came to leave the pit-lane after the first pit-stop, at the end of the second lap, the bike wouldn't even start. The battery was flat. It turned out the broken crank had shorted the regulator out and the battery wasn't being charged. My feeling was the team should've checked it.

Back in British Superbikes things weren't any better. I was in the top ten at the first race of the year, but before the end of the season I went back over my results, both on the roads and in BSB, and tallied up: 11 breakdowns out of 19 starts.

Crank sensors went, cam sensors went, stuff fell off the bike. My team-mate, Ellison, had more than his fair share of breakdowns too, but his came in practice, while I was cursed with race DNFs.

The experience turned me against BSB and short circuit racing for years. Perhaps I was wrong, but I didn't think it was helping me prepare for the big road races. It was because the season was so disrupted. Without so many breakdowns perhaps I would have been more committed to that way of doing things.

Towards the end of the season, I was really struggling with chatter at Croft, saying to Shanley, can't we try something? I was suggesting taking a couple of bolts out of the bottom yoke to allow the forks to flex more, and slackening the engine mounts a bit, but Shanley always just said it was designed to be run as they had fitted it, so they wouldn't change it. I managed to convince GP James to take a couple of bolts out of the bottom yoke, and it let me go half a second per lap quicker before the chatter came back. I returned to the pits and told James it was definitely doing some good and got him to slacken the 12-mm bolts that fastened the front of the engine into the frame. That change let me go quicker again. It proved that I knew what I knew. I still wasn't winning BSB races, but I was going in the right direction.

The highlight of 2008 was finally winning every race, except the last one, at the Southern 100. I would've won that too, if hadn't got a puncture. I won the Scarborough Gold Cup, too.

I'd spoken to Philip Neill of TAS Suzuki, but not seriously, and it wasn't going to come to anything. I'd had a shit TT in 2008, but the potential was there. We'd led races by miles, but I felt the team wasn't doing the job I needed from them and Shanley and I just couldn't see eye-to-eye.

Going into 2009, Shaun agreed to give me two of the bikes to prepare with mechanics of my own choice. It would be like my own team under their banner, but SMR would look after the 600 because it had a fancy Pectel ignition system on it.

We agreed on the plan. Cameron 'Cammy' Whitworth, a mechanic I'd worked with at AIM Yamaha in 2006, would come on board. So would my old mate Johnny Ellis. On paper, the most important member of the team was Buckle, who'd been my mechanic in my first year with SMR. He would be in charge of building the Superbike and Superstock 1000, bikes we were going to take on the world with. It seemed to all be sorted till Buckle sent me a text message to say he couldn't do it. He couldn't take the pressure. From that moment on, even though I didn't realise it at the time, we were buggered. Not because Buckle was the best bike builder in the world, but because the pressure he couldn't cope with had just landed on me.

At the last minute Shaun sorted out a new mechanic, a Yorkshireman called Danny Horne. He had been working for the Parkalgar team, but he fell out with the boss there, an ex-racer called Simon Buckmaster who I would have my own disagreements with the following year. Danny is a bit of a poseur, a pretty boy, who likes his sunglasses and hair gel, but we got on like a house on fire.

I don't feel I set the world alight at the 2009 TT. It was a poor TT by the standards I was setting myself. Because I had to prepare the bike, I was running around at the last minute to get hold of everything I needed to get the Superbike built, commissioning Spondon Engineering in Derbyshire to make a special swinging arm and then Mehew to do the engine. I'd learnt about this Fireblade and I knew it was fast. Against the advice of SMR, I ordered some specific cams to give it even more power.

I set the way the team would work at the TT. Cammy, Jonny, Danny, Kate and I all stayed in a house in Douglas that Kate had sorted out for us, but we did all our preparation well out of the way in a friend's garage. Danny remembers it just like I do, in that we all worked together well and had the best craic at a race any of us would ever experience. We'd be up working at six in the morning, music going, then come down to the paddock, get the bikes scrutineered, then go back to the house and chill out.

When it came to racing, I was third in the six-lap Superbike, behind McGuinness and Plater, one place ahead of Hutchinson; and second in the Superstock, less than ten seconds back from Hutchinson and eight ahead of Keith Amor. Then I was second in the Supersport, to Hutchie, just six seconds back in the shorter 72-minute, four-lap race, edging out Keith Amor again. At that point of the week, although I'd had no wins I was the only rider to be on the podium three times, but that year's TT was about to go bad for me.

I had a DNF in the second Supersport when the engine blew; then the chain broke in the Senior when I was somewhere on the podium, but not realistically on for the win. I've always reckoned it was a fault with the chain, while the chain manufacturers said it was the way we'd fitted it. Whatever it was, I'd shown racing-winning potential without bringing home a win. It still wasn't enough.

I went to my favourite meeting of the year, the Southern 100, and my Honda 600 threw a con-rod, splitting the case and letting oil spill onto the exhaust, setting the bike on fire. Race fans at the roadside poured beer and bottles of water over it to put out the flames. After the TT race failure I'd had with the bike I wouldn't have been bothered if they'd let it burn. SMR were building that bike in-house, while I was looking after the Superbike and Superstock. Mehew's stepson was building the engine. It broke down or blew its head gasket regularly all year.

Even though it was my job to prepare the Superbike, after the TT it had gone back to SMR's headquarters for some reason. I collected it for the Southern 100, and when I got it back on it, it felt slow. I said to Shanley that it felt less powerful, and he reminded me it had raced at the North West 200 and all the TT. I could see what he was saying. Perhaps it had become a bit blunt and needed a freshen-up. I won the big race on it, but I had to ride it hard.

After the Southern 100 I took the Superbike home to prepare it to go on show at the Goodwood Festival of Speed.

When I took the engine to bits to check it and discover what wear it had suffered, I noticed someone had taken the cams out of it, the ones I'd dug my heels in to have and the team didn't want me to use. These HRC cams made big power, and while they weren't user-friendly, they were good for the TT. SMR had seen how well they worked and had nicked them to put them in my team-mate Karl Harris's bike for Snetterton! I wasn't bothered that they'd taken them, the team had bought them after all, but I felt they hadn't been straight with me. I told Shaun, and he didn't know his mechanics had done it.

Mick Shanley is a very good mechanic and crew chief, he's proved it with great results, but we didn't see eye-to-eye. He wasn't used to working with a rider like me and didn't seem to want to give way to me. From my side of things, I wanted to make some decisions about the bike I was racing that he disagreed with. It happens.

There was still plenty of racing to be done. I went to the new Armoy race in Northern Ireland. Me, Danny and Bob Wharton, a mate of my dad's, in his late-sixties, went in the van. Wharton doesn't get his hands dirty. He doesn't even make the tea. He just sits there giving us worldly advice. He's quite high maintenance.

I finished second to Farquhar in the feature race, but I loved racing that track. Me and Ryan agreed that one particular corner at Armoy was the quickest corner in the whole of road racing. When you're crossing the start–finish line on your first flying lap, you're hitting sixth gear on the Superbike, so accelerating to well over 180 mph. And the straight is not even straight, it's a bit of a left-hand bend, then you just ease the throttle ever so slightly, no brakes, and peel in. There are no walls, bushes or trees directly next to the track here, so you can have your tyres right in the gutter and be hanging over the verge. Usually, in road racing, you can't use all the road, or your body, that's leaning off the side of the bike, will hit something. So you position the bike slightly in from the gutter.

The bike is settled through a corner like this. On the exit, when you're winding the throttle back on from 80 per cent to 100 per cent it gets the bike squirming a little bit. If you got the entry to this corner wrong, by tipping in too early or too late, you would have to roll the throttle shut and adjust your line, and then you'd lose your momentum for the run down into Armoy.

It's corners like this that separate those who can run in the top five at a modern road race from those further down the order. It's a man's corner. Road racing isn't about how late you can brake into a corner, like I tried in my first race at Kells back in 2002. You're not going to make up time at corners that way. It's about going through corners like this flat-out, inch perfect, and knowing, but not considering, that if anything went wrong it would be disastrous.

My racing calendar had gone through a big change when I joined the English-based teams, AIM Yamaha and SMR. With them, I didn't go back to Ireland except for the big International meetings like the Ulster and the North West 200. Going to Armoy brought it home how much I loved racing at the smaller national meetings in Ireland. Because Armoy was a new race, the organisers paid my ferry and put me up in a B&B. I finished second and earned a few quid. I've still never won at Armoy. It's Dunlop country – their backyard.

Former racer Rob McElnea has complained about the Irish fans being against him when he was racing local favourite Joey Dunlop, Michael's uncle, back in the 1980s, but the Irish fans have always been spot-on with me. I think they remember I learnt my trade over there.

At the end of 2009, I had to make a decision. Shaun Muir is a top bloke, but I'd been there three years and in that final year nothing went to plan. We weren't moving forwards with the job, in fact we were going backwards. I had faith in the team structure, running without a foreman, but the last-minute let-down didn't help. It wasn't a case of thinking the grass was greener. Despite three podium finishes, I felt I was further away from winning a TT than I had been in my first year with the team. It was time for a change.

CHAPTER 11

PUSHBIKES

'"You sad buggers, have you got nothing better to do with your life?" It looked so grim. The solo riders just looked like death. I had to try it.'

I'M NOT A fan of gyms. I'm not against them, I just don't fancy going to them. During a busy time with work and the TV job I had a week where, because of work, I hadn't been out pushbiking or anything, and then I had to go Birmingham for the filming job. I was in the hotel and thought, 'Bloody hell, I'm going to have to go in one of these here gyms.' I went to the hotel's gym and I couldn't believe what was going on. There were people flailing their arms and legs about, and blokes blatantly watching themselves in the mirror, with stern looks on their faces, while they were doing stuff. I couldn't take it in. It all seemed to be about what you looked like. All very vain. Look at me, here I am. But, each to their own.

A lot of motorcycle racers use personal trainers, but I think if you need a trainer to spur you on there's something wrong. The drive should come from within, but if that's what people need to get the best out of themselves, then fair play. Again, each to their own, but I set my own goals.

If I lived closer to a fellow racer on a bit of a similar wavelength, like Leon Haslam, I wouldn't mind doing a bit of training with him. I think he's a top bloke, but I don't have time to take half a day to go training. My training is part of my everyday life.

I was with Hector Neill, the owner of the Tyco TAS Suzuki team, one time when we were being interviewed for Irish TV. I was asked how I trained, and I said I didn't really do any, but Hector disagreed. 'Well, you could say that,' he said, 'or you could say you train 14 hours a day, six days a week.' And I could say that.

While I'm at work I'm exercising all day. It's not like being a car mechanic, I'm constantly jacking stuff up and lifting 70 kg truck wheels, truck drum brakes, back axles, truck cylinder heads – it's all heavy stuff. It's such varied stuff too, lifting, twisting, jacking, hammering – it's oily, greasy cross-training.

One of the hardest job is changing Scania mid-lift pins on a three-axle truck. This is on the six-by-two trucks. That means it's got six wheels, and two of them drive. The middle two steer, and also lift off the ground when the load is light or the truck isn't pulling a trailer. Anyway, these pins hold the axle to the truck. To replace them you have to burn a cut in the bush and knock it out with a ballpeen hammer and a punch. It takes a hell of a lot of doing. Then you've got to knock another one in while it's still hot.

I have the biggest ball-peen hammer Snap-On make, a BP 40 B+40 0z. I bought my first one when I was 16, but I wasn't man enough for it. I was always blacking my fingernails with it.

I'm all right with it now. I used to strangle it, hold it too close to the head. A person confident with their hammer holds it right at the end.

It'll take 100 flat-out knocks to drive the bushes and pins in. You have to do it while you're stood in the pit, so you're doing it all above your head. To do them all it takes 40 minutes, non-stop. You know you've finished. You're sweating. Every truck needs it doing every year or two. So I probably do one a fortnight. Jobs like this, and jacking cabs up, is all upper body work. The truck stuff is more anaerobic, and the bike is all aerobic.

When I joined the TAS Suzuki team I went to Queen's University, Belfast to have my fitness levels checked. They confirmed what I knew, that I'm fit enough to race motorcycles. While I was there I got more advice on training, both for road racing and mountain bike racing.

I'm regularly up at 5.30 and on my bike for 6am. The end of Radio 4's *Farming Today* is my flag dropping, then I set off pedalling to work. The shortest way is 12 miles, but I normally only do that one in winter. I've left home and it's been so cold my Camelbak has frozen before the top of Caistor Hill, a mile away from the front door of where I was living at the time. The coldest I remember it going down to was minus-11. I take the easy route on a day like that.

Most days I'll take a 20-mile route, with 1,000 feet of climbing, there and back. I love cycling down Immingham Docks on the way home. It doesn't matter what time you go, it's like the M25. All the coal tankers, the oil tankers, the cranes ... I get a bit of buzz cycling that way.

When I was training for an Austrian mountain bike endurance race in 2011, I'd go 30 miles, call in for a brew at a mate's house and get home for 11, then get up at 5.30 again. I'm not training for the sake of it. I was being technical about it, trying to increase my VO2 levels, to improve the anaerobic threshold. Basically, the harder your heart can beat before you go into the anaerobic state is a measure of how fit you are. Mine was pretty high, which is good, because you wouldn't believe how hard your heart beats during a motorcycle race. My heartbeat is reaching well over 180 bpm at times. I can't understand why, because I'm not out of breath.

To keep fuelled up during all this cycling I eat a lot of pasta and chicken. I'm not much of a Jamie Oliver and I'm not even really bothered what it tastes like. If I have time I'll chuck in some Dolmio sauce, but normally it's just plain chicken and pasta. Sometimes I'll throw some mince in. I'm getting more exotic with the spices and veg. Lasagne is my signature dish. And my mate Tim Coles is a beef farmer and sorts me out with some good cuts of steak too. For breakfast, it's cod liver oil and a massive bowl of porridge every morning.

I've put a bit of weight on since 2011 and I'm happy I have. I'm about 11 stone four pounds and better for it. When I broke my back, in 2010, I was 10 stone seven pounds, and during some road races I was like a flea on a dog's ball-sack. When I signed for TAS I knew I had to be heavier. I was OK on a 600, but I wasn't man enough for a 1000. I'd lost a bit of upper body strength. I was too lean, with a physique more like a cyclist than a motorbike racer.

I'm more into cycling now than I ever have been. Some weeks I'm cycling 250 miles, just to work and back, and I race bicycles too.

My first downhill race was an urban downhill in Scarborough, the week after the Gold Cup in 2008. The organisers of these races would find a town built on a hill and riders would race over the man-made obstacles, like flights of stairs. I went with Kate and Mark Davis, who a few years later would make the

TV show *The Boat That Guy Built* with me. I don't know where I finished in the standings, but I remember I crashed a load of times. I enjoyed it, though.

It led to a magazine called *Mountain Bike Rider* entering me in a national downhill race in Ae Forest, near Stranraer, Scotland. It was daunting, and I didn't do very well, but I learnt a lot and enjoyed just going to do something by myself, and sleeping in the back of my van.

I had been up to Fort William previously with Mark, riding the downhill course, but not racing. Maybe I should explain what downhill is.

Mountain bike competition, back when the popularity of that style of bike exploded, used to be cross-country. The races go through hilly and mountainous countryside that involves climbing and descending a long route, sometimes over 100 miles in a day. Cross-country involves loads of pedalling. It's the mountain bike sport included in the Olympics. Downhill is totally different. Basically, you've got a bicycle that looks like a motocrosser without an engine. It has loads of front and rear suspension travel, a massive alloy frame and huge knobbly tyres. You jump on a ski lift to the top of a mountain, not usually when there's snow, but there are exceptions, and then you ride down the mountain on a specially made course. There's not a lot of pedalling involved, but it's bloody hard. You wouldn't think riding a bike downhill would be so physically demanding, but the course makes it tough. From the ski lift, you can look down on sections of Fort William's course and the thought goes through your mind, 'You cannot ride a bicycle down there!' There are huge six-foot-plus drops onto rocks and boulders at all sorts of angles. But, as I'm still learning on a downhill mountain bike, speed is your friend. You hit them hard enough and you clear the gap. But it takes commitment. And it doesn't always work ...

There's a world series of downhill racing, the UCI World Cup, and Fort William would be one of the most challenging courses.

An organisation called No Fuss organised a six-hour downhill mountain bike race at Fort Bill. Instead of doing one run, as fast as you possibly could, you had to do as many runs as possible in six-hours. I finished something like fifteenth in 2008, though I wrecked myself, because I was always crashing. I was so tired, my arms so pumped up, I couldn't pull the brakes, so to lose speed I'd crash on purpose. It didn't occur to me to stop and have a rest.

Downhill offered another challenge, another buzz to fit into the weekends when I wasn't racing a motorbike.

I promised myself that if I had a good TT in 2009 I'd take some time off work and compete in the Megavalanche downhill race at Alpe d'Huez in France. But I thought I had a poor TT, I was on a bit of a downer, so I went back to work on Monday. Then again we weren't too busy at the truck yard, and I couldn't shake the idea of going to the Megavalanche, so I got on the works computer, found out that an easyJet flight wasn't too much, and it wouldn't cost a lot more to take my pushbike, so I arranged with Dad to disappear for a few days.

I took my bike to bits and stuck it in a box, flew from East Midlands to Geneva and went to pick up my hire car. The trouble was, I didn't have a credit card. I'd never had one, agreeing with my mum that if you can't afford, you can't have it. Even though I'd paid for the hire car they still needed a credit card to use as a guarantee. They didn't want my passport or cash, just a credit card number. I was close to turning around and going home, but a Frenchman next to me, who could see I was having a bit of bother, put it on his credit card. What a legend! I've no idea what would have happened to his credit rating if I'd driven off the side of a mountain.

The Megavalanche is infamous in the mountain bike world. It is a cross between a downhill and a cross-country race. You start at the top of the alp, on the glacier, and you come down however you can. Some people try to ride it, others hold their bikes and just slide down on their arses. Once you're off the snow you're on a single track, and it swaps between cross-country, then a downhill section, then some uphill cross-country, then more downhill. When you see aerial photos of the start it looks mental, people just tumbling down the mountain. It's hardcore.

I got to Alpe d'Huez and did the two days of practice, then on Friday I crashed and broke my big toe. I was racing the Southern 100 the next week, so I changed my mind about doing the Megavalanche race, but it was still a great experience.

The next year, 2010, after I broke my back at the TT, the motorcycle racing governing body wouldn't allow me to race a motorbike for a while, so I went back to Fort William for the six-hour downhill endurance. To compete, of course. I wouldn't go all that way to watch other buggers doing it. It almost goes without saying that I properly spannered myself, again, just six weeks after breaking my back.

Before that, I had my first 24-hour mountain bike cross-country race back in 2009. I did this first one in a team of four, with some of the lads I'd ride with in Lincolnshire on Tuesday and Thursday nights. We did all right. Then I did it in a team of four with the lads from Hope Engineering, a mountain bike parts company based in Barnoldswick, Lancashire who I'd become friends with.

Next I did it as a team of two. I was a guest at a motorcycle show in Aberdeen and met a couple of blokes up there and we got talking about pushbikes. They were two brothers, Francis and Forbes Dungait, who I met because they were mates with Alan, one of the Isle of Man TT scrutineers. Francis will have been about 60, and Forbes was in his mid to late fifties. Francis told me his brother was into bikes and had done the Strathpuffer. Anyone who is into mountain bikes knows the Strathpuffer is as tough as it gets. Forbes had been on the podium in the two-man class, so I knew he wasn't a messer. He said he was planning to do the next one, but his team-mate had pulled out. Did I fancy it?

After that one meeting Forbes and I had a phone call to arrange where to meet and that was it. The next time we met was at Ullapool. It's so far north only the hardcore actually manage the drive there.

I'd been training like hell, because I didn't want to let Forbes down. We would complete a 50-minute lap each, but by two in the morning, I'd finished my lap and had to do another because Forbes wasn't up to it, so I'd double up a couple of times. I wasn't bothered about the result; my whole focus was on not letting Forbes down. In the end we finished third out of 100 or so teams of two and we beat most of the four-man teams too.

I'd seen that there are some who ride the full 24 hours solo, not as part of a team. I'd look at them and think, 'You sad buggers, have you got nothing better to do with your life?' It looked so grim. The solo riders just looked like death. I had to try it.

In 2012 I rode the Relentless 24, again with Forbes, and we came second, though we should have won it. I had a bad cold. Blood was peeing out of my face. I must've ruptured something blowing my nose so hard.

Then I had the notion of doing the Strathpuffer solo – the ultimate challenge – and finished fourth out of about 80 solo boys and beating loads of the two-, three- and four-person teams.

Every six hours I'd stop for four or five minutes, maximum, to have some warm porridge and sugar. Every lap I'd have an energy drink and energy gels. You're burning so many calories, cycling for 24 hours, that you're eating all the time, and by the end of it you're sick to the back teeth of eating, but you've got to eat, because if you start to feel hungry it's already too late.

I was second at three in the morning and my bike broke, so I had to push back and get my spare, losing time.

I enter these events because I like pushing myself, seeing what I can do. I actually like the pain. I'm not doing it for pats on the back, but I get a lot of personal satisfaction from the races. By physically pushing myself I can get a buzz similar to what I've always got from racing motorcycles on the roads. It's not quite the same, but it's getting there. And the more I do it, the more I get into it. The harder the challenge, the more I'm interested. That's how I got around to entering a 24-hour cross-country mountain bike race and riding it solo. It's my thing now.

I raced another 24-hour solo, at Fort William in October 2013. I came third, and was on the podium with the world champion. That race taught me that, even when your body is screaming, 'Stop, you bastard!' it will still produce power. I'm now having to recalibrate my mind to what it's possible to do. I had said that if I ever got on the podium in a solo 24-hour mountain bike race, that would be that box ticked, but now I'm so close to winning one, I don't want to stop.

The biggest crash I never had was on a fixed-wheel bicycle. Fixies are quite trendy in a lot of cities, but they're originally track and training bikes. Fixed wheel means the back sprocket has no freewheel, so if the bike is moving the pedals are moving, you can never stop pedalling. The bikes they race in velodromes, like Chris Hoy in the Olympics, are fixed wheel. They don't have gears, just one chainwheel and one rear sprocket, as simple as it gets.

It was the week before the 2013 TT and I was out cycling with my girlfriend Steph for a hilly ride. Those of you who are paying attention will have noticed straight away here that my girlfriend's name has changed from Kate to Steph. Well done. I'll be filling you in a bit more on that later.

Back on the hill, Steph decided that she'd had enough before me, so I went to do one more climb on my own.

When we set off, the plan was for just a steady ride, so I wasn't wearing a helmet, but when Steph went home I ended up riding a lot quicker. Coming back down the steep hill, near Double-Decker Lil's, I must've been doing 40 mph, on the fixed wheel, single-speed, when the bike got away from me. I wasn't in control and my legs couldn't keep up with the speed the back wheel was making the crank spin. I had my cycling shoes clipped into the pedals and if my feet hadn't been flung off the pedals it would have been messy. Very messy.

CHAPTER 12

JUMPING SHIP

'I'm not even bothered about being paid to ride, but the bikes have got to be right.'

AS I'VE EXPLAINED, I have never thought too far down the line or planned a career progression. I wasn't like most UK National racers, who had a dream of winning the British title, being picked up by a World Superbike team – moving to a tax haven, winning the World Superbike title in their second year and then going on to compete in MotoGP. I had no master plan. Thinking about it, there still isn't one. I would like to win a TT, but I have always been more motivated by the fun I can have racing a motorbike at tracks I love.

I enjoyed Junior Superstock, because I was ignorant of the alternatives. When I raced at Oliver's Mount and Kells I realised there was another way to race and I preferred everything about it.

I was part of Finlay's Team Racing till something that suited me better, namely Uel Duncan's set-up, came along. The same with AIM Racing, and they approached me, I didn't go out looking for a new team.

I am keen to better myself, but enjoying racing is everything. As soon as I stop enjoying it I'll pack in. I have always wanted to improve my results, because I am competitive and I'm not having much fun if I'm not up the front; being on the pace and having fun are tied together. I have never done a big PR job on myself, gone knocking on doors, promised to do this or that, or bent down to kiss anyone's arse to get a ride. Teams have always had to take me for what I am and what I thought was best at the time. Fortunately for me, some very good teams have wanted me to ride for them.

Because I never thought of motorcycles as my job, I don't have to keep racing to maintain some kind of lifestyle or even just to have a wage coming in. After a win I have sometimes said things like the result was 'not bad for a truck fitter'. This might sound like a throw-away comment, but it gets to the very core of everything. Fixing trucks is my trade. It's my big picture. I can do other things, but if everything goes to shit, I'll happily be up at dawn to cycle to work preparing Scanias and Volvos for their next MoT test and truly not worry about what could have been.

I know there are those who think this is an act, all a story to detract from results, when I might have come second best, but after virtually every big race, I travel home the night of the race to be at work at 6.30 the next morning. No one is making me do it. I never wanted it any other way. Yes, I might have bought cars that not many truck fitters could afford, but I paid for them all. And not with inherited family money or bank loans.

So, with this background of a steady day job, if something wasn't working out with a team, or a good offer landed in front of me, I'd react to the situation. I'm not short of ambition, but neither was I ever driven by a dream of being Valentino Rossi's team-mate in MotoGP.

That all goes to explain some of the thought process going on at the end of 2009. After three years with Shaun Muir I was looking for a change. Other team managers had been in touch, and I had said I would join Rob McElnea's Yamaha team. We had agreed everything and done all but sign on the dotted line. The physical signing for me is normally nothing but a formality. I prefer to do things on a handshake, but this time it let me back out at the last minute.

I really like Rob Mac. He was originally from up the road in Humberside and when we were going to work together he lived even closer to me, near Coningsby in Lincolnshire. When he started racing, in the early eighties, he was a steel erector. In the racing world, where riders often spend hours every day in the gym, but are often short and slim, Rob was built like a brick shithouse. He looks like he could eat Dani Pedrosa between two slices of bread.

As a racer he'd achieved plenty, winning in Britain and racing for a few seasons on top factory teams in GPs. He was fifth overall in the 1986 500cc World Championship on a Yamaha, and two years later was the more experienced Pepsi Suzuki team-mate to Kevin Schwantz in the Texan's first full season in 500s. Schwantz would come eighth that year, Rob Mac was tenth overall. Rob scored a hatful of fourth places in GPs, but never a podium. He was a TT rider with an excellent record, too. He did his first TT in 1979, coming second in the Newcomers Junior. Then he raced from 1981 to 1984, winning three TTs from a total of ten starts. That's a bloody good wins to starts ratio. Rob was the last ever Grand Prix racer to compete in an Isle of Man TT while having a current GP contract, and he won the big race that year, the 1984

Senior. He actually missed some of practice for the French GP he was entered to race for Suzuki, because he was winning on the Isle of Man. He really was the last of a breed.

McElnea packed in racing in 1993, a leg injury forcing him to retire, and then became a team owner and manager. He always ran Yamahas in British Superbikes and also organised the Yamaha R6 Cup that helped some of Britain's best young riders really get noticed, riders like Tommy Hill and Cal Crutchlow – who I'd raced in Junior Superstock in 2002.

With Niall Mackenzie, another former GP rider of a similar age who'd returned to race full-time in Britain, Rob Mac's team won three back-to-back British Superbike titles. After those Cadbury Boost-sponsored years Rob's teams were regularly in the hunt for titles, but always missed out. Eventually the podiums dried up too and Rob retired from team management to concentrate on his other business, a courier company.

It was in the very lean period of his history that he contacted me to race. I'm not sure if there's a coincidence there, but it was at the time the profile of real road racing was growing. I wanted to try something different for 2010 and told him I'd race his Yamahas. It was even mentioned in the press that I was joining the team. Then a friend, someone you'd call 'a racing insider' told me it might not be the best move for me, and my feet went colder than a penguin's ballbag. It was suggested the team had a champagne mouth but lemonade pockets. They always looked great, through the Boost and Virgin Mobile days, but I was given the impression they didn't have the money to make the bikes as competitive as I expected them to be.

I wasn't looking to get rich, but I didn't want corners being cut when it came to bike preparation. I don't give a monkey's about a fancy race transporter or staying in a nice hotel; I'll happily sleep in my van, and regularly do. I don't expect to fly anything other than in the cheapest seat, and I'm not even bothered about being paid to ride, but the bikes have got to be right. If not, everyone is wasting their time and I'm doing a bit more than that. The smallest errors become very costly at places like the Isle of Man and the Ulster GP. There was enough doubt to make me panic and look for an alternative in a hurry.

Mehew had a hand in my plan B, as he had suggested me as a rider to the Irish-based Wilson Craig team, that he had been tuning engines for.

Wilson, a short, grey-haired Irishman, in his sixties, had been running road racing teams since 2008. Before that he'd been one of Uel Duncan's sponsors, and was when I raced for the Irish team.

When I met Wilson to talk about the 2010 season, I liked his enthusiasm. He had approached me before, offering lots of money for me to race, but then I didn't want to leave Shaun's team. Wilson told me his set-up had help from Honda for 2010, with Honda Racing's top men in the UK, Neil Tuxworth and Havier Beltran, on Wilson's side. The Irish team would obviously be playing second fiddle to the official Honda squad of McGuinness and Steve Plater, but Wilson's connections would make sure his team got the right bits for the engine and that they were built properly, ready for racing. Wilson also explained that Simon Buckmaster's Performance Technical Racing (PTR) would prepare the bikes. Although PTR Hondas hadn't won a World Supersport title, they'd done everything but that. They seemed to be a well-respected, world-class outfit.

Buckmaster was a former Grand Prix privateer, between 1989 and 1991. He had lost his leg in an endurance racing accident in the 1990s, became a team manager in British Superbike and was now managing the Parkalgar team in World Supersport.

During the short time we were discussing whether the Wilson Craig Racing team and I were right for each other, I met

Buckmaster and thought we would get on well. That would be a lesson in not trusting my first instincts.

It wouldn't take long for Buckmaster and me to start disagreeing about how the bikes I was going to race should be prepared. From what's been reported you'd get the impression the bikes his company delivered for me to race in 2010 were competitive and the whole problem was my attitude. This is my side of the story.

Wilson said he would let me have the team structure I wanted. After leaving SMR my idea was that I'd run the mechanics. It had worked up to a point in 2009, but I put the failings down to me having to organise the building of the bikes at the last minute, when we were let down.

I would choose the team members and I'd be in charge of them – there wouldn't be a crew chief, or whatever title the foreman wanted, between the mechanics and the team boss, like there is with most big teams. I was riding the bike, I knew how I wanted it to be, and I didn't want to waste time and energy disagreeing with someone in the middle who didn't see it my way. So, the bikes would come from a highly regarded race team, ready for the first session of any race meeting, and from there, me and my mechanics would tweak and try to perfect it for the track and conditions we were dealing with. Wilson said he was happy to work that way.

My mechanics would be the same as the previous season. Danny Horne left SMR to stay with me; my mate Johnny Ellis would take time off work to be my mechanic again; and Cammy would work at the bigger races like the TT.

I was excited. It seemed to be exactly what I was after. I thought we had been trying to reinvent the wheel at times when I was racing for Shaun. To me, keeping it simple was the way to go about the job. We wouldn't be based in the paddock at the TT.

We'd do all our spannering in my friend's garage again and we rented a house near Bray Hill. That meant we could stay out of the way, concentrate on the job in hand and only arrive in the pits when we were due out on track. If I stayed in the pits we'd never get anything done for people asking 'Have you got a minute?'

It was going to be a bit like the old days. Not entirely, though. Top road racing bikes had become so complicated – some of the Superbikes were £200,000 bits of kit laden with electronic systems – and the racing itself was so competitive, that it couldn't be like it was when Johnny and I would drive around in the old race truck and he was my only mechanic. This Wilson Craig team structure was as stripped-back as I thought it could be and still allow me to be in the hunt for international road race wins. It was the way I had wanted it to be for the last couple of years. It all sounded good. Better than good really, but it soured very quickly.

Wilson Craig is a wealthy Irishman who has made his money from trading in potatoes and some canny buying and selling of land. He's obviously a very good businessman, but, as far as I could see the principles he must have applied in his business life, all the rules, experience and skill, weren't carried over to his hobby, that is, running his motorcycle racing team. To be as good as he is in business you must have to be ruthless up to a point, but when it came to his team I felt he wasn't getting what he paid for. He didn't seem to be aware that he needed to apply the same principles to his team.

I was going to be running Honda CBR1000 Fireblades and CBR600s, bikes I was familiar with as I'd been on them for the last three years with SMR. So I was carrying quite a lot of specific set-up knowledge into 2010.

So far, so good, but the organisation fell at the very first hurdle. Instead of being given bikes prepared for early season shakedown tests I didn't get to ride the Wilson Craig bikes until the Pirelli tyre test in April. Some riders are out in Spain for pre-season testing from February. I had done that with SMR and would do the same later with the TAS Suzuki team, too. If you're staying with the same team and the bike hasn't been updated, it's not crucial to test too early. I don't think so, anyway. But if you're going to a new team with bikes that have been built from scratch, it's important to get on them early, to start getting them dialled in and flush any bugs out of their systems. It's reassuring for everyone. Don't test early and you can be chasing your tail when the season starts.

The bikes weren't ready for early season tests, but I still wasn't losing sleep over it. It wasn't until I rode the Hondas at the tyre test that I began to realise that all was not going to go smoothly.

Castle Combe is regularly used by Dunlop and Pirelli for TT tyres tests. It's about the only short circuit track in the UK with corners quick and bumpy enough to feel anything like a fast Manx or Ulster road corner. Obviously you can't test on the tracks I race on, because they're public roads for the rest of the year, so you're looking for a compromise – somewhere you can rent, but which is fast and not as smooth as a motorway. I test at smooth, shorter, slower tracks too, but that's to work out other issues with the bikes, to improve set-up, simple things like the position of the bars and footrests, or for setting up the electronics packages: traction control, anti-wheelie and fuelling maps. At Castle Combe it's all about assessing the performance and characteristics of the newly formulated rubber.

I arrived at the Wiltshire track, which is just a few miles from Bath, excited to be riding these 600s that had been built for me. In my mind they would be world-beating bikes. In reality, I found they fell far short of that. I knew that to be competitive in World

Above: Nutts Corner, 2003. That's an Irish Superbike race and I'm on the GSX-R1000 my dad bought me, in the Team Racing colours. I've never had a problem racing in the wet.

Left: From left to right are Richard Britton, Martin Finnegan, Darran Lindsay's mechanic, Trevor, and Uel Duncan. This could be a scene from any Irish road race, but I'm sure it's Dundalk, 2004. My team-mate Darran had crashed and broken his wrist but he could still win the Irish championship if I took a win away from Ryan Farquhar, so I agreed to ride his 250.

Right: And that's me high-siding Darran's 250 at the same meeting, with Ryan Farquhar arriving on the scene. I didn't hurt myself and tried to get back on, but the bugger wouldn't start. Obviously, I didn't beat Ryan that weekend, but I won at Killalane and Scarborough to give my team-mate the championship.

Left: Another one from Dundalk that shows how wild the Irish road circuits are. They're like motocross on tarmac. I'll have hit this jump at over 130 mph.

Below: This is the first photo a lot of people saw of me because it was used in a few British bike mags. It was taken by Stephen Davison, at the Scarborough Gold Cup meeting in 2004.

Left: You can tell I was green, I'm even wearing the team's shirt. 2004 Isle of Man TT awards with my bronze replica. I'm not sure where it is now. Maybe my dad's got it.

Right: Mid-Antrim 2005, I had finished second to Ryan Farquhar all day, but in this last race, the grand final, I won. I've raced Ryan hundreds of times. That's the last time I raced this hardcore track. It took so much learning, because there are so many places you need to be fully committed.

Above: Me and Trellis – my old mate, Johnny Ellis – in the pits at Macau, 2005. We are relaxing on the shipping containers the bikes are sent out to the Far East in. This was the first year I rode there.

Above: Ireland's Corner, Ulster GP, 2006. I won every race besides the Superstock race that day.

Left: 2007 TT on the Hydrex Honda Fireblade, at St Ninian's crossroads, on the way to second in the Superbike TT.

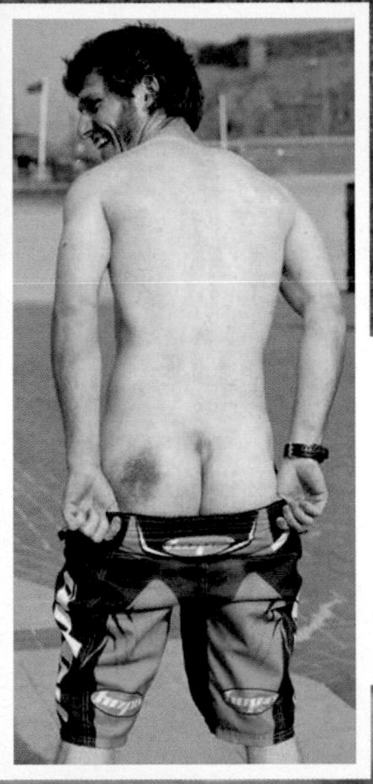

Above: This is the 2007 Superstock TT and I ran out of petrol because of a fault with the bike. This is Tower Bends, before you get to the Gooseneck. I look really uncomfortable in this photo, not in my normal riding position.

Left: Showing my bruises a few days after a big crash at the North West 200 in 2008. I'm wearing one of my first pair of Hope shorts. I've probably worn the arse out of ten pairs of them.

Above: I led both the big races at North West 200 in 2008 before mechanicals put a spanner in the works. First time, the brakes went; next race, the hose clip broke, both when I was out in front.

Above: The Pre-TT Classic races, 2008, on the Billown Circuit. I came off in this race when the battery fell off and jammed the back wheel on the last lap, when I was leading the race by a minute. I shouldn't be here now, really: that accident should've been the end of me. I spannered myself, and I had to tell my team boss, Shaun Muir, who didn't even know I was racing, what happened.

Above: With Valentino Rossi. The man's a legend.

Above: Going past the Memorial at Scarborough's Gold Cup in 2009. That's Stuart Easton's bike, because the team had sold mine. A lad called Michael Pearson is behind me. He was a bit wild, but he never bothered me.

Right: In the gutter, because the road's all there for using. 2010 was a bit of a disastrous year. This is the North West 200 on the Wilson Craig Honda Superstock Fireblade.

Above: This is what can happen if you crash at 170 mph at the TT. That's the petrol tank in the top left and my foot in the bottom right. When I was in hospital I couldn't understand why my fringe was burnt. I don't remember the explosion, so I must've been knocked out for a second.

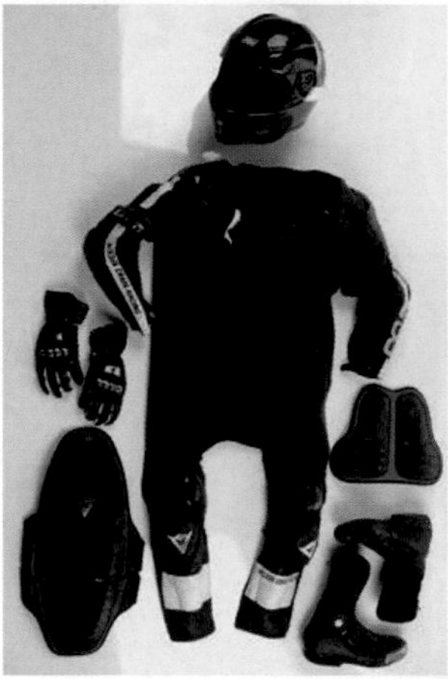

Left: Dainese and AGV took this photo of the kit that did a great job of saving my skin in the Ballagarey crash. The paramedics cut the suit off me, but other than that it looks bloody good considering what it saved me from.

Right: That won't polish out. The remains of the Wilson Craig Honda Fireblade that exploded after I crashed going through the 170 mph Ballagarey corner at the 2010 TT.

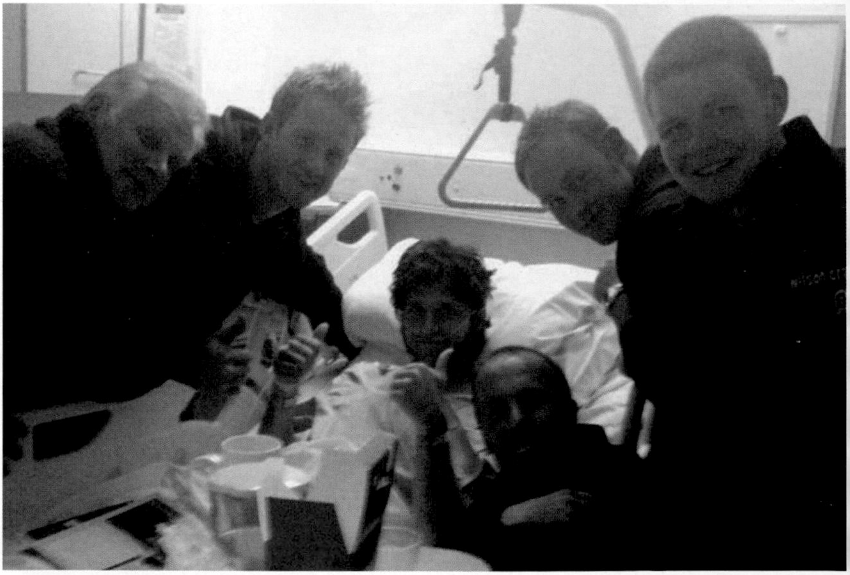

Above: In Nobles Hospital with the team on the evening of the crash. Everyone's smiling even though I broke my back and there's still smoke coming off my eyebrows, because they know how bad it could've been. I was racing three months later.

Supersport, the PTR Hondas had to be mustard. The excitement soon disappeared. Never mind being at a private Castle Combe test session, as far as I'm concerned, I could've been riding around a supermarket car park and told you these bikes weren't going to win anything.

The PTR mechanic who had been sent looked to me to have no experience in top-level motorcycle racing. He'd built Transit vans or something and helped a mate who raced a bike, but he didn't seem to have much of a clue about preparing a bike to finish a TT. Lovely lad, but some of the stuff he did made my blood run cold. If I have to explain the point of lockwiring stuff to the person who is building my race bikes, I don't have a lot of faith in him.

I felt basic things, like lockwiring, were simply not right. Every race bike, from that of a first-race novice in club racing right up to Rossi, Lorenzo and Marquez, has to have certain parts lockwired. The one many people know is the sump plug. You drill a tiny hole in the sump plug, thread some thin stainless steel wire through it, then twist the wire up, poke the two ends through another hole in either a fin on the engine case or another bolt and twist the ends together tightly before snipping the excess off. You arrange the lockwire in such a way that when it is all twisted up tightly, the bolt cannot move because the lockwire is in tension, effectively pulling the bolt tight. We had it wired the other way, so when the wire was twisted with the pliers it was pulling the bolt slack.

With few other choices, and a pile of tyres to work through and give feedback on, I climbed on the Honda and started riding. It didn't take long for the 600 to shit itself. The bike hadn't even survived the first morning of a pre-season test before blowing up. It was my very first day riding for my new team and I was already getting wound up. I rode the Superstock Fireblade for the rest of the day, because the Superbike still wasn't ready. That night we loaded up the 600, drove back to Lincolnshire, swapped the engine over, then got up at three in the morning, after a couple of hours' sleep, and drove the 230 miles back to Castle Combe, to do the second day of testing.

I can watch the way someone wields a spanner and tell if they know what they're doing or not. Danny Horne, who has worked with me for years, can handle a spanner. He likes his hair gel and sunglasses, but just watching him as he fettles my bikes fills me with confidence. That's the kind of confidence you need in whoever is spannering for you – your life depends on their work. When I was swapping the engine over with PTR's lad, any lingering doubts I had about him were confirmed. It was clear to me, when it came to top-level racing motorbikes, the fella wasn't up to scratch, and wouldn't be in time for the first race. I remember he numbered the plugs caps back to front. To me, this was basic first-week-in-a-bike-shop stuff. He made me nervous. What else might he have done wrong? I didn't want him working on my bikes.

I have been asked if I would ever work with a complete arsehole if they were the best race mechanic in the world, but I don't think it would ever happen. Based on my 30 years of experience, the two things go hand-in-hand: if you're a good mechanic, you're normally a good bloke; maybe a bit of a weirdo, but still all right. You can be an all right bloke and a terrible mechanic, but it rarely, if ever, works the other way around.

After this test I told Wilson the situation I was in. To me, it was as plain as the nose on his face that he was having his trousers pulled down. I made it clear I couldn't ride bikes in that condition because I felt they weren't safe to race, but nothing changed. Perhaps he thought I was making it up.

Because we'd had next to no track time I pushed to race

at two British Superbike meetings. We went to Thruxton first, which is a fast track as British short circuits go, but nothing like the TT or Ulster obviously.

I think I qualified on the front row on the Superstock 1000 and inside the top ten on the Supersport bike. And I'm not a short circuit man, but I thought, bloody hell, when I put my mind to it I can do it.

I was running in the top six in the race, then I crashed. I lost the front end going into the chicane and didn't know why. I didn't think I was doing anything wrong or pushing too hard. I haven't had many of those. I was obviously too hard on the brakes for those conditions on those tyres. The crash didn't do much damage to the bike; it just scraped the side.

It was still a constructive weekend. I had some time on the bike, but not loads. The big problem with using a British Superbike race as a test is the fact that you are there for three nights and three days for very little track time. On Friday you get two 20-minute sessions, on Saturday you get one 20-minute session, and on Sunday you get a morning warm-up and one or two 20-minute races, depending which class you're running in. So, you get less than an hour and a half of track time for three days at a circuit. I could enter a few classes at a one-day club race and get more time on the bike. At that stage of the season a club race would be as useful, because I'm using the race as a test, getting stuff dialled in, not seriously looking at lap times. It's more about the feel than the times.

Then I went to Oulton Park on the first of May to race during a British Superbike weekend. The North West 200 was ten days away, the start of the TT two weeks after that. Wilson got me an entry for the Supersport and Superbike class in the same weekend. It was going to be a busy weekend, but I needed it. I needed time on the bike.

When the most important bike of my year, the Honda Fireblade in Superbike specification, which I would cane around the island to try and win an elusive TT, was wheeled out in front of me at Oulton Park, I could hardly believe what I was seeing. When I walked around the right-hand side I immediately saw that its exhaust silencer was sticking right out at a stupid angle. The exhaust silencer bracket had been put on the wrong way round. I could have given it to my grannie, Double-Decker Lil, and she would have worked out the bracket was the wrong way round. I had to take a photo of it, because it was such a bloody daft thing for anyone to have done.

Danny remembers the race meeting as an absolute waste of time. He was working on the bikes and coming across all sorts of problems. The clutch levers that had been fitted resulted in two burned-out clutches – two wrecked races. Another engine blew up as well. It was a case of put them in the van and let's get out of here. We had to strip the bikes and start again. We left Oulton Park early to get the bikes ready for the North West 200.

I told Wilson that I didn't want anyone else working on my bikes. He could organise getting all the parts, but I would sort out preparing the three of them – Superbike, Superstock and Supersport – with my dad and Johnny helping. I explained everything that I thought was wrong with the bikes to Wilson, but there were others telling him that there was nothing wrong with them and that everything was my fault. I was not happy.

Unfortunately, and confusingly, Wilson was believing them, not me. Why would I be criticising a world championship team before I'd even ridden the bike in a race I was employed to compete in if there wasn't something badly wrong? It didn't make sense. Danny, Cammy and Johnny were saying to me, 'We can't have them saying all this, because everyone thinks we're useless.' I felt the reputation of my lads was suffering because of the actions of others.

Oulton hadn't shed much light on anything, because the bikes were so far off. Much too soon, it was the middle of May and time for the North West 200 – a vital race to help set bikes up for the TT, because you could really get them wound up to top speed. There are other Irish races before the North West, like Cookstown, but you don't get the same clues to set-up and performance. The 2010 North West would be a disaster. I crashed the Superstock bike in practice. I tipped in to the last corner too early, clipped the kerb and lost the front end. It was 100 per cent my fault. I reckon my eye wasn't on the ball. I had so many things to think about and was distracted. I do like to build my own bikes, but I'd taken on too much this time, out of necessity. I couldn't race these bikes if I didn't think they were right. All the racers have two arms and two legs, that means so much of racing successfully is in the mind. And mine wouldn't be on the job if I didn't have my own lads rebuild these Hondas. This was the first time it struck home that I was making too many decisions and trying to race at the same time. The way the bikes were being delivered to us meant that I had the added pressure of either stripping them to a bare frame and starting again, or at least organising someone that I trusted to do it. Perhaps I wouldn't have minded this situation if I'd known what I was getting into, but it had been landed on me too close to the TT and I was on the back foot. Also, me, Johnny and my dad were doing it for free while someone was being paid to build what we were spending days and days trying to fix.

I'm someone who likes to have a lot on his plate. I'm happy to have distractions, but this was one too far, and I felt the buck stopped with me, because I'd set up this structure without a crew chief. I was thinking about gearing and gearboxes, concentrating on what I was going to change when I got in the pits, rather than thinking about what I was doing on the track, when I clipped the Coleraine kerb.

The day went from bad to worse. The clutch went in the Superbike, the 600 blew up and I can't remember the rest of the results. It was a race meeting that was memorable just for being bad. There wasn't a single positive to come out of it except that I hadn't injured myself badly crashing. I got back from Ireland on Sunday knowing there was just one week before we'd leave for the Isle of Man TT.

During all this, the pre-production of the film *TT3D: Closer to the Edge* was going on.

My involvement in the film began around the end of 2009. The boss of North One Television, the company who had taken over the contract for producing the Isle of Man TT highlights programme for ITV, had been approached by an outfit called CinemaNX. This Manx-based film production company was funded, in part, by Manx government money as an investment for the island. CinemaNX were talking about making a film of the TT and approached North One because they had all the footage and rights to the race action shot during the fortnight, action that was crucial to the film.

I was down in London talking to North One Television about their plans to make me a TV presenter. I didn't honestly think anything would come of it, but if it did it might be fun and I'd earn a few quid, which would oil the wheels money-wise. As far as money goes, my opinion is that you're better off looking at it, than for it.

The London meeting had been scheduled so that I could also go to the get-together about the film. Andy Spellman came into the meeting with me as an adviser, but we were totally out of our depth. I didn't have a clue, and all of a sudden we are in a room with people who've made films with Christopher Walken and Zac Efron.

When I first met him, I thought Andy worked for North One, because he'd been one of the TV directors that filmed a lot of riders for the 2009 ITV coverage. It turned out he was a freelance producer fresh from the world of Formula One cars – who also had his fingers in other TV projects and businesses of his own. Road racing couldn't be much further removed from the F1 world, but he must have liked what I said, or how I said it, because he got all revved up to try and get me involved in a TV programme. After the TT in 2009 we met at the Goodwood Festival of Speed and he explained he was keen to act as an agent for me on the TV side of things, before I even had a TV side of things. He said it would be a learning curve for both of us, but he knew the TV and commercial world better than me and he promised he would make sure I didn't get shafted or involved in anything that would make me look like a dickhead. He added that if I was being a dickhead he'd tell me. I said, 'You'll do for me, boy,' still thinking nothing would come of it.

Back in the meeting, we sat listening to Steve Christian, who was the executive producer of the proposed TT film, and the director, Richard De Aragues, who were doing all the talking. De Aragues had filmed adverts and small projects and I picked up on the fact that this was going to be his first film.

The original plan, as outlined at this meeting, was for *Closer to the Edge* to be a two-part documentary. The first part was going to be a dramatisation of the 1967 race between two of the all-time greats, Giacomo Agostini and Mike Hailwood. It's a race that has gone down in history. The film production company wanted me to be a stunt man for it, dressed up as one or both of them. The second part of the film was going to be a documentary of the 2010 TT. In that first meeting they were talking of budgets of 30–40 million quid. Even though most of the talk was going over my head, I was picking up enough to know it was massively ambitious. I was in nod-smile-agree mode. I came out of the meeting thinking, 'As long as I've got a hole in my arse, that's not happening.'

With this film job and the interest from the TV production company people who thought I could become a TV presenter, I started thinking I was in some kind of *Truman Show*; like I was the Jim Carrey character, being secretly filmed for others' amusement, with everyone laughing at me doing these things. The difference between me and the Jim Carrey character, of course, was that everything that happened to me was happening for real, in the real world – sometimes it just didn't seem like it.

Over the coming months the *Closer to the Edge* plan was scaled down, but still moving along. In early 2010, I got a call from Andy Spellman saying he thought it was going to happen, but the budget had shrunk a lot. Someone said it ended up costing a couple of million quid, not the mega money they'd been talking about at the start.

As the planning of the film started, the production company said they wanted the bike I was going to race, Wilson Craig's Honda Fireblade, to have a simple, classic paint scheme. The Agostini and Hailwood part of the project had been dropped, but someone clearly wanted to shoehorn in a visual link to those days.

The problem was, Wilson had a lot of sponsors lined up for the season and the producers didn't want their logos on the bike. I was also asked if I needed to wear any logos on my leathers, and I must've been getting a truck ready for an MoT or something when the call came in, because I just said 'No' and signed a contract to say I could ride in plain leathers. I'd forgotten Dainese, Pirelli,

Red Torpedo, AGV, Elas ... That caused a bit of a headache for Andy Spellman, who was trying to sort it all out.

I don't know if it was because of the director's background in adverts, but it was De Aragues who was obsessed with the whole look of the bike and the leathers. There were a thousand emails going back and forth, between the film company and Andy, about these leathers. Dainese weren't happy about the lack of logos, while De Aragues wasn't happy with any logo at all. The film director wanted the number 8, that was to be stitched on the back of the leathers, tweaking this way and that. I kept being reminded, by Andy, that I was in breach of two contracts I'd signed – one with Dainese and the other with the film people. I'd shrug.

At times like that I just think, 'Fuck it, it'll be right.' And it normally is. Someone will bail me out, and it's better to seek forgiveness than ask for permission. If anyone had taken the hump and said they didn't want to deal with me any more, then it wouldn't have been the end of the world. The people at Dainese are so nice, the kit is mega, and I don't want any of them to get into trouble at work over me, but when it comes down to losing a sponsor or something, I'm just not bothered.

Part of me thinks these sponsors have got involved with me and they know what I'm like. In the last couple of years lots of stuff would've fallen apart if it wasn't for Andy, but I would still have had the trucks to go back to and I'd still be racing bikes. When those are the most important things in your life, and they are to me, then it's difficult for people to hold me over a barrel. I don't worry about any of the other stuff – TV, sponsors, or whatever – crashing down. In fact, there are times I almost wish it all would.

On the eve of the 2010 TT, because of the state of the bikes and the work needed to ready them, the film wasn't on my mind. I knew I had to do a few bits and pieces, but I was concentrating on what was right in front of me – three motorbikes that needed sorting.

We got on with preparing the bikes for the toughest test in road racing. The TT can find any weakness in a bike and hammer it till it fails. I was so busy prepping the bikes, right up until the last minute, that I hadn't even thought about racing them, or how I was going to challenge for a win, until I was on the ferry.

CHAPTER 13

THE FATEFUL SENIOR

'A death can happen in a race meeting and it barely sends one ripple through my part of the paddock.'

WHEN WE ARRIVED on the Isle of Man we had to drive straight to one of my long-term personal sponsors, Gary Hewitt of ELAS, to borrow parts out of a bike he had on display in his house. Gary had bought my 2009 Fireblade race bike, from Shaun Muir, to put on display in his house, and I wanted to borrow the swingarm out of it for the Wilson Craig bike. It was the same swingarm I'd bought from Spondon. We went to Gary's directly from the ferry, and then it was finally time to ride ...

After the first night of practice, I told the lads we had a lot to do. I knew then it was going to be a long and tough fortnight. The lack of high-speed stability made the Superbike very hard work through places like the 170 mph right-hander at the end of the Cronk-Y-Voddy straight. The bike was dead nervous and lacked accuracy. I had to fight it, and that, in turn, was making me suffer from arm pump.

When you're hanging on for grim death on a bike that isn't handling right, the muscles in your forearms are doing a lot of work and they demand a lot of blood. Because you're tense, the blood can flow in, but it struggles to flow out. This means your muscles go absolutely rock-solid and your hands go numb. You end up with no feeling in your hands and fingers, so you can't judge how hard you're pulling the brake lever, or how hard you're gripping your handlebars. Arm pump also alters your position on the bike, as you can't fully commit to hang off the side of the bike through corners because you can't feel the 'bars. It's not a nice feeling, but I hadn't suffered with it for years.

Riding the bike with a full tank of 24 litres of fuel on board totally changed the bike's character too.

My idea that year had been that I'd make all the decisions so I didn't have to explain everything to a middle-man. It sounded like a great idea, but the decisions were coming thick and fast as we'd been dropped in it, having to prepare the bikes ourselves, because of how we felt about PTR's preparation. The lads, Cammy, Danny and Johnny, were asking me everything about set-up – stuff they'd normally ask me about, but I had my head full of all the prep I had to do as well. They knew exactly what they were doing, but mechanics need guidance for set-up. That comes from the rider, but it was taking too much time and thought to explain everything when we had so much else to do. Do we put another clutch in it? What's the gearing? Do we change the rear ride height? I was racing three bikes – Superbike, Superstock, Supersport, as usual.

At many race meetings I'll race a Superbike, with over 210 bhp running on slick tyres. I'll also race a Superstock 1000 on treaded tyres and the Supersport 600, a really trick bit of kit, with fancy ignition, but much less power and weight than the 1000-cc Superbike, meaning it needs a very different riding style. The Supersport 600 – that all of us in the team refer to as 'the little bike' – runs on treaded, road legal tyres, not slicks.

Some of the other real roads riders will also compete on a Supertwin – the 650-cc, two-cylinder racers, like Suzuki SV650s or Kawasaki ER-6s – or 125s and 250s, little two-strokes.

To be competitive in all the classes, you need to be able to switch from one riding style to another without even thinking. A rider must be able to deal with braking markers changing – literally where you have to brake to make it around the corner in one piece. The racing line and turn-in points alter. Even the overtaking opportunities can differ. And the way to set up each of these bikes to get the best out of them is different too.

Having said all that, we put the hours in during practice week, and by the end of it I was feeling some kind of confidence. I had done a 128 mph lap, but Hutchie and McGuinness were doing 130s.

My girlfriend, Kate, had sorted a house for us to all stay in: me, her, the three mechanics, but I ended up sleeping in a mate's camper van in the bottom paddock and, some nights, in my own van, down on the Southern 100 course. All my mechanics are top lads, but I needed my own space. They all knew me, and that I was weird, so I don't think they took it personally.

The first race of any modern-era TT is Saturday's Superbike, now a six-lapper for the 1000-cc bikes, machines that are more powerful and using more advanced technology than British Superbikes do on comparatively safe short circuits.

After the grief of the season so far, working so hard to get the bikes something like ready, I went into the first TT feeling all right. I finished the race in second place behind Ian Hutchinson on the Padgett's Fireblade, but was given a 30-second penalty for breaking the new pit-lane speed limit. I wasn't happy.

I started asking where the calibration certificates were, and when the equipment had been calibrated last, but no one came up with any answers. It seemed like they hadn't operated with a tolerance. We'd set our bike to run at 60 kph, calculating it to the gearing and the tyre size, and had it checked by Brains, Mark Woodage, who had the formula, but their speed gun was reading 60.112 or something. They repeated that the limit was 60 mph, and I wasn't doing 61, so surely I was doing 60. There was no tolerance. It was the first year of using that system and I don't think they'd thought it through. There was no way we could check our speed against their radar gun, and their gun could have been slightly out. A penalty of 30 seconds was added to my race time, for being 0.18 of a per cent faster than the limit. When it's that close, surely it makes sense to do what even the police do and run a tolerance. Yes, we could've have set the speed limit below 60, to be on the safe side, but we're trying to win a race, and when TTs have been won and lost by three seconds you don't want to give the opposition any breaks, so we set it correctly.

We'd worked our bollocks off and second would have been a good start to the week. I wasn't going to beat Hutchie that day, but a podium would have been some return on the effort the lads had put in.

Kate kept me calm. She didn't try to reason with me, she just called them rude names like I had been doing.

I thought, I'll win a race and show them. I didn't, but I came close. In the next race, the first of two Supersport 600 races, I came second by three seconds, again to Hutchie, and didn't go to the podium. I rode up the slip road, past the parc fermé where the podium placed riders are supposed to stop, and went and had a cup of tea in the awning instead. I wouldn't have gone to the podium at all, but Wilson's wife Esther told me I should go for Wilson, so I did. I still think I'd made my point. I was being awkward. Perhaps people thought I was being childish, but I didn't care and still don't. I had my reason for thinking what I thought. I'd have done the same if I had won.

On the plus side, after a disastrous start to the season our bikes were holding up well. We should've had two second places if it wasn't for the 30-second penalty that dropped me to fourth. I came fifth in the Superstock on Thursday and fourth in the same day's second Supersport race. Meanwhile, Hutchie had won all four solo races so far.

Then came the Senior, the biggest race of the week, the one I and every other racer really wants to win. A six-lapper, not four laps like the Superstock and Supersport 600 races. The fateful Senior, as it turned out.

Going into the race I was still feeling annoyed about the penalty. It wasn't the best frame of mind to be in at the start of a TT. The anger would give me a push going into it, but would it give me the focus needed for two hours of tough racing?

The Senior was, as it traditionally is, the last race of the TT festival, meaning it would be another year before we all got the chance to try to win a TT again. It's not like a MotoGP or World Superbike race, where if you have a bad one you only have to wait a fortnight or even less to make up for it. I had to make it count. I wanted to do it for Wilson and the boys.

There's always one extra lap of practice for those doing the Senior, just after the second Supersport race, this year on the Thursday, and we'd made a couple of minor changes to the bike, a slight alteration to the rear ride height. The bike now felt spot-on and I was full of confidence. I felt I could go and do the business.

Two racers had died during the second Supersport race on Thursday, the New Zealander Paul Dobbs and an Austrian racer,

Martin Loicht. I didn't know either well. It might be hard for people outside the world of road racing to understand, grasp or even believe, but a death can happen in a race meeting and it barely sends one ripple through my part of the paddock. It doesn't make the slightest difference to me. Someone may mention it to me if I was stood next to them in a queue. They might be taking it to heart but I wouldn't.

I'm not trying to delude myself by not recognising it. Some people could regard it as heartless, but I'm that focused on what I'm doing I don't think about anyone else. I knew it was Dobbs's own fault, by which I mean no one else had made him crash by dropping oil or petrol. And no one twists anyone's arm to race the TT. From all I've heard Paul Dobbs loved racing the TT and did everything he could to make sure he could afford to go back there to race. He went doing what he loved. A lot of people would say that was a good way to go.

I knew he'd crashed at Ballagarey. It's the kind of corner where, if you come off, it's game over. Everyone who raced at the TT believed the same.

Friday 11 June, Senior day, and I didn't do anything differently to any other TT race day. I was still staying in the camper van while the team, Kate and her cousin Fay, who is Johnny's missus, were all in the rented house I was paying for. Perhaps they were wondering what they'd done wrong, but most likely not. No one mentioned it. They hadn't done anything wrong; they all knew my strange ways and realised I was under some kind of pressure.

All that TT I would run number eight on my bike. In 2008 I had tried number one. At most races, wearing number one on your bike means you're the champion, or you won the last running of that annual event, but not at the TT. Because the TT is run like a time trial, with riders leaving at ten-second intervals, there is no need for a traditional grid. Times from practice don't affect the start order, it's all decided in advance. The fastest riders get to choose what position they want to set off in. I think I had the third or fourth choice that year. You consider who is around you and pick your spot. John McGuinness never liked me going directly behind him, so there was a gentleman's agreement to avoid that.

Though I liked starting at number one, out at the front, running my own race, I hadn't had too much luck with that number at the TT, so I thought I'd try a different approach. I thought perhaps I needed a carrot to chase, so I went for number eight, with plenty of carrots in front of me.

Michael Dunlop was in front of me. When I'd caught him during races earlier in the week he'd played silly buggers, trying to pass me back.

In the first Superbike race, I'd passed Dunlop, who then did everything he could to pass me on the straight, but I was already ten seconds ahead of him on corrected time. He was holding me up and it wasn't safe. Before the Senior I walked up to him and said, 'When I catch you, play the white man.' Perhaps that was a bit cocky, already assuming I was going to catch him, and he said something cocky back, so I thought, 'Bloody hell …' Anyway, I caught him on the first lap up the Mountain Mile, he heard me coming and put his foot out to show he knew I was there and I could pass. If you're catching someone on the first lap they're better off tucking in behind you and seeing where they can make up time for their next race.

I caught Bruce Anstey and Cameron Donald too. It was obvious I was doing something right without needing them to pull me along. When I'm in that position I have to keep my focus on what I'm doing, not focus on them. As soon as I get to them I have to pass them, by any possible means, because if I pause for a second I'm travelling at their pace, not mine; I've lost the rhythm and that takes some getting back. The race has gone. So, go over the hedge, up the kerb, whatever you have to do to get past. Multiple TT winner Phillip McCallen told me that.

When you're going off in position one, you're only passing backmarkers in the fifth and sixth laps, and a race-winner is so much faster he should always be able to find a way past. So it's easy to see that going off number one suits some racers, who can get in a rhythm and set a high pace without needing a carrot to pull them along.

I had friends and family holding up pit boards around the track to give me information letting me know how the race was going. In a grand prix, the riders are passing the pit once every two minutes, and they are mass start races so they can see who is ahead of them. In a TT, you don't pass the pits for over 17 minutes, and you can be racing neck and neck with someone who is two miles up the road from you, so having pit boards out on the track is even more important.

I was seeing P1 and P2, telling me I was leading or in second place. I was in a fight, but holding my own. The first board was held by Uncle Rob, who, like Uncle Rodders, wasn't my uncle. Anyway, he was doing the signalling at Ballacreg. He does it in the driveway of a house. The next board is Rhencullen 2, which is where Andy Kershaw, the radio DJ, held the board for me.

You come out of the village of Kirkmichael, go through Rhencullen 1, over a jump, then right, right again and there's another jump with a wall on your right-hand side. Next to it is a bit of a walkway up the side of a house and I have a pit board there. In 2005 I saw that Richard Britton had a pit board at that position. Before that I'd never heard about anyone having a board there. I must have been near Richard on the track just going through that section and spotted it as it was held out for him. I thought it was a mega idea, and decided to have one there myself.

The people who are doing the pit boards are listening to the commentary on Manx Radio. The commentators have screens that tell them who is leading and by what time through different timing points. My mates are positioned far enough away from the timing section to have a few seconds in which to put the numbers on the board and hold it out as I come by. The board is like those used at MotoGP or Formula One, but it'll only give the minimum information because you can't read it otherwise. So it'll say P and a number, and that's my position in the race. Then it'll show a plus sign and a number, and that's how many seconds I am in front of the rider behind me. It'll also show a minus sign and a number, and that's how far I am behind the rider in front of me. This is all on corrected time, not on the road. At the TT, the winner could be in eighth or, theoretically, thirtieth place on the road. The pit board doesn't tell me who is in front or behind, like a GP one would. That's too much information to try and take in. You're pretty busy going through a section like Rhencullen 2, but it's just good to get a glimpse of where I am in the race.

Some people are a bit confused about the usefulness of a pit board, because you're surely trying the hardest you possibly can. But sometimes, if you get the set-up of the bike just right and all the stars are lined up, you can be riding at lap record speed, yet it feels slow because everything's working so well. At times like this, the bike isn't getting out of shape, so you're not trying hard to keep it under control and you're not tensing up and tiring yourself out, so it feels slow. The other side of the coin is, you can be trying so hard, that the bike is shaking its head, you're up on the kerbs and two-wheel drifting into corners and you think you must be riding faster than ever, but you're not. The pit board takes the guessing out of your performance, at least in terms of position in relation to the other riders.

If you're seeing a pit board that's saying P1 and the numbers keep growing, then you know whatever you're doing is right, so you don't have to change anything. If the board says -2, +1, then I'd think, I might be able to get him in front, but to be honest I don't have a lot to spare in a TT. Unless there's a problem with the bike, I'm racing to win from the time the starter waves me off. I can't go faster than I'm going at any point, but it might keep my mind on the job a little bit more. It can sometimes be hard to stay completely focused for 100 per cent of a two-hour race.

A mate called Tom does another board at Sulby Bridge, on the right-hand side, just before Ginger Hall. The pit boards at Rhencullen and Sulby are close together, but the timing points they're referring to are far apart. The first board is for the timing point at Glen Helen, nine miles into the lap, and the Sulby Bridge board is telling me the times at Ballaugh, 17 miles in.

My little sister used to do my board coming out of the Gooseneck, but since she became a mother, Steve, a mate of mine, does it. And that's the last one I have. In later years, if the TAS lads have any mechanics coming over that aren't working, ones who are just over for the craic, they'll do a board at the Nook, about half a mile from the pits. That one is used to tell me to come in for a pit-stop. A local lady, Yvonne Murphy, who visited me when I broke my ankle at the Southern 100 in 2003, did that board for me for years. Sometimes I can forget if I'm on the third or the fourth lap of a six-lap race, so I start wondering about it. Not coming in to the pits on the right lap is a disaster, because these bikes won't do three 38-mile laps on one tank of fuel. So, in a four-lap race, the Supersport 600 races and the Superstock TT, you do four laps with a pit-stop at the end of the second. For the six-lap Superbike and Senior TTs you have to pit twice for fuel and a rear tyre. A pit board at the Nook means me not having to think about it.

I was pushing like hell in the first two laps of the Senior, seeing either P1 or P2 and time of plus or minus 0.5 seconds. The board wasn't telling me who I was trading the lead with, but I had a feeling it was McGuinness. I was thinking, 'I'm in with a shout, I can do this.' I was riding the TT like a short circuit. I wasn't bouncing off the kerbs, but I was using every inch of the road. I was pushing the front into Governor's Bridge; braking so hard the back end was off the ground; turning it in with the front brake on; sliding the rear. I was really trying hard. The rule was always slow on the slow, fast on the fast: keep it smooth on the slower stuff and really make the difference on the ballsy corners, but we're talking about losing races by a second or two, so I was trying like hell everywhere.

I came into the pits at the end of the second lap of six. In previous years Johnny had always done my back wheel, but we changed it for this TT. He didn't like the pressure and I don't blame him. I didn't enjoy it when I'd done it for Finnegan in 2003. Johnny held his hands up and said he didn't really want to do it, so Danny did it. It wasn't a problem, because Danny had done the job for the Australian Cameron Donald in the past.

Johnny filled the tank. Cammy handed me a drink bottle with a long straw to stick up the inside of my helmet, changed my visor and gave me information while he did it. I loved that, because he was always so calm and precise, it was like listening to the shipping forecast. This was the one and only time I could hear a bit of urgency in his delivery. He didn't think we had one hand on the trophy, but he knew we could win it. He told me I was leading, but by fuck-all. The pit-stop was spot-on.

The bikes obviously burn their first tank of fuel gradually over two laps, so you don't even feel the change, but then 24 litres are dumped into the tank and the bike immediately gains over 20 kg in the space of a 30-second pit-stop. You don't notice the weight difference in the fast sections, but you do in the slower parts of the track. It's harder to pull the bike up on the brakes and when you lean it over, after the initial turn-in, the bike wants to bank over further, to fall on its side. You can hear the forks bottom out when you're on the brakes, and you have to ease off so you don't lose the front end.

I was up and running on the third lap, flat knacker out of Union Mills thinking, 'I've got to make this count.' I was pushing as hard as I could go. I was at my limit, but the gap to McGuinness was nothing.

I knew where the line was. The line of performance, of skill and of grip, that I can feel and push up to and be right on the edge, but I was pushing past it – and had been even on laps one and two. But there's a time and a place for riding in this way, and the 2010 Senior was it. The bike was skating about a lot more than either I or the Honda was comfortable with. Through the faster corners I was getting two-wheel slides. My arse was nipping.

You can push past the line on certain corners and I was getting comfortable with it, like I never had in the past. Perhaps I was getting too confident pushing past the line. The line has moved all through my racing life as I've improved and got faster, but at any one time I've known that if I push past the line I might crash. Still, I hadn't had any major moments in the race. I'd had a little one near where Andy Kershaw was pit boarding, Rhencullen. We carry a lot of speed through there, a good 160–170 mph, and the bike landed with the wheels slightly out of line so it tankslapped when it touched down, but nothing too bad because I was carrying loads of forward momentum and in a situation like that, speed is your friend. The bike wants to keep going in a straight line, so the gyroscopic force of the front wheel straightens it out. You just have to be sure it can straighten out before the next bend.

Three miles into the third lap I came up to Ballagarey. It's one of my favourite corners. Another big balls one. An extremely fast right-hander. By fast, I mean 170 mph, with the bike leant hard over. It goes over a slight crest and there's a wall on your left-hand side. You don't brake, you just flick it back a gear, into fifth, and get straight back on the throttle to drive through the corner. You're on zero throttle for tenths of a second and then straight back on the power. With everything being as tight as it was in this race, I clicked it back a gear and I was back on the gas even quicker than normal. That slight crest in the road just took enough weight off the front of the bike to cause the front wheel to tuck. When this happens, the front tyre is no longer tracking round the bend, it's sliding to the outside of the corner.

If I hadn't had the experience of dozens of front-wheel slides at that kind of speed, in those conditions, surrounded by walls and telegraph poles, I'm pretty sure I would be dead. The fractions of a second where I was trying, but failing, to save the front-end slide meant I travelled further around the corner. If I'd bailed out at the time I lost the front end I'd have gone straight into a wall at 90 degrees at 160 mph plus, but I hung on for grim death, got it a bit further around the corner and glanced off the wall. I hit the wall on one side of the road, then ricocheted over to the other side. Then the bike exploded. Back in the pits, my mechanics didn't have a clue what was happening.

Danny, Cammy and Johnny remember the travelling marshal going out on his bike. Danny thought that some poor bugger had come off somewhere. He never thought it might be me. Then a red flag came out. Another mechanic, Denver, who is now part of my TAS team, walked over to Danny and said, 'It's Guy.' Danny's heart sank and his thoughts went straight back to his brother being killed racing at Mallory Park in 2006.

TT mechanics, like the racers they work with, are a bit of a different breed. Making a mistake on any racing bike is bad, but the TT turns little mistakes into bad situations. Everything went through Danny's head. Had he done the back wheel up? But it was nothing he or anyone else in my pit had done.

Kate was in tears. They asked Danny to go in the office, but he didn't want to. Cammy and Johnny had disappeared. They all said it felt like a lifetime before the word came through that I was all right, but Danny still wasn't confident. He remembered when Martin Finnegan was killed. Martin's wife had been told by someone he was up and talking.

I tried to get up and walk, but my back didn't feel right and hurt like hell. I tried moving all my fingers and toes and it seemed as if everything was still working, but I knew I'd badly hurt something. A marshal started talking to me, dead calmly, just chatting about normal stuff. A Welsh fella – I've seen him since. No one was getting flustered.

I was complaining about my back hurting, I could sense people panicking and I was strapped to a stretcher. I could feel everything, so I wasn't shitting myself. And I'd had some morphine by then, too. That keeps a fella calm. I was dazed, but I knew I was only a stone's throw from the hospital, so I didn't know why they'd sent a helicopter for me. It was concerning me a bit more that they were putting me in a helicopter to take me over the road to the hospital.

As far as I know it was the first time the Senior had been red-flagged, which is something considering what must've occurred in that race in the previous hundred-odd years of its history.

When I arrived at the hospital the staff were pricking me to make sure I could feel everything. They had cut the leathers off me by this point. I'm pretty sure I hadn't put clean pants on. I like a three-day cycle of underwear, four at a push.

I was put in an MRI scan and it showed I'd broken four vertebrae and four ribs. They thought I'd broken my leg too, but they were looking at the mess from the old 2003 Southern 100 injury. I also broke some ribs, punctured my lung and singed my eyebrows and fringe, but worse things happen at sea.

When people hear you've broken your back they think you're going to be crippled, but a large percentage of people who break their backs aren't paralysed. I was one of the lucky ones. The Dainese kit I was wearing did its job.

Johnny, Cammy, Danny and my girlfriend, Kate, all got to the hospital quickly. Cammy was in a bit of a state. Even though I had been a bit distant during that TT, not staying in the house with them, we were very close. Perhaps they were still thinking, 'Did I tighten that?' They all have the ability to work in the stressful situation of a TT pit-stop and I trust them with my life, literally, but they must've been doubting themselves a bit too. It was natural for the mechanics to wonder, because it was so soon after the pit-stop. When they saw me talking and smiling, they were straight back to normal.

My mum had been watching up at the Keppelgate, just before the run down to Creg-Ny-Baa. She knew something bad had happened. Andy Spellman arranged for the pace car to take to her straight to the hospital. He was thinking I was on my last legs. My mum's seen it all, though. My dad's broken his back, so it wasn't new to her. I'm sure Big Rita wouldn't have been panicking.

Maybe I'm selfish, but it never even enters my head the worry that I'm putting those around me through by racing where and how I do. The only reason I'll stop racing motorbikes is when the bullshit outweighs the buzz I get out of it, not the amount of pain I'm going to put my family through. The crash didn't change a single thing about my attitude to racing. Not one thing. All I wanted to do was get fit and race again.

When I was in hospital I couldn't work out why my eyebrows were singed. Then I was shown a photo of an explosion, with orange flames as high as the top of a lamp-post, and thought, 'That was nothing to do with me, was it?' A full tank of fuel is going to make a mess, given half a chance.

I was put on the ward and later in the day they brought in the local Manx rider, and TT front runner, Conor Cummins. He had a massive crash at the Verandah, on the Mountain, in the afternoon re-run of the race I'd crashed out of and caused to be stopped. He'd been pushing for the lead too when he went off the side of the Mountain, literally. Because he and his bike left the road, the race carried on.

McGuinness, who I'd been racing nip and tuck for the lead when I crashed, broke down in the re-run and Ian Hutchinson won the race. Hutchie told me, a while later when I interviewed him for *Performance Bikes*, that he was about to retire with a mechanical problem when the race was red-flagged. If I hadn't crashed when I did he'd have been out and not taken his fifth win of the week, a clean sweep which I don't think will be repeated.

Simon Buckmaster, the PTR boss, sent out a press release while I was lying in hospital with a broken back, telling anyone who'd listen that the bikes were more than competitive and that I had been unprofessional. The statement accused me of courting publicity. It seemed like he was telling me how to win a TT, but I don't remember him winning one. From what I've heard, he started three TTs, finished two of them with a best finish of thirty-first, according the Isle of Man TT's own database.

It didn't annoy me, because, as I said to the lads and as I've repeated many times since, those that know know, and those that don't know don't matter. I knew what the people who really mattered to any of us knew would think, and if some people wanted to believe something else, then we wouldn't want to work with their kind anyway. I don't think any of the shit that people might throw in my direction makes any difference to my career chances. If they have anything about them they know the truth, or they'll make an effort to find it out. I've never given a damn about what's written in *MCN* or on internet forums or what other racers thought about me. In a way I like all the bollocks and bullshit that's spouted about me. It gees me on a bit.

At the end of 2010 I was still considering riding for Wilson the following season. I told him it was dead simple – I would ride for him if he gave me the bikes from the off and we'd do it ourselves with more time and less panic. Wilson said that wouldn't work, Buckmaster must have the bikes, so I left Wilson Craig to join Hector and Philip Neill's TAS Suzuki team.

Wilson stayed with Buckmaster and PTR, and signed the Australian Cameron Donald and William Dunlop, Michael's older brother, to race for them for the 2011 season. William doesn't get the same attention as his younger brother, but he's quick, and a race winner on the roads. A few years later we'd be TAS Suzuki team-mates. Cameron is spot-on, he's a TT winner, he understands how bikes work and he's fast. He went one way, leaving the TAS team to join Wilson Craig, and I went the other.

It took a year, from my crash at Ballagarey, for the shit to hit the fan but it eventually did.

At the 2011 TT Cameron was on it, out to prove a point, and Wilson's bikes were fast, but they kept breaking down, when the camshafts would fail. The cam they were using had a radical closing profile that was putting a lot of stress on the camshaft. The rules limited the amount of lift, so tuners look at ways of lengthening the duration the valve is open. Legendary tuning guru Phil Irving came up with the theory, or at least explained it in his famous book, *Tuning for Speed*, back in the 1950s. A cam is normally roughly egg-shaped, but Irving had the idea of putting a flat top on the cam. This way the valve would 'jump' after being flicked off the flat edge of the cam, giving more lift than the cam actually measured. But doing this puts a lot of strain on the cam, and if any race is going to find an engine's weak spot, it's likely to be the Isle of Man TT.

Cameron should've won two races that year. Some websites and reporters called it cruel luck, but, to me, there was no luck about it. In any event, Wilson Craig and PTR fell out too. Before the end of the 2011 TT all the fairings of Wilson Craig's bikes had the PTR logo covered up with pieces of black tape. Wilson didn't want to give them any more publicity.

I felt the bikes weren't right, and any team manager looking to sign me will have seen enough to feel the same as me. It all came back to the saying, those that know know, those that don't don't matter.

CHAPTER 14

DOWN WITH A BANG

'It's probably the last time I cried. I lay there, not having the strength to lift myself up, thinking, "What are you doing?"'

AFTER THE 2010 TT, I spent a week in Noble's Hospital on the Isle of Man, and Kate stayed out there with me. The amount of get-well-soon cards and messages of support was amazing. When I got back to Kirmington I had another week off work while I limped around the farm, getting looked after by the Lancasters.

I had been prescribed some strong painkillers and after a couple of weeks I was really struggling to get off them. In the past I'd watched *Trainspotting*, looked at the stories of heroin addicts not being able to kick their habits and thought, 'You weak-kneed bastards. It's only drugs, what's up with you?' And now I was addicted to these tramadol painkillers. When I needed one I would be shaking and had no energy. I had to have them.

As soon as I took them I just felt normal, 100 per cent. Not high or feeling any kind of altered state, just normal, with a little bit of pain.

At that point, so soon after breaking my back, I could hardly lift my arms up and I was constipated. I hadn't had a shit for over a week and I was tearing myself another arsehole trying to move something. Nobody ever put more effort into having a dump, but all that would come out was a pea, or less. It wasn't a good time.

I was straight back on the fitness trail and borrowed a turbo trainer from my brother just to do something, to try to keep active. You bolt your bicycle to the turbo trainer rig, so when you pedal, the back wheel spins a roller, and you can increase or decrease its resistance. I couldn't bend down to hold the bars, so I'd have it set up outside the farm and I would grip onto a drainpipe while I pedalled – just to be doing something. Anything. I was struggling mentally and physically.

Once, during this week off work, I slipped over in the shower and started crying to myself. It's probably the last time I cried. I lay there, not having the strength to lift myself up, thinking, 'Fucking hell, Martin, what are you doing? Man up!' I managed to get up before Mrs Lancaster had to come and help me.

I went back to work, or at least trying to work, at Dad's truck yard, but I was still not managing to get off the prescription painkillers.

It got to the stage where my doctor wouldn't give me any more of them, but I had some left. They came in little capsules and I had to open them, take some of the grains of painkiller out and mix some aspirin in. It took me a month of this to get off them.

Around the same time it came out that I'd been seeing another woman behind Kate's back. When I first met Steph she was a salesperson for a pharmaceutical drug company. She was doing an Open University course and, in 2009, she came to my dad's to interview me for some part of it. She kept popping in and I eventually fell for her, then it all got messy. One hundred per cent my fault ...

It would lead to me splitting with Kate, leaving the Lancasters' farm in Kirmington, where I'd lived for years, and moving in with a mate in Caistor.

During this very low time, when I felt not much was going to plan, a mysterious and unusual character came onto the scene. I didn't want to change any names in this book if I had a choice, but I had to alter this one. Mr X is a very serious bloke. He is deeply involved with a specific charity and had trucks to transport donations around. He approached my dad to fix one of his trucks and I ended up doing the job.

My dad had met Mr X before I had, and told me he was very religious. The first time I met him he said, 'I've been sent to see you. He's not ready for you yet. He has big plans for you.'

Perhaps it was because I was still coming off those painkillers, but I felt vulnerable. I must've done, because I took it all in.

Mr X would regularly turn up at my work. He would arrive in Bentleys, Aston Martins, other sports cars and a very rare five-cylinder Transit that I thought was the best of the lot. I didn't even know they existed. It sounded like he had fingers in a lot of pies, but he reckoned he spent a million quid a year keeping his name off the internet. It must have worked. When his real name is typed into Google nothing comes up. That's bloody unusual on its own. He said he was involved with the SAS, but I had a strong feeling he had a shady past. He made me think he had links with the underworld, yet his charity now had contracts with the UK government.

He knew my dad was into World War II and military history and he would bring him presents like random bits of Spitfires and Lancaster bombers.

Eventually, it came out that Mr X wanted me to work for him, indirectly. He wanted my earnings to go to him and then he'd distribute some of it to me. It became clear, from the things he said – he even admitted it – that he was having private investigators do background checks on the people I trusted, like my accountant and Andy Spellman.

I don't know if he was running some kind of cult, but it seemed like he had followers giving him a lot of money, perhaps for religious reasons. I'm not saying there wasn't a lot of good being done with the money, but Mr X had a lot of very nice stuff too.

I went to stay at his house for a night. He had loads of servants. One of them would follow him with a glass ashtray as Mr X walked around smoking a huge cigar. When he got in his Jacuzzi, someone would appear with his slippers and put them by the side of it.

It sounds ridiculous, writing about it now, because normally I'd run a mile, but he had a way about him that somehow sucked me in. And it wasn't just me. It seemed like he worked on people in a psychological way. He told me that he saw me the racer and me the truck fitter as being both in awe of each other and looking down on each other and in conflict. It struck a chord. I didn't feel brainwashed at the time, but with hindsight I think I was.

I was certainly coming around to his way of thinking, starting to believe that maybe everything I earned should go to him. Mr X knew I was mad about the Britten, the extremely rare New Zealand-built, V-twin race bike – my favourite motorcycle of all time – and told me he knew where one might be for sale. He was flicking all my switches. Making me think, 'He's not a messer.'

He'd helped a lot of people through his international charity work, but there were a couple of things that put doubts in my mind about him. He was rude to the people around him, the servants he would have following in his wake with a glass ashtray or slippers or whatever, and I didn't like that rudeness.

He said stuff like, 'I hate myself for buying new cars, but I can't help myself because I love them so much. I see such poverty, but I buy these cars, so the only way I can get around it is to give them away.'

Andy got on well with Mr X at first, and they seemed to talk regularly. Andy has told me since that he was given some good advice on how to deal with me when I was acting like an arsehole towards him. Mr X offered Andy an Aston Martin V8 Vantage, but he turned it down. Wisely.

Mr X was good to talk to. He is very intelligent in lots of ways. You could have a yarn about all sorts of things and he'd know about them. I like people like that.

During this time Mr X was getting more and more interested in my finances. He was requesting copies of contracts I had with sponsors.

Meanwhile, I'd been doing any kind of exercise I could from the time I got out of hospital, my injuries were healing and I was feeling much stronger. I missed the Southern 100 in July, but I was fit for August's Ulster GP. I did all right in my first race back. I got on the podium in one of the Superbike races and it showed I could still race at fast road circuits – the Dundrod is the fastest, with lots of man's corners. I wasn't in any doubt, but the proof of the pudding is always in the eating, and I proved I still had the balls for it, even after the crash I'd had. I wasn't scared of dying at a road race. I was more scared of running out of teabags.

Then came the Gold Cup meeting at Scarborough. It had been a terrible year, but a win at Oliver's Mount would be a good way to end the season. The bikes had been back to PTR, Buckmaster's lot in Louth, and to me they were unrideable in the wet due to the way the ignition and fuelling had been mapped, and apparently no one could, or would, do anything about it. It felt terrible off the throttle, jerky, not allowing me to feed the power in with the finesse you need on a circuit like that in those wet conditions. The weather was miserable. Any dreams of winning at Scarborough, just three and a half months after breaking my back, were knackered. I felt doomed.

For that Gold Cup, and other meetings in 2010, a friend of mine, Shaun the Sheep, would drive his camper van to the races and zip on the awning, and that would be our base in the pits. The bikes would arrive in the back of a van and Shaun would look after me, Danny and whoever else was spannering that weekend, keeping us fed and watered.

I'd known Shaun from the SMR days and got on well with him. He is an older bloke, in his fifties at the time and blunt, blunt as you like, but you knew where you stood with him. Mr X must have thought Shaun was the hired help, because he was being rude to him – when we were basically guests of Shaun, in his private camper van, and good friends beyond that.

Shaun had a rule: if you were going into the motorhome itself you had to take your shoes off. I did it, everyone did it. Prince Philip could have come by for a brew and he'd have been told, politely, 'Shoes off, your Highness.'

When Shaun told Mr X this he flipped his lid. The very calm and calculated exterior fell away and he started shouting, 'Next year we're not going to be with you! We've got plans!' The mask had dropped.

While I was watching this all develop I was in the corner of the awning cutting my slicks, slicing extra grooves into tyres with a special tool, to go out in the wet conditions. Then Shaun got Mr X by the scruff of his neck and shoved him out. I had a race to try and win, so I just kept my head down. I didn't need to be dragged into a fight on a race day. They seemed to be dealing with it themselves.

Meanwhile, this was far from the only relationship going to shit. I wasn't getting along with Andy Spellman, having shut him out when he'd put some kind of F1 driver's contract under my nose. I realise now he was just trying to help me and move the whole job forward, but it all seemed too formal. Mr X had done a bit to muddy the water, but it was my decision. Mr X wanted to take over all the dealings that Andy had helped set up and was keeping on track. Being under the spell of Mr X meant I was messing Andy about. And I was messing the North One people about. I was all over the place. I had all these opportunities, but, back then, I would probably have been happier just getting up at 5.30am, as usual, and doing five and a half days' graft at the truck yard.

Before the set-to with Shaun, the whole scene at Oliver's Mount had become even more weird when Mr X explained to Andy Spellman that he'd been under surveillance since he'd appeared in Scarborough. Mr X even went as far as to introduce Andy to the two huge, ex-military blokes who were spying on him. He was basically saying,'I'm the man, don't mess about with me.'

Seeing the way he treated Shaun made my mind up, and I've never had anything to do with Mr X again since, though he still tries to get in touch with me. It didn't take long for it all to feel like a lucky escape.

I left a disappointing and disturbing Scarborough without talking to Andy. I hadn't spoken to him all day. I got it into my head that filming *Closer to the Edge* and getting involved with a TV company had turned my life to shit. I'd lost my girlfriend, which was my fault. Lost my home, because I had been living with her at her parents' farm. My racing had gone to shit. I wouldn't go home and mope and cry, I just got on with it, but I was being an arsehole to Andy.

The next day, right after the Sunday of the Gold Cup, was to be the first day of location shooting for *The Boat That Guy Built*. I'd done some bits in Kirmington, but this was the start, proper. Andy met me in the reception of the hotel, in the north of Manchester, where the film crew and Mark Davis had stayed, and I was telling him I could take or leave the whole TV programme. I was being selfish. I hadn't thought how much work had gone into the pre-production of the show, the research, buying the bloody boat – I was just down on it all.

I was about to start six weeks of filming, working on my first-ever TV show. *The Boat That Guy Built* was a six-part BBC TV show with my name in the title, but I was feeling so negative about the whole job, I wasn't bothered if it happened or not. I still wasn't in a good place mentally.

CHAPTER 15

THE TV JOB

'I thought I was spitting teeth out, but it was actually pieces of my top jaw.'

THE BOAT THAT *Guy Built* and all the rest of the TV job all came from being interviewed for ITV's 2009 TT coverage. The first year North One got the rights to cover the Isle of Man TT they contacted some of the racers and arranged to interview them before the racing started. A researcher rung up and told me they wanted to film me training or whatever I did. I told her I didn't really do any of that, I just fixed lorries, so they came and filmed that instead.

North One is a production company. They make all sorts of programmes and sell them to various TV channels, like ITV, Channel 4 or the BBC. One of North One's directors was asking me all sorts of questions about engines and then started asking my views on electric bikes. I began telling him that I reckoned until they sort out nuclear power stations the electric bike is burning the fossil fuel a different way, further away from the end user.

They filmed me at work, then at the farm. I got talking about tea, explaining the theory Russell Benney had told me back at the end of 2007, about how putting the milk in first made an emulsion and the molecular reaction made for a tastier cup of tea.

Anyway, I was rambling on and it must have triggered something in someone's head at North One, when it eventually was shown during one of the highlight shows for the 2009 TT. The boss of North One, Neil Duncanson, came to see me in the pits, and told me I could be on TV. I didn't think anything of it, but if they wanted to do some legwork and have TV channels tell them, 'Thanks, but no thanks,' then it was no skin off my nose.

Weeks went by and nothing seemed to be happening, but Andy kept reminding me North One were pushing hard. I was hardly losing sleep worrying about when my TV career would take off, but in January 2010 North One got in touch to say they'd like me to do some film tests up in Kirmington. Andy and a lad called Dan came and filmed me at work, talking about the Suffolk Punch piston tattoo on the back of my leg, my tool-box and loads of other stuff. That day's filming was edited down and mixed with me yarning about tea and shown to Jay Hunt, the lady who was in charge of commissioning at the BBC. I didn't think of it as a waste of time, because I still wasn't going out of my way to do anything. The film crew came to me and sat about until I'd finished what I was doing, then they went away and pulled strings, leaving me pretty much ignorant of what was going on and liking it that way. I've been told that the BBC made the decision that they wanted me to do a series for them on the strength of my videoed ramblings. It was a pretty big risk on their part, as I was totally unknown in this line of work, and apparently it was very unusual for them to work this way.

A while after that North One got in touch again, because they had a BBC1 project they wanted to involve me with, but I'd need to do the show with a co-presenter. Honestly, I wasn't that bothered. I explained I had enough work and didn't really want to take a day off. Andy twisted my arm, saying it was my big opportunity. The BBC were under the microscope at the time. Listening to Radio 4 at work, it sounded like every man and his dog were complaining about how they were spending the licence fee, and here I was, a truck fitter, being offered the chance of a TV show. You can see why I was thinking, 'Not as long as I've got a hole in my arse ...'

Andy added that North One would pay me some expenses, so I ended up taking a couple of days off work to do screen tests with established TV presenters.

The first was in Brighton. I met Andy Spellman and travelled halfway there in some noisy Porsche he had at the time. He changes cars more often than I change underwear. We got nicked on the way and, for some reason, when the copper asked, 'Where are you going?' Andy replied, 'Off to see a man called Jem.' He made us sound like a couple of drug dealers. Why didn't he just say Brighton?

We did go and see a trick ex-German Fire Service Mk2 Ford Transit that Andy had found. It was still on its original tyres. I asked the salesman if he'd take an Aston Martin V12 in part-exchange. He looked at me like I was off my head, but I meant it.

When we made it to Brighton, the test was with Jem Stansfield from the BBC show *Bang Goes the Theory*. Clever bloke, lovely bloke, but we didn't hit it off. He knew all these maths formulas and he was a sound bloke, but not my kind of fella. He wasn't trying to show off that he was cleverer than me or anything, we were just very different.

The next screen test was up in my dad's shed with Jason Bradbury from *The Gadget Show*, who was another lovely bloke. Andy Spellman turned up to operate one of the cameras, along with other fellas I didn't know from Adam, but, it turns out, people I'd work with later.

I didn't realise what a big opportunity this was for TV folk, those whose only career was in TV. Bradbury was a Channel 5 presenter and keen to get on the BBC. Maybe that had something to do with the way he behaved. It was the day the iPad launched and he was all revved up about that, but it was a bit lost on me and my Nokia 7210.

He'd talk away normally, like me and my mates would, until a camera was put on him, then he became the most enthusiastic bloke in the world. He kept picking up my 18-volt Snap-On nut gun to pretend it was a machine gun. He did it four times to make sure at least one camera got it.

For this screen test, we had to pretend to build a hoverboard out of old leafblowers. It was all make-believe, but I got these knackered leafblowers going, something the crew didn't think was going to happen. You'd think I'd turned water into wine, the way the TV folk reacted. Just when I was about to try and start them up, Bradbury went into a big spiel about having to open the shed's windows and doors to make sure we weren't poisoned by the carbon monoxide or something. I was thinking, 'Get a grip ...'

Still, after the screen test I must've thought it had gone quite well, because when they quizzed me I said I thought the test with Bradbury went the best and that he got the best out of me. The crew who were filming the tests and those who were judging them can't have agreed.

The problem was, they reckoned, that I looked like someone who was just interested in what was going on, while the two professional TV bods looked like they were presenting a TV show, and because of the way I behaved it made them look even more exaggerated. It was chalk and cheese.

The whole idea of the screen tests was to see if I was any good and if I could work with anyone. Unfortunately, the experienced TV presenters didn't get me and I definitely didn't get them. People might say we had no chemistry. They weren't my kind of people. They didn't think like I thought. They didn't come from a background where a perk of the job is reading a truck driver's porn mag. They were all right people, but not my cup of tea.

North One got the gist that the tests hadn't really worked because I struggled to hit it off with the people they suggested, but for some reason they were still keen on me doing something with them. They asked if I knew anyone. No one came to mind until I was mountain biking in Wales with my mate Mark 'Mavis' Davis.

I have known Mave since I was about 18. We'd go mountain biking together a fair bit and we'd always have a good craic. I asked him if he'd be up for trying to present a TV show with me, and he was. So I texted Andy, he got the wheels in motion and another screen test was set up at Mave's house. He's a carpenter and we made something for his kitchen, in front of the cameras. It all went well and we got the job.

It had taken a year from being told that something might happen to actually getting it off the ground. I'm sure there was loads of paddling going on below the surface, most of which I knew nothing about.

A few weeks later we started filming the BBC TV series. I booked a block of six weeks off work, which my dad was sort of all right with, starting right after the Scarborough Gold Cup on 20 September. I still went in and worked weekends at the truck yard.

The show would become *The Boat That Guy Built*. The idea was to buy a knackered old canal boat and for me and Mave to do it up and kit it out using technology and methods from the Industrial Revolution. It would include stuff like making a steam-powered shower, the china and stainless cutlery, the cotton bed sheets ...

In the time between signing up to make the show and filming actually starting, the wheels came off a lot of aspects of my life. That meant, right from the off, Mave was more interested in it than me. I was all over the shop. He was behaving professionally and I wasn't.

I came round slowly, but I still needed to escape from it, so even though I had a hotel room booked I would sometimes sleep in my van. I wasn't having big heart-to-hearts with myself. I'd go to a pub and have something to eat, then when I'd get back in my van I would just feel, *Aaaaah*. A feeling of relief and relaxation. I love my van and I like being by myself – but it was an absolute godsend to have Mave with us.

Two weeks before the Gold Cup and all the Shaun the Sheep and Mr X weirdness coming to a head, and two weeks before I saw the boat for the first time, we were filming the title sequence for the show in Lincolnshire. It was beginning to feel like the same old interview stuff, in my dad's shed in Kirmington, at Mave's house or at the truck yard. North One had said they wanted to do a bit of personal stuff: people who knew me giving some soundbites. I don't know what the thinking was behind it, but I just nodded along.

The show was originally going to be *The House That Guy Built*, and they were going to have a lot more input from people I knew. They planned to talk to Kate, my girlfriend at the time, and her mum, Mrs Lancaster, who knew me well because I'd lived on her farm for so long. But just before filming began, me and Kate split up and I moved out.

Before we started work on the boat I was in the shed in Kirmington, doing the first bits ever to a proper broadcast camera, other than interviews on the grid of the TT or whatever. Before then it had all been handheld cameras.

The time came for them to interview Kate. I obviously hadn't made the situation clear and reverted to my default setting of, 'Oh, it'll be right, worse things happen at sea, let's just get on with it.' I might have played down the seriousness of the break-up and the hurt I'd caused Kate. Looking back, I can understand how the film crew assumed we'd just had some change of plan and gone our separate ways, so they still planned to ask Kate if she'd come and do the bit to camera for us.

When Andy walked over the road and knocked on Kate's door, she explained I'd been sleeping with someone else behind her back. Something I might not have explained to the TV crew at this point. She added she didn't think she had too much positive to say about me at the time, but still asked if I was over in my dad's shed. Andy admitted I was and then spent the short walk from the farm to the shed desperately trying to think of anything to say to make the situation better.

Kate, always a very calm, laidback woman, came into the shed and asked if she could have a quick word with me. I walked outside with her and once we were around the corner she lamped me, slapping me hard across the face, and started shouting at me at the top of her voice.

Next she stormed back into the shed and asked the film crew why they were wasting TV licence payers' money on a See You Next Tuesday like me. It was quite an introduction to their new presenter.

Some of the directors of the shows were new to this kind of show too. They were experienced in TV, but *The Boat* was a different kettle of fish for them too and we'd bang heads.

The crew were all used to working with professional presenters, and I was far from it. They dealt with the likes of Jason Bradbury, Jason Plato and Tiff Needell. These were people who could say things again and again, changing it slightly if the director thought it would be better a different way, but I just wanted to do it how I'd do it naturally and wouldn't budge.

There were three different directors on the series, each doing two programmes. That isn't unusual in TV, I'm told. One of the directors, Jess Matthews, would ask me to say things a particular way and I'd tell her, 'No, I'll say it like I say it.' I didn't get on with her at all to start with. She was as stubborn as I was. We were like two rams butting each other. I bet she thought, 'Why have my bosses chosen this dickhead to be a presenter when he doesn't even want to do it?' I'd have agreed with her.

From my point of view, the problem was she was trying to direct me, she was a director after all, but I didn't want directing. She'd say, 'Can't you say it like this?' And I'd remind her I wasn't an actor. I didn't have any diva moments, but I look back and pity her for having to put up with a dickhead like me. We've worked again since and got on really well.

If you'd asked me at the time I'd have told you, 'I should never have done this.' Getting up on a Monday morning to go filming wasn't a good feeling. I was struggling to get going, a problem I'd never had with the trucks. I'd finish a day's filming and not have the usual feeling of job satisfaction I'd always had. It didn't feel like proper work to me.

I thought Mave and I would have exactly the same outlook when it came to the TV, but he liked the camera a lot more than me. I can't look into a camera and talk, I have to talk to the person next to the camera, not an imaginary audience. Mave was spot-on and, without doubt, the best man to do the first series with. He was more switched on to the whole job than me. As the series went on, I felt he became more and more like a TV presenter, and was going away from the character that he was at the start.

Even though it sounds like I could take or leave the whole thing, we had some laughs. We built the steam-powered shower for the boat, and I had hand-made a bar of soap. When it came time to test the shower in front of the cameras, the crew said I could keep my pants on or get some swimming trunks, but I thought, 'Sod it, I don't wear pants in the shower.' I looked at Mave and he said, 'Get on with it.' So in the boat, crowded with five or six crew, men and women, I stripped off and got in the shower. The water went from freezing to scalding while I was trying to get washed and I managed to get soap in my eyes. There wasn't a lot of room on the narrowboat at the best of times, the clue's in the name, and I remember Nat the cameraman shouting at me to keep my John Thomas out of the shot.

I was laughing and swearing at the same time, while everyone except Mave kept quiet. I don't think they were used to their presenter's meat and two veg swinging in the breeze on a Tuesday afternoon. Maybe if they'd asked me to lie in a warm bubble-bath listening to Mozart I'd have been the awkward one. What I found much harder was being told I had to walk up to a complete stranger and ask what he thought about the huge Boulton & Watt blowing engine in the middle of a roundabout on the A38(M) near Birmingham. The idea of talking to someone random, rather than someone random talking to me first, made me more on edge than waiting for the flag to drop on a grid.

I didn't mind that filming was pushing me out of my comfort zone, in fact I enjoyed that. I want to learn new stuff. I want to be challenged by stuff that is out of my league. And I wasn't worried if I was no good at it. I'd put it down to experience and move on. I was embarrassed at times, but most when I had to go and speak to the public. It was awkward, but I did it.

I don't have a TV or internet at home, but I listen to the radio a lot. That's come from living on my own for a while. I bike home from Grimsby, leaving at six or seven o' clock, and pass house after house where people are just staring at the 70-inch plasma TV screens. It makes me think, 'You don't get that time back at the end.' I can honestly say I've only seen one episode of the boat series. We were still finishing the last programme when the first was edited and ready to watch, so one of the crew showed me it on an iPad at lunchtime.

The lion's share of the filming was done, certainly all the main bits, but the production company wanted me and Mave to go back and do a few fill-in pieces to link certain parts of the show together, to smooth it out a bit.

By this stage I was even quite enjoying it. I'd done my six weeks solid. I was back working with my dad and this was me and Mave, a couple of mates, taking the odd day off to do something different.

On this day, they had me jumping from the dock edge onto the side of the narrowboat, like I'd done a hundred times before. The filming stopped and I did one last jump onto the boat from the towpath. That would be the last time I jumped onto that particular boat. The oil-soaked sole of my rigger boot slipped on the edge of the boat and I fell into the water. That wouldn't have been a problem if my front teeth hadn't caught square on the boat's steel tiller, the steering handle, on the way down.

The impact knocked my two front teeth under up into my nose cavity and smashed my side teeth out. I lay in the water for a while, then managed to pull myself out. I walked up to

Mavis and asked, 'Am I all right?' He pulled a face and just said, 'Fucking hell!' Coming from Mave, that was very bad news. He'd broken tons of stuff riding mountain bikes and BMX, and for his face to turn like it did after looking at the wreckage of my gob wasn't good.

I thought I was spitting teeth out, but it was actually pieces of my top jaw. It had shattered. There was a lot of blood, but, strangely, it wasn't that painful.

I went to the local hospital, and after looking at the X-ray they told me there wasn't much they could do for me. They actually told me my teeth might push back down! What were they thinking? I had demolished my top jaw, leaving bits of it on the towpath of a canal.

Next, I visited an emergency dentist. There they dried their teeth, sucking in breath – like when a woman takes a car to a garage and the blokes stand around drying their teeth, telling her it's a big job, when all it needs is a spark plug. Anyway, I needed more than a filling, that was for sure.

I got up the next morning, and went to the local dentist in Brigg. He told me I had to go and see this man to sort the jaw, then go see that man, to do this, then go see this man for that, and come back in two days.

Luckily, Steph's mate is a dentist in Newcastle. He met me on a Saturday morning, and he cut my jaw right open and cut the teeth out, under a local anaesthetic. I could see the rack of front teeth coming out and being placed on a tray next to the chair.

He stated the bleeding obvious when he told me my face was a mess. I was sent away till the swelling went down. When I returned he made a pattern for some false teeth. After that I went back again to have a bone graft to rebuild my jaw. They used a certain kind of cow bone that took about six months to knit together.

Through all those months I had a plate glued in with Fixodent. It changed the way I talked. The shape on the back of the false teeth must've been slightly different to my own teeth, and it made me talk with a short tongue. Now, I have permanent false teeth, not on a plate, and they're as good as new.

At one point in that first series, we were making some cotton bed linen, and I was asking how it got from the sheep. I now know cotton doesn't come from sheep, but I'm not embarrassed to look daft and I'm not sorry they left that in the programme. If it makes me look thick, then I'm thick, I'm not bothered. The show would regularly get five million viewers on its two showings and has been exported around the world. It's also shown in schools in Britain.

Through connections with North One, and their contract to cover World Rally, I was invited to drive a Ford World Rally car up in a Cumbrian forest. It was November, snow and ice on the ground. Ford's top driver, the Finn Mikko Hirvonen, was there, and so was Ken Block – who'd become famous for the drifting videos he'd made that had squillions of views on YouTube.

I'd stayed in a hotel in Cumbria the night before and filled the works Transit up in the petrol station next door, on the way to the forest. As I was pulling out of the forecourt a woman was indicating to pull into the petrol station, so I rolled onto the road and she ploughed straight into me, damaging the front suspension.

I managed to get the van fixed the same day, and drove a World Rally Ford Fiesta in a Cumbrian forest, but the accident would cause problems at work. It came after I'd done a daft thing, trying to be a bit rum by sneaking under a car park barrier behind Mave's van, so I didn't have to pay for parking. The TV company would have paid the expenses if I'd asked them. Someone took the phone number from the side of the van and rang up my dad.

Left: The Southern 100 takes place on the Isle of Man, but not on the TT circuit. It's probably my favourite race of the year. It's mid-week, the track is proper hard-core and when you sign on with the organisers they give you a handful of tea vouchers.

Right: Pit stop at the 2011 TT. Having done both, I can honestly say I'd rather be racing than changing the back wheel. Pressure? You can't imagine it.

Above: The Dundrod circuit, home of the Ulster GP. I love it round there. This is the 2011 Superstock race.

Left: I had a few podiums during the 2011 TT, but McGuinness did the winning. I have massive respect for him.

Below: I'm trying here. I can't do wheelies on purpose. All I'm trying to do is get the front wheel down on the ground.

Left: Me and Mave, Mark 'Mavis' Davis, just before we started our first ever filming day for *The Boat That Guy Built*. Spellman took the photo and we'd just had a decent sized row about calling it all off. You can see by my face I was still more than half thinking of going home.

Right: Filming *The Boat That Guy Built*. We crashed *Reckless*, as she was called, a good few times that day. Didn't feel like a real job then and still doesn't now.

Left: Getting my John Thomas out in front of the crew for the shower scene in the boat series didn't bother me one bit. Here I am trying to show Mave I didn't have skid marks in my boxers. What a couple of pros.

Above: I think this is the biggest crash I ever had, and I came away unscathed. It's the North West in 2012. I've crashed a lot of motorbikes and I always know why; I've been trying too hard or I've done something wrong, but the cause of this crash is still a mystery to me.

Left: The TAS Suzuki team at the Ulster GP in 2012. Team owner, Hector Neill; me; team boss and Hector's son, Philip Neill; and my team-mate that year, Conor Cummins.

Right: I've had some battles with Michael Dunlop at races like the Southern 100 and Ulster GP. Sometimes I come out on top, sometimes he does. This is one of the times, in the Superbike race at the Ulster in 2012, that I did.

Above: Like a spaniel with its head out of a van window. This is the locomotive 5164 I had a hand in restoring for the *How Britain Worked* series. I need to be involved in TV where I'm getting my hands dirty.

Right: The MacMillan, a pioneering bicycle with wooden wheels and metal 'tyres' that me and Mave helped make a replica of for the telly. Not suited to crossing cattle grids at speed.

Above: Welding a gear for a Victorian lawn-mower. Mowing used to be the thing that helped me relax, getting all the lines dead straight and then tidying up the headlands. Now I don't even get time to do that.

Right: And sometimes I even have to get my feet dirty.

Above: Tower Bends, TT 2013. That bike never ran right, it took everything for me to scrape into the top ten. Look at those beer bellies! Proper.

Above: Without doubt the most scared I've ever been on two wheels. 113 mph on a pushbike, an inch or two from the back of a racing truck. Riding blind and tearing the muscles off my bones to keep going. A hell of a buzz, though. I'm still amazed it didn't go pear-shaped.

Left and below: The engineering department and students at Southampton University were the brains and I was the brawn, pedalling like hell to get our HPA – human-powered aircraft – off the ground. It worked, too. More people have been into space than have flown under their own steam.

Above and right: The sledging record in Channel 4's *Speed* series was the perfect mix of cutting-edge engineering and danger. Flying down the side of a mountain in a carbon-fibre sledge, designed just for the top speed record. I crashed on the practice run, then did 83 mph, smashing the existing record that stood at 62 mph.

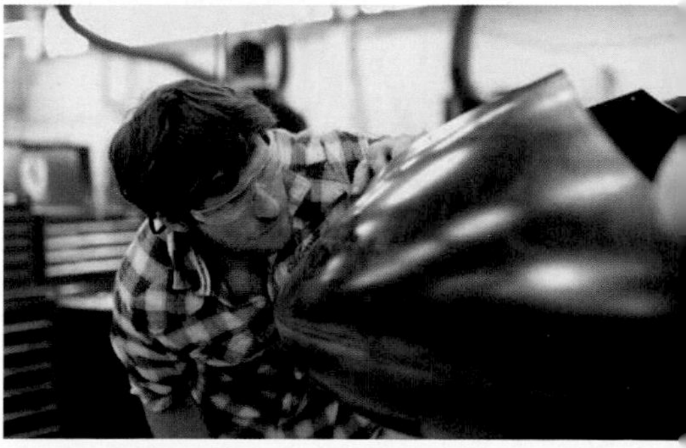

Above: The 2013 Le Mans 24-Hours stands out as the best thing I've done with motorbikes. I just love racing bikes and to do it for over eight hours in two days is great.

He was on the rev limiter when he rang me up. I apologised, but it didn't make any difference.

Over the weekend, back home at the house where I was living in Caistor, Dobby, my mate who owned the house, came in and told me he'd just seen my van driving off. I thought it had been nicked, but it turns out it was my dad repossessing it.

He hadn't knocked on the door, he just took it, using the spare keys. I took that as a sign I was sacked from the family business. I think I'd have preferred it if he'd knocked on the door and lamped me when I answered it. I'd have thought a million times more of him if he'd come up to me, face to face, and told me that he was taking it and that I was an arsehole. He was well within his rights. I was taking the piss. I held my hands up. I didn't bother calling him to see for sure if I was sacked, and the rest of the family say I wasn't, but in my mind, that was it, I was out of the village I grew up in. I was out of the family business. Me and Dad didn't talk for months. I didn't speak to my mum either. Me and Kate split up. I'd been flicked out of the Kirmington bubble.

With no job, I thought, 'That's it, I'll become a professional motorbike racer.' I went out 'training' on my pushbike, but as much as I love riding my bicycle, by lunchtime I thought, 'Bugger this.' I rode to Grimsby and went to see a couple of mates who knew a couple of mates who worked on the banks of the Humber. I was offered a job working on the maintenance crew of a big factory, Blue Star Fibres, labouring for a contracting firm. I'd lasted one morning as a full-time motorcycle racer.

That job, labouring with my mate Paddy, who'd driven me back from the North West race when I spannered myself and also paints my racing helmets, was the first time I had a job that finished at a reasonable time. I'd be done and dusted at twenty past four. When I was at home, work would not enter my head until I got up the next morning. I could do my own thing. There was no job satisfaction, and it was physically hard graft, but it was the first time I had no work worries niggling at me when I wasn't there.

I was living at Dobby's flat, for £350 a month. He was supposed to be living there, but he was always at his girlfriend's. It was all right, but I was missing fixing things, so I applied for a job at A Plant, the plant hire place. We used to rent our jackhammers and diggers from them. The manager said they were snowed under and needed another fitter. I went in for three interviews, biking there on my way home from work. They couldn't get their head around me wanting to work for them. I told them I would need time off to race bikes. It was a big depot, because they supplied all the Humber refineries. They offered me the job at the same time North One offered me another TV series.

When talk of the second series came up, I told North One their best bet was to just use Mave, not me. Or we could change roles. He'd be the main man, and I'd do the odd day. He loves all that stuff. 'Get Mave to do it, he's a bit slack at work,' I said, but they didn't.

The Boat That Guy Built aired in February 2011. The month before, Andy Spellman got a call from someone at the BBC saying that the channel were looking for a new presenter of *Jimmy's Food Factory*. It's the show where the presenter, Jimmy Doherty, investigated what went into supermarket food and tried to make his own versions using Heath Robinson, home-built looking machinery in a barn in Suffolk or somewhere. Jimmy must have had enough of it, or had a better offer from another channel, and they wanted me to audition. It was all set up, but I blew it out on the morning of the audition, ringing up the BBC reception and leaving a message with the security man at 5am before I set off for work.

When North One found out I'd been offered an audition on a series that was nothing to do with them, they drove up to Lincolnshire and offered me a retainer to stay exclusive to them. I signed a three-year contract on the spot, when I should have sat on it and asked Andy for advice, which we later had quite a lively debate about. Signing the contract meant I had to do a programme a year, but only programmes I was happy with, for the next three years. It seemed like money for old rope. The offer was rushed because Neil Duncanson didn't want me to take the job I'd been offered at A Plant, where I'd have less flexibility to take time off. Or maybe he thought I was going to get poached by another TV production outfit, but I wasn't looking to do that.

North One went back to talking about doing *The House That Guy Built*. They said was there was no 'legacy' to the boat. It was all done for TV's sake. The boat got sold, no one knew what happened to it. I wasn't keen on doing all the same stuff again, so they came up with another idea.

The next series would be *How Britain Worked*. The researchers found stuff that was due to be restored, or there were people who wanted to restore it, and the TV's show and budget helped make it happen, in some cases saving special things for years to come. We were highlighting the work other people were doing and getting historic old things working for other people to see and enjoy.

One big difference was that the series would be six one-hour shows, rather than six 30-minute shows. That involved 50 days' filming rather than 30, but the filming was spread over six months, rather than in a solid six-week block, because I was desperate to keep my hand in at work, proper work, getting my hands dirty, plus race motorbikes too. Six weeks of filming was too much of the same stuff. At that stage of the TV business I still wasn't feeling like I'd achieved anything. Perhaps it was related to something Mr X had said, that had stuck in my mind: that the truck mechanic looked down on the TV presenter side of my personality.

Another difference was that North One decided to break away from the BBC and go to Channel 4, who were offering a bigger budget, to make a better programme. Jay Hunt, the lady who'd commissioned the boat series, had moved to Channel 4 and was still interested in me making more programmes.

The new show would have something like a £1 million budget, I reckon. Expensive programming, I'm told. The BBC wanted another series, but they didn't want to pay any more, and the idea was to make the next programme better than the one before. Anyway, that was all down to the production company, North One, of course, and nothing to do with me.

I was a lot more involved in *How Britain Worked*, visiting the projects as they progressed and getting my hands dirty on a regular basis. *The Boat* was more of a fleeting glance over stuff, while *How Britain* made me realise that I could enjoy the TV projects if I was actually doing stuff, not just talking about what other people were doing or had done.

The idea behind *How Britain Worked* was to 'rediscover our industrial past', to show inventions from the Industrial Revolution, and to explore both the mechanical and social side of things like the introduction of public parks and annual holidays to the seaside. The series was about the innovators and the grafters who changed the world. Not just the likes of Stephenson, Davey and Brunel, names nearly everyone knows. It would tell about the men who designed and built the high-speed Brixham trawlers, and those who went out to sea to catch fish to feed the exploding population of workers; about the miners and how difficult the work was for men, women and children. It was genuinely interesting. I loved seeing the passion of the 20-year-old lad who worked at Birmingham

Botanical Gardens. Herbaceous borders aren't my thing, but the passion he had rubbed off on me. We met another teenager who was restoring a steam train. It was just good to see younger blokes interested in this side of things.

The best and most memorable part of filming that series was being involved with a crew that travels round the country repairing and maintaining the old Victorian cast-iron piers. The programme was about the introduction of the workers' holiday and the way it transformed the British coastline, with holiday resorts popping up. We filmed most of the episode in the North Wales resort of Llandudno.

The town's 2,295 ft pier was opened to the public in 1877, and is an amazing piece of civil engineering. It goes without saying the metalwork is in a hell of a corrosive environment, battered by the sea and freezing winds. The fellas who I met have working lives that revolve around replacing damaged parts of Britain's cast-iron seaside landmarks. And, I found out, there's no easy way to do it.

When a cross-member has corroded to the point where it's potentially going to affect the structural integrity of the pier, it needs to be torn out and replaced. The thing is, it's riveted together and the way to remove the rivets is to burn them out with the 3,500°C oxy-acetylene cutting torch – while you're dangling from the underneath of a pier above the Irish Sea. Everything's cold, wet and slippery, and you're hanging from climbing tackle, so you don't have much to steady yourself against. You're working to a deadline with a torch in your hand that could do some serious damage if you got too close to the hot end. I cut one of the cross-members out. At the time it was the only job I'd done that I could consider packing the trucks in for. It had the mix of hard graft, job satisfaction and an added element of danger to keep you on your toes. Plus I liked the fellas who did it for a living – we had a good craic. They could drink too, but were all up at the crack of dawn to get the job done. Proper.

By the end of *How Britain Worked* I'd made two series about the Industrial Revolution, and North One wanted to choose another era and make a similar series. The Edwardian age was talked about, but I wasn't interested in repeating the same idea. It seems like the TV way of doing things is to find something that works and flog it to death.

The experience of presenting two series taught me a lot about what goes into the shows, what is needed to make an hour of television. If the TV lot get five minutes of telly out of a ten-hour day they're happy. And after filming's done a programme can take six weeks to edit. I pity the poor sods watching me for that long. I also learnt what I enjoy doing and what kind of jobs wouldn't interest me. I realised that I could do some amazing stuff, like the experience of fixing the pier, a job I didn't even know existed and one that I'd have never tried. I also got involved with the restoration of a Spitfire for another TV show. Proper dream stuff.

The filming took me all over England, Scotland and Wales, and the long drives to and from filming gave me plenty of time to think over what I was involved with. It made me realise I don't want to be the person who is talking about interesting stuff that other people have done – I want to be doing the interesting stuff. And because I'm willing to try things that a lot of other presenters maybe aren't, and couldn't do, then perhaps between me and the production company we can come up with some new ideas or at least new takes on old ideas. After having an attitude of take it or leave it, I'm getting quite into that whole side of things and thinking about schemes that could be great fun, give me a hell of a buzz and hopefully make something memorable to put out on telly.

CHAPTER 16

IN TROUBLE

'The next minute a riot van turned up, two coppers jumped out and handcuffed me.'

EVEN WITH A TV contract and racing for a decent-sized motorcycle team, I still want a proper job, and labouring, though it had its plus points, wasn't hitting the spot. I was working with a good group of blokes and was home early to get on with building engines or training for a mountain bike race. I could forget about work the minute I left too, but that was part of the problem. It wasn't testing me, so when I heard a Grimsby company was interested in me running the truck maintenance side of their business, I was interested too.

Mick Moody used to run a refrigerated transport business, and my dad would do a lot of repairs for Moody International. When I was working for Ian Martin Motor Engineers I used to end up doing the oddball work that Moody would send to us. After packing in that side of his business Moody concentrated on selling used trucks. He had built his own garage to service the trucks ready for sale, and to maintain a fleet for customers. I'd been recommended to him and was asked if I would visit the yard to talk about working for him. This was in March 2011, not long after *The Boat* had been shown on the BBC. We arranged to meet on a Friday afternoon after I knocked off work. When I was labouring I would finish early on a Friday. I told Moody I would be with him by two.

On the day of the interview I was out on a job in a Transit van with a tipper back, picking up hardcore, rocks and broken-up concrete, and taking it from one site to another. The tipper bed was loaded by the digger driver, then I set off. On the way back to site I got pulled over by VOSA, the Vehicle and Operator Services Agency, who are the enforcement arm of the Department of Transport. They're the inspectors who check that MoT stations aren't cutting corners and also do roadside spot checks to make sure haulage firms and drivers are sticking to all the rules. If you just drive a car you never really come in contact with them, but haulage firms do.

I was sent to a weighbridge in the lay-by and then told the Transit was overweight. Each van, lorry or trailer has a safe working load, and the hardcore I was transporting was over the legal recommended weight for the Ford tipper I was driving. It meant I would get a fine, but work would pay it, because I didn't load the van and there was no real way for me to know if it was under or over the weight limit. I was just couriering it from one place to the other for them.

The VOSA man took all my details and told me to wait a minute. Then wait a while longer, then a bit longer and a bit longer … Eventually, I said, 'Look mate, I'm on a job. I've got to get going,' but he wouldn't let me go.

After an hour, I had another word, pointing out that the load was off, the van was legal and I had to get to work to tell them what had happened. The next minute a riot van turned up, two coppers jumped out and handcuffed me.

'There's a warrant out for your arrest,' the Grimsby coppers told me. For speeding. Kind of.

It all started from being caught a year or so before, on the road past Cadwell Park race circuit. Doing 70-odd mph in a 60-mph limit in my red VW Transporter, GEZ 5649. No arguments.

On my day in court for that offence I took a letter from my dad and one from Mr Lancaster, who I helped out driving tractors during harvest, saying that if I lost my licence I'd lose both jobs. I got a whacking fine and some points added to my licence, but I wasn't banned, so I could continue driving.

The next time I got pulled over was when I was driving from a dentist in Brigg to the hospital in Grimsby the day after I'd knocked my teeth out on the tiller of the narrowboat. I was rushing to the hospital. Again, no excuses, except the bottom half of my face was a broken mess dripping blood down the front of my T-shirt. The copper wasn't having any of it. Perhaps he thought I was making it up.

A week later, a letter came through the post and I thought, 'That's it, I've had it this time.' I replied saying yes, it was me driving the vehicle at that time. Then I was sent another letter, a Notice of Intended Prosecution, giving me the choice to attend court or have it dealt with in my absence. I ticked the box saying I didn't want to go to court. There was no point. I knew I'd had it, or at least my licence had. I'd accepted my fate, a ban was coming, and didn't see the point in taking the day off work to be told I was losing my licence, so I ticked the option for them to deal with it in my absence.

It turns out the court date was on the Wednesday, two days before I was pulled over for being overweight in the tipper van on the Friday. I'd been waiting for the letter to come telling me I'd lost my licence. When it hadn't arrived I just carried on. I had buried my head in the sand. If no one had officially told me to stop driving, I wasn't about to. I was keeping calm and carrying on. Or I was till the handcuffs snapped shut. I wondered if there was any need for that. I was only doing a day's work, with part of the tax I would pay at the end of the week going towards paying coppers' wages. I might have reminded them about that fact at the time. They always like that ...

I don't get on with coppers. I'm sure there are some really nice ones, but I still prefer not to deal with them. Once, I was driving when I saw a police car waiting to come onto a roundabout and one of its headlights was out. I drove around the roundabout again and it took a lot of self-control not to park in front of the car, blocking its route onto the roundabout and do a citizen's arrest on the driver for being in charge of a car with a defective headlight. I was desperate to give him a lecture.

I was arrested near Grimsby, but when we started driving I realised I'd been in the van a lot longer than it took to get to Grimsby police station. I was eventually put in Scunthorpe nick. These coppers who handcuffed me were all right, to be fair. The handcuffs were going a bit far, I thought, but they let me take my pushbike from the back of the tipper truck into the police van with me.

When I was booked in they did the whole business: took my fingerprints, scraped my mouth with a DNA swab, took my mugshot. They stopped short of the finger up the backside, but they did everything else, then they locked me up. It was Friday afternoon and they told me it would be a struggle to get me in front of a judge that day, so there was a chance I would be in all weekend. I think they knew I wasn't a dickhead, but they weren't kidding.

Luckily, they managed to squeeze me in before the court shut. I stood in front of a group of magistrates in my overalls, telling them exactly what had happened. I was told I'd been arrested because I hadn't attended court when instructed. They were threatening to do me for no insurance on the van too.

I told them about the letters I'd been sent, and me ticking the box to say I would prefer not to attend court. They got hold of the letter and it showed I was telling the truth. The magistrate doing the talking told me I shouldn't have been sent the form giving me any options, so it was their mistake. They could also see that I was insured.

The magistrate asked me if I needed my licence for work, obviously not knowing I'd been to court a few months earlier, so I told him I did, and that I'd actually been driving the tipper truck for my daily work when I was arrested. He explained they'd made some mistakes, listened to what I said – and I wasn't telling any porkies, he just didn't ask if I'd been in court before. He gave me more points and another fine, £200 I think, and let me keep my licence. Again. I tried my hardest to keep a straight face, knowing I'd flown by the seat of my pants and got away with it.

By this stage I was very late for my very first meeting with Mick Moody. I knew he'd been locked up in the past (for working too hard, as he'd put it, or tachograph offences, as the authorities would see it), but I didn't want to start on the wrong foot with him, so I said I'd been tied up on a job. Again, it wasn't exactly a lie.

Mick Moody is a legend in the haulage business. He's rum, but not a rogue. He is a grafter. He pretty much offered me the job there and then and I became his only employee. I now run the maintenance side of things. Once I had my feet under the table I told him the full story about being late for the interview.

With my licence loaded with a lifetime's worth of penalty points I was driving like a saint, most of the time, but things still managed to go wrong.

I was up in Dumfries, driving to a museum to film something for *How Britain Worked* in the works Transit, when I was pulled for doing 64 mph in a 60-mph limit. I couldn't understand why I'd been stopped. I thought the police usually worked to a ten-per-cent tolerance, on roads that aren't in built-up areas, to keep things sensible. By that reckoning I should've been safe up to 66 mph.

Without even saying a word to me the copper walked up to the door of the van, opened it and looked at the VIN plate, the vehicle identification number, to check the kerb weight of the van. Because it was 2.2 tonnes, the speed limit was 50 mph for this van, not 60. That meant, even with a ten-per-cent tolerance, the limit would be 55 mph.

On that road, there were signs saying anything over 7.5 tonnes was limited to 40 mph, but then there were national speed limits. Anyway, I was wrong, the copper was right. I had another day in court coming up.

When I told my boss about where I was pulled, he dried his teeth. Dumfries is notorious among lorry drivers. If you get done there you've had it. Moody gave me the number of his solicitor. Even though Mick had been locked up, this solicitor had got him out of a lot of scrapes.

Before the day arrived I'd spent two grand on legal fees and got to the stage where I decided I wasn't going to fight it. I was sure I was going to lose my licence and felt I was just throwing good money after bad. The TV bods at North One said I needed help on the legal side, so I had to change plans, but saving my licence wasn't going to be easy. In fact, I thought it was impossible. I'd pleaded my truck job to keep my licence once, then got away with it when I was taken straight to the magistrates' for missing my court date. I had already pushed my luck beyond breaking point.

The only defence I had left was related to how banning me would affect other people's livelihoods; if I didn't have my licence I couldn't make the series I was working on, *How Britain Worked*. That meant the TV production company and all those people involved in the show would be out of work. Of course, all the magistrates had to say was I should've thought of that before, but we were clutching at straws.

I'd almost convinced myself it wouldn't be that bad losing my licence. I could still ride my pushbike to truck breakdowns for Moody with a mobile tool-kit. The reality was a truck driver having to wait three hours for me to do a 50-mile trip. I doubt it would've gone down well.

The week before the court date I was told by the solicitor to buy a smart shirt, and that was what made me realise I was trying to be someone I'm not. I was happier to just walk in, as I am, tell them my side of the story and see what happened. If I wasn't even willing to dress up smartly, what was the point in spending another £800 on top of the two grand, to take someone to defend me? I rang the solicitor up and left a message telling them not to bother sending anyone, I'd take my chances on my own. The solicitor rang me back, convincing me we had a good case, for this, this and this reason.

The night before the court appearance Andy Spellman stayed at my house. He was going to be a witness for the defence and had a load of carefully thought-out arguments. We left home at four in the morning and drove to meet Moody, in Grimsby, for the long drive north.

Moody chain-smoked all the way there. Still, the atmosphere was all right. He didn't say it until later, but he was thinking I would be given a two-year driving ban and a big fine. If I was very lucky, I'd get a 12-month ban. I was thinking along the same lines while I was signing hundreds of photos in the back of the Range Rover for the 2013 calendar Andy had just ordered. I still hadn't bought a shirt and tie, and ended up going in my Red Torpedo chequered shirt and jeans.

I arrived with all these letters from the TV company, and one from Moody stating that without a licence I was not much use to him, even though I'd used a similar defence before and it's something you can only use once in a blue moon. It was a desperate roll of the dice.

I was supposed to be seen in court at ten, but was told my hearing had been put back. The three of us went for a coffee, then returned to the court to be told my case had been put back again.

Members of the public are allowed to sit in on the hearings, so I walked in and sat down to get a feel for how things were going on other cases. Lots of the accused had dead-end lives, and there was story after story of misery. There were details of heroin addicts attacking people. It was an eye-opener, all of it reminding me how lucky I am.

The local brief, who had been assigned by Moody's solicitor back in Lincolnshire, didn't give me much of a steer on what I was supposed to do or say. Then, after four in the afternoon, we got the shout and the panic started. I walked into the court and was pointed into the dock, behind a glass screen. Before the hearing even started I had 18 points on my licence. I was hardly full of confidence.

Andy, being the chief witness for my defence, was sent to another room outside the court and across the corridor so he couldn't hear what I was saying. The brief had been sent notes by Moody's legal representative, but as things got underway whatever he was saying didn't seem to be cutting much ice with the magistrates, even though he was charging like the Light Brigade.

Moody sat at the back of the court. Andy could look through a toughened glass panel in the door of the room he was in, through another square glass panel in the court room and just see my truck boss sat in the public gallery.

I was giving evidence, and out of my line of vision Moody was trying to signal to Andy how things were going. At this point I was, in the words of Mick, a quivering wreck, but the proceedings started well. Andy saw Moody give a subtle, but clear thumbs up. Then the chairman of the magistrates asked why I needed my licence and I told him it was for my regular spud-picking job on a Wednesday night. With that Mick threw his head in his hands and started rocking back and forth. I was spouting nonsense. Then I blurted out that the TV show I was filming, the one I needed my driving licence for, was called *Speed*. Hearing that, Moody started drawing his finger across his throat, to show Andy how well it was all going. Mick was sure I'd had it. I was totally out of my comfort zone. I was isolated in the dock. Shitting it.

Eventually, Andy was brought in. He was wearing a suit. He laid out the arguments, explaining I needed my licence for the TV work, because it involved driving long distances all over the country to do stuff. He explained that I would lose my TV contract, and that would have a knock-on effect on Andy's own company. He went on to say I'd lose the profile that he'd worked hard to build up (which wouldn't be a disaster from my point of view); I'd be dropped from North One and Channel 4, and therefore other people who made programmes I was in would lose income because of it. Andy added that Channel 4 would lose commercial revenue they'd worked hard to get in these tough economic times. He made it sound like the world would stop spinning if Guy Martin lost his licence. He had also organised letters to be sent from charities I'd helped, including Spinal Research, to say nice things about me. Andy wasn't lying, but he wasn't holding back either, and things would certainly have gone tits up if I lost my licence.

The prosecuting solicitor said he knew who I was, mentioning the motorcycling and the TV show he'd seen. 'That's the last thing I need,' I thought, 'that they know I'm a motorcycle racer as well.' He said he was an advanced motorcycle instructor.

The magistrates then argued, as we knew they would, that if the TV job was so big the production company making the show could supply a driver to ferry me to the filming locations. It was hard to argue against. Andy, who was speaking on the side of the TV lot, said he was only here to help me keep my licence so it didn't affect the earnings of other people, and my licence was essential to the filming and the jobs of the crew. Andy came back to them with an explanation that I had to drive in the series, to give the idea of the journey and my everyday life, so a taxi wouldn't be any use. He said this wasn't *Top Gear*, all handbrake turns on an airfield. He pointed that I didn't ever ride motorcycles on the road, only when I was racing.

Then a weird thing happened. From where I was sat, and it's clear I'm no legal expert, it seemed the prosecuting lawyer started saying stuff to back up our argument, agreeing with us rather than trying to nail us. At that point the chairman of the magistrates started throwing his head around saying, 'This is ridiculous! Mr Martin has 18 points on his licence already! He's obviously a total liability on the road.'

When all the questions had been asked and answered, the magistrates left the court to deliberate. With everyone else remaining in the court, the prosecuting solicitor came up and said, 'I saw you at the TT. The way you boys race around there is amazing. I ride a motorbike. How do you get your knee down?'

A few minutes later the magistrates all came back into the court and the judge gave the verdict, saying, 'In all my time,

I have never known anyone have this many points and keep their licence. I won't ban you, but I'll give you another three penalty points and a fine of … At this point, me, Andy and Mick were all expecting it to be thousands. Then he said 'One hundred and sixty pounds.'

He added, 'I've been a magistrate in this area for 20 years and I've never let anyone with that many points keep their licence, but for the reasons you've given I'm going to let you.'

The three points took me up to 21, a winning hand at black jack, but not ideal to have on a driving licence. Normally, reaching 12 penalty points means an instant ban.

I just mumbled back that I was genuinely sorry and I genuinely didn't know the speed limit was 50, when it would've been 60 in a car. I was very sorry. There wasn't a lie told.

When I walked out of the court I was still a bag of nerves. I couldn't deal with the atmosphere or the situation. I like to think they'd seen sense. Yes, I'd been to court for traffic offences twice before, and I should've known better, but I had been driving like a saint, just 4 mph above the limit really.

The last case of the day was lad who had been caught doing 81 in a 70 and he got banned. Apparently, he tweeted like mad that I'd been in court and got away with it, just because I'd been on TV. Having a high profile wasn't always a bad thing. I was lucky I had people to argue my case, while the lad whose case followed mine didn't.

CHAPTER 17

THAT FELLA OFF THE TELLY

'Then I noticed I was beginning to have weird thoughts.'

WHEN MAGAZINES FIRST started writing about me and asking me to contribute by going on road tests and new bikes launches, it was still unusual if I was recognised at anything other than a road race meeting, and then it was only the race fans who noticed me. I remember going to see an exhibition of TT photos in London. I had just parked my van, and was looking for a parking ticket machine when someone recognised me from my column in *Performance Bikes* – I was amazed. It was a magazine I'd always read, and if people read *PB* they were right folk. When the TT coverage grew and began to be shown on ITV. and then the film *Closer to the Edge* came out, I started to get mobbed at the TT and bike shows.

I don't regret doing *Closer to the Edge*. I've watched it twice, at a screening and then at a premiere in London, and it is me, I come across how I am. The film also opened a lot of doors. But until I saw the film I didn't realise how much I was in it. I went to a private screening with Steph and Andy, and before I got on the tube to start going home, me and Steph had to call into a nearby pub and have a drink. We were both speechless, just shaking our heads in disbelief. They were filming a bunch of riders at the TT, but everything that happened to me must've made them choose to focus on me a bit more. If I hadn't crashed, perhaps things would have turned out differently.

The boat programme went out on the BBC in 2011, twice a week for six weeks, and that meant even more people recognised me. The first programme was due to go on at seven o' clock, but I was flying to Spain for a week's testing in Cartagena at exactly that time. It couldn't have been timed better. I landed in Spain, switched my phone on and there must have been a hundred text messages. I was glad to be out of it. After that people started recognising me in Tesco.

I was working as a labourer in Grimsby at the time and we'd going to the local supermarket to buy our butties. If someone said, 'I know who you are,' one of the lads I worked with would stop dead, look at me and laugh, saying, 'You're right, he does look like that fella off the telly, loads of people say that.' Then we'd just walk off. They got brilliant at it.

Since back in 2010 I've been suffering with these strange thoughts. It came on gradually and I don't know why. I'm not rude, but if I'm at a big race and I stop to sign one thing, another person always wants something, and then someone else wants something, and I'm trapped, and I have a job dealing with it. Mentally, I mean.

I began to feel uncomfortable. Then I noticed I was beginning to have weird thoughts when I was in the middle of a crowd. And, from my experience, a crowd attracts a crowd. It's not Chinese water torture, but it triggers odd feelings, and my mind goes adrift.

At a race in Ireland I met a lass called Andrea who has two sons that she regularly brings to the racing. I got talking to her about stuff like this, the problems I have in crowds, because I found out during the conversation that her sister was a psychiatrist. Towards the end of the chat Andrea said, 'You need to see my sister.'

I made an appointment, and me and Steph travelled over to Ireland. Steph really encouraged me to see the psychiatrist. She wanted answers, to find out why I am like I am, but I don't know if she accepted them.

We sat down with the specialist, and spent all day filling out forms and answering questions, while we drank tea and ate biscuits. It wasn't like a doctor's office; we were sat in comfy seats, no desk between us. She didn't have one of those mirrors strapped to her forehead either.

I explained that I can be sat talking to someone, nodding, smiling and agreeing, and a thought will enter my head, like, 'What would happen if I smashed this cup around the side of someone's head and went crackers for five minutes?' The people who come to see me are mega folk on the whole, but I could be talking to the Queen and I don't think it would stop me having these thoughts. I'm just wired up wrong. I weigh it all up logically in my head before I snap out of it. Small talk triggers it off. People are talking to me like they know me, because they've read something in a magazine or seen me on TV. And I'm being polite, because always I try to be polite, but my mind starts wandering. I've even done it myself when I met one of my heroes, Mick Doohan at the Goodwood Festival of Speed one year. I blurted out, 'I've read your book three times,' but it wasn't even his book – Mat Oxley had written it about him. He just nodded and smiled. Perhaps he was looking for a cup to smash me around the head.

I had the cup-smashing thoughts a couple times in the practice week of the 2013 Isle of Man TT. I was sat with my friend and sponsor, Gary Hewitt, boss of the company Elas, at his house on the Isle of Man when Steve Parrish, the ex-racer and TV presenter came to visit. It was all very pleasant. We were just sat having a cup of tea, but Parrish started talking about Twitter, saying stuff like he does it to keep his profile up. My mind drifted off and I started thinking, I wonder if I should start smashing cups and take all my clothes off and go crazy, running round for five minutes.

I picture myself doing things and it's quite vivid. That was the first time I'd had the naked thoughts, though. I visualised myself, John Thomas in the breeze, jumping off the sofa onto the sideboard. Normally, it's still the cup around the side of someone's head. I never have acted on the impulse and I am pretty sure I never would, but I realised I'd better go and see someone before I do.

At the end of our day with the psychiatrist she said, 'There are no ifs, buts or maybes, you have Asperger's Syndrome.' It's a type of autism, but there's a massive scale and I don't know where I fall on it. I haven't even looked up Asperger's Syndrome on the internet. I'm not denying I have it, just disregarding it. Other than trying not to be at the centre of a crowd, when everyone's looking at me, I haven't changed anything I do. I'm not famous in my garage at home. I'm not famous at Moody's truck yard or my mates' houses either.

The psychiatrist reckons the Asperger's shapes the way I look at everything. While I've not been brought up to be rude, I'm not bothered about offending people by saying what I think is the truth. Which is, I suppose, why people want to interview me and have me write columns for magazines. The psychiatrist made it clear that it would be a good idea not to put myself in the kind of positions that trigger the thoughts that cause this tension. That's one of the reasons I try to stay out of the way at the TT and why I really don't want to do media days at shows like Motorcycle Live at the NEC, Birmingham if I can help it.

Lots of people, from race fans to team managers, marketing people, sponsors and race organisers think I've been awkward for not wanting to do all the PR stuff, but the truth is, I can't stand dealing with. Some of the other riders are happy to do it. They even enjoy it. On the surface, it's not difficult to sit and sign stuff for people who like me as a racer or have enjoyed the TV shows, but that's just the surface – underlying it are these weird thoughts and emotions bubbling away. I'm not trying to be different or awkward, but I can't help the way my brain has been wired up.

The problem is all to do with this tension, not pressure. The pressure of the race or pressure of work doesn't do it to me, even if a boss and five drivers are at work all asking for their truck to be finished right now. I can deal with that.

I'm not turning into a recluse, I still do signings for sponsors, because they really want me to, and they're loyal supporters who I've worked with for years, but we set it up so I only do half an hour. More than that and things start to get on top of me. People might think, 'Who does he think he is? I've been waiting here for an hour,' but I hope I've explained it. If I have or haven't, there's nothing I can do about it. I know I could sign stuff at the TT for 12 hours and someone would still slag me off for not signing stuff for 13 hours.

The psychiatrist also said she thought I could love tools and machines as much as I could love a person, that I see them in the same light. I do know that people can shout and scream and have tantrums at me, and I don't give a shit – and perhaps that's unusual. I'm looking at them, but thinking about the next cylinder head I have to port.

CHAPTER 18

THE £20-PER-MILE CAR AND OTHER WAYS TO SPEND MONEY

'I told myself I wasn't having any more fast cars.'

SINCE I STARTED earning a few quid racing, I've spent a big part of it on flash cars that I usually keep for a while, before waking up one day thinking, 'Martin, what are you doing?' Then I sell it and go back to whichever van I have at the time.

I have owned BMWs, a Porsche and an Aston Martin, but the car I've owned the longest is a 1972 Saab 96 that I bought for £300 when I was 21. And I've still got it.

When I bought it, the car was a dysentery brown, but I could see the potential. Me and my mates Matt, Benny, Johnny and Jonty all painted the Saab. We gave it a coat of matt black and then added hot rod flames on the bonnet and front wings. We re-trimmed it with leopard-print fake fur too.

It was all done so we could take it to the local hunt ball. Fox-hunting is a big thing round this area of Lincolnshire. In fact, it seems bigger now than it was before they banned it. They don't call it fox-hunting any more, just hunting. They put a trace out for the dogs to follow. They still get foxes, though.

I've never been on a hunt, but we did visit the kennels when I was at junior school. Fox-hunting keeps all the Yah-Yahs happy, but the hunt ball was on our social calendar because all the farmers' fit daughters would get dressed up and go.

We finished the Saab just in time and it must've worked, because I ended up meeting a girl, Charlotte – a horse trainer, who I went out with for three years.

The Saab wasn't my first choice, though. I really wanted a Volvo Amazon, and the whole desire for an old Swedish family car came from a bloke called Stuart Clifford. He was a truck driver, who worked for Bill Banks's BB Haulage. He was really into hang-gliding, and he would live over in Tenerife for most of the year doing that, but he'd come back and drive for a few months to earn some money. When he was in England he'd drive around in an old matt black Amazon saloon with Swedish number plates on it. ESO 172, I think the registration was. If he was ever pulled over by the police he'd start talking in a made-up language that must have sounded like Swedish, because he would get let off without the coppers ever realising he had no UK tax or insurance. He was a cool dude, in his early forties when I was in my late teens.

The story turned bad for him when he developed cancer and went through a couple of operations to try and sort it, but the job was buggered. He'd been told it was terminal, so he went to Kirmington airport, or Humberside Airport as it's known now, and rented a car. Next, people reckon, he bought a gallon of fuel in a can, and drove flat-out down the A46, between Nettleton and Market Rasen, aimed the car straight at a tree and that was it. Lights out.

My mate Dobby, whose house I lived in when I moved out of the farm in Kirmington, is a retained fireman who was called to the scene. He pulled him out of the car, but it was already much too late. Stuart didn't want to make any mistakes with this job and it wasn't a nice scene. Dobby thought he knew who the driver was straight away because Stuart had had a finger missing for a few years. If you're going to go out, go out in a blaze of glory. I had admiration for him, though I'm glad I didn't have to clear up after it.

A while later Stuart's Amazon came up for sale. Someone else had got hold of it, but I couldn't afford it and the engine was a bit knackered, so I ended up with the Saab 96 instead. I still always wanted an Amazon, though.

I bought my first proper fast car at the end of 2005, a year I'd won a lot of races in Ireland. I'd always fancied a fast car and the limited edition BMW M3 CSL caught my eye. It was the stripped-out version with a carbon-fibre roof and 3.2-litre, straight-six engine. I thought it was mega. It blipped the throttle when you changed down the gears using the semi-automatic gearbox. The induction roar sounded a treat. I did a few track days in it too.

Then, halfway through the following year, 2006, I had a mad yearning for something faster for track days, so I bought a Porsche GT3 RS. I'd have only been in my early twenties.

The RS was the stripped-out, non-turbo 996 with a full roll-cage and a whale-tail spoiler. It was white with red stripes on the bottom of the doors, that said GT3, and red wheels. It looked like it had crashed into Halfords. I had 204 mph on the clock and thought that was probably enough and sold it. As long as I have a van, I don't need a car, but I do like them.

Then, in 2007, BMW came out with the V8 BMW M3. I went to the local BMW dealer in my lunch-hour in rigger boots and dirty old trousers held up with baling wire. I think part of buying that car was to show the salesman that he shouldn't judge a book by its cover, but it was me who made the bigger mistake. I got the first V8 M3 in the area, but I didn't like it. It was a big comfy thing, totally different to the CSL. It was set up more to be loaded up and driven to the golf club than hammered around Donington on a track day. I sold it and lost a fortune on it, saying to myself I'd never have another fancy car ever again ...

Still, while I'd owned the Porsche and BMWs I had always really wanted an Aston Martin. If I had nothing better to do in my dinner hour I'd look on the internet at my dad's work. I used to visit the Pistonheads website, where I saw the V12 version of the Vantage had been released and there was one registered and on sale. That meant I didn't have to order it and be on the waiting list. I had known this version was coming out for ages and had rung a dealer called JCT600 in Yorkshire, asking when they could get one. They didn't even ring me back. Even though it was over £120,000 I was really tempted.

For a few years, I'd been getting financial advice from my mate Mad Nige, and I thought I'd give him a call about the car. I'd met Mad Nige when me and Kate were in Colours Night Club, on Douglas seafront, during the 2004 Isle of Man TT. We got talking and he invited us to meet him the next day, when he'd take us up in his plane. It was my very first TT, so he didn't know me from Adam, but we just hit it off. I loved talking to him and he looked out for me up until he died in 2011. He was an advertising salesman, but he became my financial adviser, even though he had no experience in it.

When this V12 Aston came up, I rang Mad Nige and told him I wanted to buy the car, asking him if he thought I was stupid to buy it. He said, 'Fuck it. Get it if you want one.' As I said, he wasn't a qualified financial adviser.

I had the car for two and a half years and did just over 3,000 miles in it. The novelty soon wore off. The seats jammed. The electric windows jammed. There were faults with the paint. It suffered from bad build quality and bad finishing.

When that particular box was ticked, the Aston just ended up sitting in a barn on the Lancasters' farm, long after I'd left and was no longer living there or seeing them and their daughter, Kate. I think I'd only ever wanted an Aston Martin because my dad said they were mega. A bit of the attraction was buying one to take Dad out in it.

One thing that really turned me against Astons was that I'd always thought gentlemen drove them, but then I decided it was just dickheads. What changed my view was seeing everyone drive them with the LED sidelights on. I thought they must come on automatically and you couldn't do anything about it, but you have to turn the switch for them to come on, so people are turning them on to say, 'Hey, look at me!' They want everyone to know they're driving an Aston Martin. Cocky buggers ...

When I had agreed to sell it, I was quite nervous going to pick the car up from the farm. I wouldn't have been surprised if one of the farm's fork-lifts had picked it up and turned the Aston on its roof. Kate could have, perhaps should have, tipped brake fluid all over the bodywork, but she just sprayed WD-40 on the windscreen. She wanted to pee me off, but was still too nice to do anything too bad.

When I sold the Aston, I lost an absolute fortune on it. With the depreciation it cost me about £20 for every mile I did in it, so I told myself I wasn't having any more fast cars. That lasted only until a friend who I stay with in Ireland, Paul Dunlop, no relation to the racing Dunlops, showed me a film of a Volvo Amazon estate that was faster than a Ferrari 458 Italia. And it was for sale. There and then we started looking for the code for Sweden and rang the owner. Two more phone calls and we'd done the deal.

This car won an award at the SEMA show, the world's biggest modified car show, in Las Vegas, and was voted Sweden's coolest Volvo. It's a 1968 Volvo Amazon, but it's a two-door – and Volvo never made a two-door estate. The builder of the car, who works for Swedish supercar maker Koenigsegg, cut the B pillars and doors out of an Amazon saloon and welded them into the four-door body. The front doors are longer, so it gives the car a much nicer look and it's easier to get in and out of. The back doors are welded up and filled in. The roof has been subtly lowered too, meaning all the glass has had to be trimmed. It has a NASCAR rear differential and one-off 19-inch wheels. The paintwork is better than any Ferrari I've ever seen. The front grille is hand-beaten and took two weeks to make. The red leather interior was made by the same people who trim the interiors of the £900,000 Koenigsegg Agera R.

The AP brakes, the hubs and the suspension struts are all from a Koenigsegg supercar. It has Öhlins suspension; FIA bucket seats; five-point harnesses; a fire extinguisher system; full roll-cage; a racing ignition ... The fuel filler has been moved to the roof. The engine bay is so tidy, because things like the battery are all hidden away. It has a Sparco steering wheel and a dash out of a P1800 Volvo, because it's slightly better looking than an Amazon's.

The engine is a 2.6-litre turbocharged, six-cylinder Volvo T6. The car is an extreme Volvo Amazon, but it's still a Volvo Amazon. It makes 780 horsepower and runs on £3.80-a-litre E85 race fuel. I love it, even though at the end of 2013 the timing pulley stripped off the end of the crank and wrecked each of the six pistons and all the valves. I'd had 3,000 trouble-free miles out of it and it was going to be the last drive of the year. It definitely turned into that. Luckily I was only on the way to Caistor for a pint of milk when it broke.

The only thing that is disappointing, other than the crank problem, is that I've peaked. It's impossible to have anything better than this car. It's the fastest car I'll ever go in.

When I bought the Rolls-Royce Merlin engine, one of the engines out of a Lancaster bomber, the fella I bought it from had a Ferrari F50, worth a million quid; a Ferrari F40; a Lamborghini Countach; a Ferrari 355 GTB ... He had all the gear, and as lovely as it all was, I wouldn't swap any of them for this Volvo.

The Merlin engine is something else too. It's a 27-litre V12. Each cylinder displaces over two litres per stroke. It makes 1,600 horsepower.

I have to prime the engine before I start it, getting the oil pressure up. If it's cold I have to warm the oil, with a hot air blower on the oil tank, to thin it. It is mounted on a specially made trolley.

It can sit it at 2,200 rpm without it wanting to move on the trailer it's mounted on. Every exhaust stub has a constant glow of flame out of it, running onto the front of the exhaust stub directly behind it. It's angry. It's difficult to put into words what it's like having a hand on the throttle of this thing. I'm like a dog with ten dicks every time I start it up.

It cost £35,000 and is out of a 1942 Lancaster Bomber, the first year of the Lancaster. It's the same engine they used in the Spitfire. Before 1942 they used a different design of engine for the Manchester and Stirling bombers, and I've heard the RAF lost more planes through engine failure than enemy fire. The introduction of the Lancaster changed that very quickly.

Mine will run on normal petrol station pump fuel, that's held in tanks on the custom-made trailer the engine is mounted to. It only needs Avgas, high-octane aviation fuel, when it's running masses of boost pressure, from the supercharger, and under a lot of load at high altitude.

The Merlin lived at Moody's for a while, before I moved it to a mates' farm. He wasn't sorry to see it go after what it did to his workshop. One day I decided to see if I could get the rev limiter out of it and run it a bit harder. I managed to disconnect it, meaning I could get the propeller spinning faster, and rang my boss, Mick, to ask if he wanted to walk over the yard from the offices to hear it going.

He came over with his phone to video the action and stood in front of the propeller – it has a full-sized propeller attached – while I was behind the seven-foot-long motor, controlling the throttle.

I got the engine cracked up, flames spitting out of the headers, then gave it a bit more throttle than I'd been allowed when the mechanical limiter was still on it. A second later my heart was in my mouth as the trolley started moving. I killed the ignition, but the propeller was still spinning and the trolley still had its momentum. There was nothing more I could do. Moody jumped out of the way and hid behind a truck that I'd been servicing, swearing loudly, his smartphone now just filming the ground and his trouser leg, as the propeller cut my beautiful hand-built Rourke bicycle in half, chopped a wooden staircase into kindling and chewed a chunk out of a concrete block wall before the propeller stopped spinning. The rubble from the wall damaged the truck I'd been working on. And I think we got away lightly.

I was a nervous wreck for a while after that. I was worried I'd wrecked the ultimate in stationary engines, that wasn't quite as a stationary as I would have liked it, but after a good look over it, the only damage was some scratched paint on the propeller. It's some kind of machine that engine.

Since I crashed the Kawasaki AR50 into the Fiat Punto at Barnetby Top, the 1997 accident that started me on my racing career, I hadn't owned a road legal bike for years. Then I bought the Martek – a turbocharged one-off Suzuki.

I first saw this bike years ago, at my mate's bike shop, Chris Gunster Motorcycles in Grimsby. I could see how well everything had been made or modified, the engine mountings, the frame and the exhaust ... It was in having some work, and even though I hadn't owned a road bike since I was an apprentice I said, 'If that ever comes up for sale let me know.' Gunster told me, 'Oh that'll never be sold.' Then six or seven years later he told me it had come up, but looking nothing like it used to. It had been sprayed with Suzuki blue and white colours and had fluorescent pink wheels and a rats nest wiring loom, but I could see beyond that.

It was running and making decent horsepower, but the work done to finish it off wasn't up to Martek's standard. The original builder, Mark Walker, had sold it unfinished and someone else had got it running. I went out for a test-ride and it was the quickest thing I'd ever been on. It made my Fireblade TT Superbike of the time feel like a moped. It was ridiculous. Even off the turbo it felt quicker than my Superbike.

When I bought it, people were surprised what I paid for it (I'm not telling how much), but the work done by Mark Walker and Richard Todd, the other founder of Martek, and the parts they fitted and fabricated themselves were the business. I wanted the whole bike to be the same quality as the best bits of it.

I took the Martek to pieces the first week I had it, which was the back end of 2009 or early 2010, and it was still in pieces in 2014. It doesn't disappoint me it's taken this long. It's been built a few times, but I take it to bits again because I'm not happy with something.

The engine is based on an oil-cooled Suzuki GSX-R1100 and it's turbocharged. I was going for 500 horsepower until I talked to a turbo expert. I liked the sound of 500 bhp, it's a nice round number, but I was told that while I could tune this engine to make 500 bhp, one run on the dyno and the gearbox and clutch would be scrap, so now I'm going for a decent 350 horsepower, after which I'll ride it a bit, then park it up and move on to the next project.

The engine made 320 bhp when I got it, but only on 120-octane fuel. I want a genuine 350 running on pump fuel. Then I plan to use E85, fuel with 85 per cent ethanol. It's good for getting big power out of turbo engines, but it's a bit of a journey into the unknown.

The petrol tank has been chopped about to leave room for one of the turbo pipes and now only holds eight litres, so the bike will pass everything but a filling station.

I know the look I want to go for, a modern café racer look. When I've finished, it'll look nothing like the bike I bought. I want it to be a bike that Mark Walker looks at and says, 'I like that.'

I've prepared and built race bikes on and off since I started, but the Martek got me back into owning and working on bikes that are road legal – or kind of road legal. I love the attention to detail that's needed. You can't daydream, everything has to be 100 per cent. But I don't tune as many engines as I used to and I don't know if I could do it full-time, because everyone wants a million-quid job, but no one wants to pay for it. With a modern Superbike you can't just do one thing, you have to do the complete engine to make any improvements. It's an expensive job and no one wants to pay, so I don't want the hassle. People cut corners, then when it blows up it's the engine builder's fault. With the trucks I can say, if you're not going to do it right I'm not working on it. It keeps things simple.

CHAPTER 19

THE ULSTER

'There are times when the side of the rear tyre kisses up against the kerb and it'll cause the bike to wheelie.'

TRUCKS, TELEVISION, MOUNTAIN biking, a lot going on, but I still take racing seriously. It's not my career – I lasted a morning as a professional racer, remember – but all the races I enter I go out to win. If I don't win them, it's not for a lack of effort.

Since the 2011 season I've raced for the Northern Ireland-based team TAS Suzuki – first with black Relentless Suzukis in 2011, then the white and blue Tyco-sponsored bikes. They've all be run by the father and son outfit of Philip and Hector Neill. TAS stands for Temple Auto Salvage, the family's original business. Hector has sponsored riders and run teams for years, and Philip was an international level motocross racer.

As a team, they've won TTs, but, famously, I hadn't won

a TT at the end of 2013. I have won plenty of other races and beaten every other TT racer of my generation in International mass-start races.

The North West 200, the Isle of Man TT and the Ulster Grand Prix are the races called the 'Internationals' in the real road racing world. Other races, like the Southern 100 and the Scarborough Gold Cup, attract the top racers and pay decent prize money, but the Internationals are the bigger and more prestigious races to win.

I'm not much of a fan of the North West course any more, but I love riding the TT and the Dundrod circuit, home of the Ulster GP.

Matt Wildee of *Performance Bikes* magazine summed up the Ulster GP's circuit well after he visited in 2006. 'The fastest racing circuit there has ever been is little more than a collection of A- and B-roads spliced together with ribbon and hay bales. For 363 days of the year these roads are used for the school run and dawdling tractors. This is about as far away from Monza or Phillip Island as you can get.' *Performance Bikes* featured a lot of road racing back then, long before any three-dimensional TT films. The same article went on to compare some of the speeds with tracks readers might know from TV.

'The fastest lap at Phillip Island [an Australian circuit famous among MotoGP and World Superbike fans for its fast corners] is 111.734 mph [now it's 112.9, set by Marc Marquez in 2013]. Troy Bayliss has lapped Monza at 121.317 mph. But Ian Hutchinson – a little known racer outside Irish circles – averaged 130.829 mph at Dundrod, while chasing *PB* favourite Guy Martin.'

Matt picked the year I won four races in a day to visit. He ended his intro saying, 'But you'd never find a telegraph pole 78 cm from the apex of the Parabolica ...'

The Dundrod is fast and flowing. It hasn't been monkeyed around with and had a load of chicanes added like the North

West has. I first raced here at a meeting called the Killinchy 150 in 2003. It used to be its own meeting, but now they run it on the Thursday of the Ulster Grand Prix meeting and call it the Dundrod 150.

The Ulster GP lap record is 133.977, set by Bruce Anstey, in 2010, making it the fastest track in the world still being used. This is what a fast lap of the 7.4-mile Dundrod circuit feels like ...

I call the start–finish straight the Flying Kilo, but I've no idea if it's a kilometre or not. In 2013, we were timed at 199 mph along there, but it's dead smooth for a road circuit. There's a really fast left at the end of the straight, called Rock Bends. In fact Rock Bends is a group of corners, all with the same name, and the first is this very, very fast left before the right. You might not think it's a corner at all, but it is at 190 mph.

I used to be able to get through the first fast left flat-out, but as the bikes have become quicker you don't actually want to be going through the first part that fast, because it sends you off-line for the rest of the corners, knackering your line through and out the other side. You're better off going slower to go faster, so I roll the throttle there now and make the rest of Rock Bends more flowing and less of a panic to get through.

For the right-hander, the beginning of the second section of the Rock Bends complex, I go back two gears, to fourth, and drive hard through a few downhill lefts and rights, all on the throttle, before I'm hard on the brakes for Leathemstown, a 90-degree road-end corner. These slow corners are all about the run out of them down the next very fast straight.

I use the kerb as a stop for my tyres on the way out. The ideal racing line uses all of the road, but instead of a nice sunken kerb, like at a MotoGP or BSB track, this is a kerb that would chew up a car's alloy wheels if you weren't careful parking. At the end of the kerb, I'm still way over on the left of the road and sometimes in the grass and dirt while I'm firing down the next straight. I'll have the bike upright enough that it doesn't give too much of a problem, but I'll sometimes feel it kicking as the tyre struggles for traction. There are times when the side of the rear tyre kisses up against the kerb and it'll cause the bike to wheelie. That unsettles the bike and means I have to roll the throttle off, or get on the back brake to calm it, and that loses time, so I don't want to be hitting that kerb on the exit of Leathemstown too hard.

It's a top-gear thrash to the uphill Deers Leap that has a 180 mph blind entry. The bike's leant over and the revs rise as the contact area of the tyre goes from middle to the side, because the diameter of the tyre is different at those two points.

In the middle of Deers Leap, I'm back two gears, to fourth. At the side of the track is the Cockwell Inn, the garage in someone's garden that turns into a pub for the house owner's mates every Ulster Grand Prix.

The road drops away rapidly here and you can see a huge part of the west of Northern Ireland from this point, if you have time to take it in. In a race we are accelerating hard down the steep hill. I'm using every inch of the road. You really don't want anything to go wrong here. The last part of Deers Leap is a 150 mph downhill right. I'm hard on the back brake, stood up on the pegs, weight over the front of the bike, all to try to stop it wheelie-ing over backwards.

My guts nearly drop out of me as the road changes from downhill to climbing back uphill to Cochranstown. I'm in fifth gear again and on the back brake for a lot of this section, trying to keep both wheels on the floor. I bet the rear disc is nearly glowing red hot along here.

Then it's over a rise going into Cochranstown. I'm back from fifth to second gear. The road is dropping away so fast that it's a job to keep the tyres in contact with the tarmac, and it's impossible to be too hard on the brakes. I'm trying to lose 100 mph to get around the 90-degree corner, so it would be dead easy to tuck the front after asking too much of the front tyre's grip.

Once you're through this road-end bend the track isn't making any steep climbs or drops, but it's undulating. I'll be high up in the revs in second gear, the Superbike delivering most of its 200-plus horsepower to the rear wheel while the front wheel is just wanting to rise up all the time, so, again, I'm calming it with my foot on the back brake pedal.

Up to third, then fourth, on the run into Quarterlands, then back two gears to second. It always seems to be damp here and you've got to be careful on the painted road markings. I've had the front tuck while I've been braking hard and gone over the white lines. When that happens I have to instantly get off the front brake, stamp the back brake to allow the front tyre to grip again, then get back hard on the front brake to slow enough to get around the corner. If you panicked you'd be off there. Directly in front of me, when this is going on, is a copse of 100-year-old trees. No run-off, just trees.

There's no gradient here, you're on a level road into third, only up to about 12,000 rpm for the short straight to Ireland's Bend. Off the throttle, still in third, no brakes, just chuck it in and run up the hill. I use the hill to lose my speed while trying to understeer through the left-hander. A barbed wire fence lines the outsides of the track.

I'm accelerating hard up into fifth gear for Budore Corner, that's been renamed Lougher's. It's one of my favourite corners anywhere. It's a difficult choice whether to be in fifth or sixth. When I'm in fifth it feels right, but the bike is revving so hard that when I lean it over, right onto the very side of the tyre, the rolling diameter of the tyre changes and this affects the gearing, making the engine spin faster and hit the rev limiter.

Bikes have had rev limiters for years. They're an electronic safety system that cuts the ignition if the engine is trying to rev past its safe limit. When the rev limiter is hit, the engine stutters slightly and loses momentum. But if I run through Budore in sixth, to avoid hitting the rev limiter, when I stand the bike up, onto the middle part of the tyre, the revs start to drop and it's not pulling hard enough. I've settled on putting up with being on the rev limiter in fifth for a moment to get the best drive out for the run to Joey's Windmill.

The road undulates through a left and right. I go back two gears and then the road goes uphill. Bruce Anstey came off in front of me there once. A very big crash.

Out of Joey's Windmill I'm in third. The road is rising and I'm using the hill to scrub off speed again, so I'm not hard on the brakes. It's the same as Quarterlands – big trees directly in front of you. Anything goes wrong and you're knackered.

Up a bloody steep hill and over Jordan's Cross. After that there's a kink. I'm normally revving hard in fifth gear, the shift lights all lit up on the dash, telling me to change to sixth. The shift lights are little LEDs that are programmed to indicate when it's the optimum time, for the engine, to shift up. I don't here normally, but in 2013 I was sure Michael Dunlop was going to put a move on me, so I put it up to sixth just to keep all the momentum and not give him a sniff of an opportunity.

When I've got someone that close behind I'm trying to ride defensively and not do anything daft while staying as fast as possible. I'm riding differently than if I was going for one fast lap by myself. If I was just going for a flying lap with no one trying to put a move on me, I'd leave it in fifth and run it on the limiter all the way.

Into Wheelers, there's a place called the Hole in the Wall, where there's a wall with a hole in it. This is all fast lefts and rights. The road is level, not really climbing or dropping, and once again I'm using every inch of the road, sweeping from the verge on one side to the verge on the other.

Wheeler's is third gear, nicely cambered and one of the only places on the Dundrod circuit with any run-off to speak off.

Then it's up two gears for the run to Tornagrough. I'm flat-out in fifth gear, so the thick end of 170 mph, and there is a dip in the road that makes the bike bottom out at that speed, the suspension completely compressed and neck muscles straining to stop the chinbar of my helmet from banging on the top of the petrol tank.

Depending on what bike I'm on, either the 1000-cc Superbike or the 600-cc Supersport, I then shift back to either second or third for the left-hander Tornagrough. The Superbike has much taller gearing, so it'll go through in second. The Supersport needs to be in third. There's a little manhole cover on the right-hand side that I use as a braking marker.

There are a couple of bumps that unsettle the bike, making the front tyre squirm and protest. Even though I'd be in second gear, and that sounds slow, I'm still going through here at 90 mph or so – that's an educated guess, like all the speeds I've quoted, because my race bikes don't have speedos.

Through this long sweeper the whole bike is squirming, the rear tyre struggling to cope with the amount of power it's being asked to deal with as I wind the throttle on, just touching 100-per-cent throttle, the twistgrip on the stop, full power, maximum revs, before getting hard on the brakes for the first gear hairpin.

The hairpin is the only point on the whole seven-and-a-bit-mile lap that we're back to first gear. The hairpin is dead tight, downhill and off-camber. You don't want that mix of ingredients in the wet. I'm having to brake over the white lines, that have very little grip. This section feels like walking pace after some of the 190-mph straights.

Accelerating out of there, I'm hard on the back brake, even though I'm hammering up through the gears, just to keep the front wheel down. Second, third, fourth, into Quarry Bends.

I have a lot of lean on, banked hard on the right-hand side, and I know I've got it right when the shift lights on the dash come on in fourth as I'm leant hard over.

Quarries is a big complex of corners. There's a lamp-post on the right-hand side and I pull as tight as I can to that. The bike isn't trying to wheelie here, but I'm on the back brake again to try and compress the rear suspension. I've gone from 100-per-cent throttle to 70-per-cent, and it's putting a lot of weight bias on the front. When I'm then going back to 100-per-cent throttle, driving hard out of Quarry Bends, there's a lot of front to rear transition as the front suspension rises and the rear squats under the power. That transition unsettles the bike, making it buck and shake. Keeping the back brake on through the corner keeps the rear shock compressed, pulling the rear shock into its stroke, and minimises the front to rear movement and stresses the rear tyre less.

The last bit of Quarries is down two gears, into third. Getting back onto 100-per-cent throttle makes the bike squirm about a bit, but it's not too bad.

Then there is another very long right-hander, Dawson's Bend, that doesn't really have an apex. I've watched a lot of riders through there, and I've tried a lot of lines myself, and keeping in the middle of the road seems to work best.

Coming out of Dawson's I'm leant over and balancing grip and throttle position. The rear tyre hasn't got enough of a contact patch to just wind the throttle wide open. At best, it would spin up, meaning less traction and less acceleration. At worst, it would spin, grip and highside me, slinging me off the top of the bike at 120 mph and more.

Then it's the run down to the start–finish line, along the Flying Kilo, for another lap. The Ulster Grand Prix is a seven-lap race, covering a total of just less than 52 miles. The whole race is run at an average speed of close to 130 mph.

I'm the third or fourth winningest rider at the Ulster, but I've never won a TT. I like the cut and thrust of the mass-start races. I like getting stuck in.

I went to the 2013 Ulster after a poor TT and came away thinking I'd been to Michael Dunlop's back garden and done him over. And not just a bit.

In the Superbike race, the big one, the one for the money, I led and Dunlop came past me. He qualified on pole with me in second. There was only me and him doing the times. It was going to be like 2012, only the two of us.

In the race, he came past me in the Rock Bends on the first set of corners, with a 180–190-mph entry to it. When he passed I knew he meant business. He always does. At those speeds I can feel someone benefiting from my slipstream, so I know they're close – then he came past. I knew he was trying hard from the very off. He was 50p-ing it into the corners, meaning he was entering corners on one line, too hot, then tightening and tightening to make it around the corner, not taking one smooth line. His elbows were touching the grass, he was having to lift his knee up to miss the kerbs. Riding ragged, but bloody fast.

I decided to sit behind and see what he had and what I could do. I was happy that he wanted to show me his cards. He's a bit like that. The thing at the Ulster is, if you're not the quickest there, you can still get pulled around by the quickest quite easily. It's rare for someone to really break away at the Ulster. If someone is leading and doing the speeds, it's relatively easy to tag on.

Obviously, Michael thought he had the speed to get away, otherwise he'd have done what he did in 2012 – stayed behind and mugged me on one of the last corners with a do or die move that made our fairings bash together.

My Tyco Suzuki had better top-end speed than his Honda Legends Fireblade, but with the Superbike I'm riding, the Suzuki GSX-R1000 of 2011 to 2014, there is only a very narrow margin where it works really well. The set-up and the way the bike works with the tyres is a small window. When it's right it's brilliant, better than the other bikes, but getting it into that narrow operating area is much more difficult than with the Fireblade. The Honda works well over a wider range of settings. You don't have to be so precise setting it up. That day the GSX-R1000 was more than a match for the Honda, though. I knew that straightaway.

Another big variable are tyres. Since 2008 I've been using Pirelli or Metzeler tyres, when virtually every other top racer has been on Dunlops. Tyres from Pirelli and its sister company Metzeler are made in the same factory, but branded differently.

'Factory' is a description regularly used in motorcycling that I used to hate. People would talk about bits on their race bike as factory this or factory that, but all parts on a bike come out of the factory. What they meant was they have the fancy parts. When grand prix riders talk about a factory part, they mean a special part that has been made back at Honda or Yamaha headquarters, not created by the team or a specialist small company. It gives the part and the bike a bit of glamour and shows the manufacturers are so interested and supportive of the rider they give them the cream.

A team like TAS Suzuki are the official Suzuki team on the roads, getting assistance in one form or another from Suzuki in the UK, and a few parts directly from Japan – factory parts. It means TAS have to find their own support for suspension, engine electronics and plenty of other things. In comparison, Jorge Lorenzo's Yamaha MotoGP team are bankrolled and supplied entirely from Japan, even though the race team will be based in Europe – they are a true factory team.

There are positives and negatives with being a factory team. In the past, the official Honda British Superbike team's Fireblade had a rear suspension issue. The shock was mounted in a certain way that made it difficult to change quickly, if I remember rightly. All the non-official teams made an easy modification to make life simpler, but the official team weren't allowed to, because it would be admitting that the factory had got something wrong.

Anyway, after saying all that, I'm on factory Pirelli-Metzeler tyres. Anyone can buy slicks from the company, but they can't buy the stuff I am usually supplied to race on. The tyres are made by hand in small batches. The carcass, rubber, compound and profile can all change from batch to batch, and we go with the ones that feel best during testing.

The carcass is, as the name suggests, the body of the tyre that the rubber is laid on to. It is usually steel wire, wound round and round, and a Kevlar belt. The way the carcass is constructed can change the feel of the tyre massively. Compounds are often simply described as hard or soft. The softest tyres are often the grippiest, but they might only last a lap or less before they start to slide every time I try to brake into a corner or accelerate out of one. Some road tyres, and most GP and World Superbike tyres, have different compounds sandwiched together. If you were looking at the back of a bike, and could see the width of the tyre, the centre section is often much harder than either side. When the bike is on this centre section, it's often travelling fast, generating a lot of heat, but traction and grip aren't usually a problem. When the bike is leant over and the side of the tyre is being punished and trying to slide, grip is crucial so the compound is softer and grippier.

For years I have regularly been the first Pirelli-Metzeler rider home in the TT. The winner would be using Dunlop. If I was behind one of the top Dunlop riders I could often see him just whacking open the throttle while I had to feed in the power more gently. It meant they would stretch a few bike lengths on me every corner, so I'd have to try even harder, go through the fast corners even faster, to get them back in.

Pirelli would say all the right things, but they wouldn't deliver a tyre that would do what a Dunlop would do. It was beginning to get me down. I'd missed out on winning a TT by three seconds – in 2010. At the end of 2011 we went to Kirkistown to test the factory Pirellis against some Dunlops. The Dunlops weren't anything fancy, certainly not 'factory', they were just slicks anyone could order and buy to run on their race bikes or even at track days.

I knew the Dunlops would be better, but I had no idea how much better. And these weren't even the best tyres that riders at the time, like John McGuinness, Bruce Anstey and Ian Hutchinson, would have been supplied.

On one hand it made me keen to get onto Dunlops for the next season. I couldn't see how I could win without them, but I also realised that if you're racing for a different tyre company, and you're all pulling in the same direction, you might have a tyre that no one else has and that makes the difference. Neither did I want to be the seagull following a tractor, doing what everyone else did. In the end we stuck with Pirelli-Metzeler.

There's an argument that it wouldn't make sense for Dunlop to supply me tyres. A fella called Gary Ryan took me on one side at Cookstown in 2013 and put me straight. Ryan is the man behind the Street Sweep company, one of Michael Dunlop's loyal and long-term sponsors. He told me that if I wasn't racing on Pirellis, choosing to race on Dunlop instead, Dunlop would have no one to beat. If everyone is on Dunlop tyres what does it prove? They'd definitely have a Dunlop winner, whoever came home. As it is, when someone wins on Dunlop tyres they're beating Pirelli, they're beating TAS Suzuki and they're beating me. I'd never looked at it that way, but as soon as Ryan said it, it made sense.

In that 2013 Ulster GP, where I was battling Michael Dunlop for the main race, we were still on the first lap, entering Lougher's, a man's corner if ever there was one, when Michael rolled off the throttle. I was flat-out in fifth, the engine bouncing off the rev limiter, and I passed him when I didn't really want to. It wasn't a calculated pass, because I'd actually wanted to stay behind him for a while, but I was back in the lead.

For the next few corners, I was taking really wide, sweeping lines. Still pressing on, but leaving enough room for him to come underneath me with some margin of safety. I gave him every opportunity to pass me. When he didn't come past at the first gear hairpin, I thought I'd just keep on doing what I was doing, riding really big, sweeping lines, but still going as fast as I could. This was the opposite of riding a defensive line. I was hitting every apex, and while I wasn't hanging my bollocks out, I was still getting a few slides. I was trying.

At the end of the first lap my pit board said P1 +0. That told me I was position 1 (I knew that), but with a gap of nothing to the bike behind. After the second lap it was +0.3, then it was +0.5 ... +1 ... +1.5 ...

For the last lap I started to run a more defensive line. The thought at the back of my mind was, I'm going to get torpedoed at the Hairpin. Dunlop and me are a very similar speed at the Ulster. It you try to pass someone after the Hairpin who is running at the same speed it is very likely you'll come off. But he never came past.

In an interview after the 2013 Ulster I was asked if I had predicted I'd win three races, but it's a daft question. I can't see into the future and know what someone else is going to do, or how any of the other front runners have set up their bikes. The whole of racing is unpredictable, and the characters in road racing add a further level of unpredictability. They're not reckless or crazy. Sometimes Michael Dunlop does something that makes me think, 'Woah, Nelly!' But I've made those moves on people in the past and may well again in the future. We're riding on the limit of what's possible. You need to be riding like that to beat the Dunlops, Anstey and Hillier and those boys. I always ride as hard as I possibly can. Sometimes I'm not willing to push as hard as the winner in the rain. Sometimes I'm willing to push harder than everyone and it's me that takes the chequered flag.

That race could have been so different, because during practice I had the biggest crash I never had. By that I mean I had every ingredient of the crash, the realisation it's all going wrong, even the impact and the damaged bike, but I didn't actually fall off.

I've come close to crashing a lot. I've crashed quite often too, but the near misses are memorable. Before this Ulster Grand Prix, the biggest crash I never had was the one on my fixed-wheel pushbike, near Big Lil's, but the escape at the Ulster beat that.

It was coming into Deer's Leap, a blind-entry, 180-mph corner. The track was wet in places, but I was out on slicks. I saw a rider in the distance, and knew I'd pass him after the corner, so I rolled the throttle slightly, so I could get on the gas and accelerate through the corner for a good run down the next straight and make the pass safely before Cochranstown.

As I was weighing all this up I entered the blind corner and was immediately on the rider, who turned out to be Dan Cooper. In a race I'll take that at 180-plus. Even though this was practice and I'd rolled the throttle I would still have been doing over 160 mph in the wet on slicks. I braked and the front wheel locked up and went hard against the lockstop, the wheel turned to the right as far as it was possible to go, so I let off the brake and the bike sat back up. I had nowhere to go. I hit straight in the side of the other bike, going, I reckon, 100 mph faster than him.

I was thinking, 'This is going to look like a plane crash. There's two bodies here. This is it ...' The next thing I know I'm riding down the road on my motorbike, I look over my shoulder and Cooper is still on his and I'm wondering, 'What the fuck happened there?'

The impact shoved my handlebar into the tank, buckled my front wheel, bent one of the steel front brake discs and ripped the front mudguard clean off. His exhaust was bent in half and pointing at 90 degrees out to the side.

Having got away with it, my brain immediately went back into racer mode and the very next thought was, 'That has screwed up my fast lap.'

I got back to the pit and told the lads I'd had a near miss. They asked where I had come off. I don't think they believed me when I told them I hadn't. There were holes punched in the side of the fairing.

That night, in bed, it came back to me how close I came. Cooper, a good rider, who has won a 125 British Championship, explained later he was going steady because he was on slicks, but so was I. The rule at the riders' briefing is: Do not tour. Riders have been killed at the TT and other road races when they come round a blind bend and hit a rider from behind, so we were lucky to both escape this time and it's not something I dwell on.

What I prefer to think about are the same faces year after year at the Ulster. An old lass, Maureen, has been bringing me rhubarb jam, wheaten bread and scones for the last five years.

Another lady brings me six bottles of Old Speckled Hen. It's just mega. The whole mood in the pits is dead friendly.

The Ulster fans are hardcore, but they're polite people. The Irish fans know their racing inside out. They're not going because it's the cool thing to do, and they don't want to make small talk; they're asking what tyre compound and gearing you're running. They're into the details and I like that. Even with everything else going on, I still love races like the Ulster and pushing the best of the other real roads men for a win on the fastest racetrack there is.

CHAPTER 20

SPEED

'I wasn't in control, I was just blind and lucky.'

I HAVE RACED, led and won road races, on circuits that grand prix racers have said make their blood run cold, but I've never been scared. I have had moments when I thought it was going wrong and I was just picking the wall I was going to crash into, but there was never fear. When I have crashed, in the moments where I hit the deck and time slows down giving me a split second to consider what's going on, fear never comes into it. If I was scared I don't think I could race the way I do.

So it might be strange to read that the most terrified I've ever been was riding a pushbike for a TV show.

After *How Britain Worked* was finished the idea was to make a series I was even more involved in. I'm not a normal TV presenter, for good or ill, but I'm not afraid of getting stuck in, and that meant North One could come up with some unusual ideas. The one everyone got behind was *Speed*.

The series was four different hour-long episodes, shown on Channel 4 at the beginning of 2014. The show followed me as I tried to break four separate records. It went into the science of making the attempt, showed the building of the kit I'd use, and then the action as I went for it. The show was made for the science and educational part of Channel 4's programming.

The records were: British speed bicycle speed record; world toboggan speed record; world human-powered flight speed record; and hydro-bike distance record.

The first we got wrapped up was trying to break the British speed record for a bicycle, that had stood at 110 mph since 1986. It was set on a section of the M42 motorway, in Warwickshire, the day before it opened. The rider was David Le Grys and he reached that speed by using the slipstream of a Rover SD1 British Touring Car racer with a special spoiler enclosure on the back.

A flat section of motorway is an ideal place to do it, because you have a good length of well-surfaced road to get up to speed and then stop safely on. We didn't have that option, so the production company approached the Millbrook Proving Ground in Bedfordshire, where manufacturers take their pre-production test cars to be put through the mill on different kinds of tracks, from the roughest corrugations to a high-speed bowl. It sounded like we had permission to use the Millbrook loop, the circular high-speed track, right up until a week or so before we were due to make the attempt, then Millbrook got cold feet, thinking that it would all end in tears, so the hunt was on for somewhere else.

The next obvious place was the Bruntingthorpe Proving Ground. It's an old airfield in Leicestershire, often used by car and motorcycle magazines for speed testing and photoshoots. It has a Cold War-era runway, now privately owned, and is 1.85 miles long. Being a runway, it wouldn't be as good as a bowl, because the never-ending loop of a bowl allows the attempt to go on for as long as the rider, me, has power. The runway, even one of the longest in Britain, becomes a limiting factor, but it was all we had.

For the attempt, I'd ride inches behind a racing truck, using its slipstream to allow me to pedal a massive gear. The bike was custom-made for the job. Brian Rourke, the Bradley Wiggins of 40 years ago, was a consultant. Jason Rourke, his son, is a bicycle frame-builder who created the special bike for me to ride. Simon from Hope Technology made all the gearing for the bike. Getting the right gearing was crucial.

On the day of the first attempt I got dressed in a set of Dainese leathers that I raced in back in 2010, chest protector, back protector, my AGV helmet, in the blue and pink Britten colours, and cycling shoes.

To start, we gave it a go, at a steady speed, to try things out, and it all felt all right, but we reckoned the runway would only be quick enough if I came around the top corner onto the runway at over 40 mph, a fair lick round a 90-degree corner when you're less than a foot off the back of a racing truck.

The truck that I was slipstreaming was a MAN TGA 440. From the outside it looks like the kind of trucks I work on, a tractor unit that pulls an articulated trailer, but this racing truck is nothing like a road-going, working truck. The engine position is different, the engine's moved further into the middle of the chassis. It has a bigger turbo and a different exhaust. The standard truck makes 440 horsepower. Dave Jenkins, the owner and racer of this one, reckons his truck makes over 1,000 bhp. Dave is an experienced truck racer, a former champion, and I trusted him from the off. It would have been difficult to get anything done if I didn't totally believe in him.

For a record like this there was a balance to strike between wanting to practise, but not wanting to shag my legs out on these two-mile sprints. After a couple of practice runs Dave and I quietly agreed to go for it.

We got round the corner and onto the runway well, and I was as close as I needed to be. Rourke had welded a bumper bar onto the handlebars of the bike so if I rammed into the back of the truck I wouldn't fly over the handlebars.

During the run the truck got away from me, meaning I began to lose the tow of the slipstream. I'd been told I shouldn't get out of the seat to pedal because it would unsettle the bike and be potentially dangerous at the speeds we were talking about, but I forgot that, got out of the saddle and pedalled as hard as I ever had. The truck had a monitor set up showing a live feed of me so the driver could see exactly what I was doing. When Dave saw that I'd dropped back, he let his speed lower slightly at the exact same time as I stood up to accelerate, so I battered into the back of the truck at 80-odd miles per hour.

I kept pedalling, thinking the muscles were going to rip off the back of my legs, until it was time to brake. I'd reached 111 mph pedalling a pushbike. This bike was a fixed-gear, so you can't stop pedalling until the bike is completely stationary. If you forget, like I did, it reminds you sharpish by nearly breaking your legs. The bike threw my feet off the pedals at over 100 mph.

I don't usually watch any of the TV footage we film, but I wanted to see some from that run. There's a shot from a Vauxhall Insignia, that's doing over 80 mph, and the truck comes past with a bicycle behind it. It doesn't just overtake, it flies past. I watched it and thought, 'That's me!' It looked mental.

After Bruntingthorpe I couldn't sleep that night because the buzz was so massive from riding a pushbike at 111 mph a fag paper's width from the back of a truck. But we wanted to go faster. As of the end of July 2013, trying to go faster than I had on that day in Leicestershire would be the most terrifying thing I'd ever done on two wheels.

The idea someone came up with was to run on Pendine Sands. This Welsh beach was a famous, then notorious, site for British land speed record-breaking. It was first used in the1920s, and chosen because the retreating tide leaves the strip of sand very flat and quite compact. Back then I think they used as much as seven miles of the beach. Back then the roads were so terrible this probably seemed liked the perfect place – a motorcycle magazine of the time called it 'the finest natural speedway', but sand isn't tarmac or concrete. It's far from perfect for record attempts.

Malcolm Campbell used Pendine Sands to set the world land speed record at 146 mph in Blue Bird in 1924. It was broken time and again until Campbell raised it to 174.22 mph in 1927. He was in a battle with the Welshman J G Parry-Thomas and his car Babs. Parry-Thomas had held the record and was trying to win it back when he crashed at 170 mph. The driver died and Babs was buried on the beach until it was dug up and restored decades later.

I arrived at Pendine Sands at 10pm the night before the attempt. I was told to meet in a restaurant, and when I got there it was totally bunged, every table full. Everyone in the restaurant was part of the record attempt: helicopter pilots, medics, runners, directors, cameramen, soundmen, cycle fitness blokes, bicycle designers, truck racer, truck mechanic ... I wouldn't have wanted the bill for Saturday.

We met on the beach the next morning. James Woodruff, the director, had done the whole risk assessment and had a laminated sheet full of plans and timetables, all done with military precision. The idea was to build up to the attempt, in 5 mph steps, like they suggested we should do at Bruntingthorpe. At the airfield it was clear that me and the truck driver, Dave Jenkins, gelled pretty quickly and we could make much bigger jumps. My legs have only got so much in them; I can't keep building up slowly and slowly.

The laminated sheet said the first attempt should be 40 mph, but I said, 'Fuck that. Let's chuck a gear in the bike that allows us to do 100 mph.' The biggest gear available on the day had potential for 122 mph.

Dave said his truck felt squirrely at 40 mph. Not unstable, but not planted either, so he thought we should go for 70 or 80 as the first attempt. I'm glad I listened to him.

We did two miles at 70 mph and I couldn't see a thing. The sand was blowing up on the inside of my helmet and covering the visor. And the slightest indent left in the sand by the truck was massively unsettling the pushbike. When you ride on tarmac, the tyres are deforming, the wheel rims are flexing, the frame is flexing too, while the road surface is remaining constant, the datum point. But riding on the beach, the sand was moving, while the bike and its tyres were staying the same. The sand couldn't exert enough force on the bike to make it flex, and it was the most alien feeling in the world. It wasn't stable and I couldn't turn it. Every time I tried to turn, the front felt like it wanted to tuck. And this was at 70 mph. It turned everything I knew about feel on its head. It just wasn't right.

I told the crew, 'That's mental. And not in a good way.' I even gave one of them my mum's phone number. That's how sure I was that I was going to crash. It wasn't the pressure of there being over 20 people on the beach, just for this attempt, or the money that had been spent. The TV people would've stuck to my decision. If I'd said, 'No, it's too dangerous,' they would have known I'd said it for a good reason. The final decision was purely down to me, but if I hadn't tried it I wouldn't have been able to live with myself. It was a five-hour drive home and it would've been torture if I had given up on it.

I pulled on my helmet, 100 per cent sure I was going to crash. It wasn't a matter of if, but when and how bad ... I asked the bicycle mechanics to put the big gearing on the bike so we could have one go at it, adding, 'Because this is going wrong.' I knew that the more attempts we made the more indents we would press into the sand, and that would make riding even more dodgy.

While the gearing was being changed on the bike, I taped up all the underneath of my helmet to stop the sand finding its way up.

I had a quiet word with Dave, the truck driver, saying, 'When I crash you need to get your foot down and get out of the way. Let me crash by myself.' The monitor in his cab meant he could see what I was doing and I knew his gut instinct would be to back off, but that would have been disastrous.

I wasn't comparing myself to Evel Knievel at Wembley in 1975, when he knew he wasn't going to make the jump but still went for it anyway because so many people had turned up to see him, but I do think I had an idea of what Evel was going through.

We set off and I've never pedalled harder in my life. I wasn't getting any kind of buzz. I was just shitting myself. It was a horrendous feeling. I was told by Dave Le Grys, who had helped with training advice for this record, that I should never stand up to pedal because it unsettles the bike as you're pulling on the bars and swinging the bike from side to side. Stay in the seat was what the expert said, but again, I couldn't help it. At 40 mph I had to stand up, because the truck was getting away. I couldn't let the truck leave me, because I didn't want to do another attempt, so I just had to stand up. I stood up four times on that run. The last time was at over 100 mph.

Again, when Dave the driver saw that he was getting away he'd slow down, just as I'd stood up to catch him, so I'd bump into the back of the truck. The difference in speed when we hit might have only been 5 mph – the truck slowing to 78 mph while I had increased my speed to 83 mph to catch back up – but I could feel the whole bike flex as it tried to chuck me over the bars.

Taping up my helmet did stop the sand finding its way in, but it caused the inside of the visor to steam up, so I could hardly see a thing. The back of the truck had boards at the side, at an angle, to try and stop some of the sand pelting me, but if I went off line and nudged them with my handlebars it would be game over. So we put big lines made of white tape at the edges to show me how far I could safely move either side of the centreline of the truck. My vision was so obscured I could only just see the vague outline of the white lines as I was pedalling like hell along the beach.

In the end I was clocked at 112.94 mph, 1.5 mph faster than on the concrete at Bruntingthorpe. The beach course was three and a half miles long and I was pedalling at over 100 mph for two miles of it. I've no idea how I survived it, because I was not in control. It doesn't matter how wild the TT and other road racing looks, because I'm still in control. I wasn't in control on that beach. I was just blind and lucky.

Instead of thinking I'd got away with it, I left Wales with ideas of wanting to do 200 mph. As long as the lead vehicle could do 200 mph, and we had the room to do it, doing 200 mph is no harder than doing 100 mph. In fact, the faster the truck went the easier it was, because the air being pushed around the truck would curl around like a wave and fill the low pressure area behind the truck, where I was tucked in. So it felt like a tailwind: 200 mph – it's got to be done, hasn't it?

Another episode of *Speed* concentrated on a human-powered aircraft, the HPA. It was another tough challenge, but not quite as dangerous to my life or limbs. I was told, before filming, that 530 people have been into space, but only 450 have flown a human-powered aircraft. So it wasn't going to be easy.

The aircraft was designed by Alex and Ben, a couple of proper boffins from Southampton University. Ben was a mature student, Alex was a lecturer, and they got three students involved in helping to make the plane for the attempt.

The main wing structure was foam cut with a hot wire machine, that Ben had made himself; material like thick clingfilm, and carbon-fibre wing spars. A pushbike was strapped to the bottom of it. Southampton University have been involved in attempts like this for decades and I loved seeing the science and history behind it. I even got to fly a glider as a practice for piloting the HPA.

We first tried the HPA at Lasham, near Southampton. The finished plane weighed 27 kg, but it had a massive 20-metre wingspan. We made the attempt at first light, when the air is best for flying. The plane got off the ground, about two feet, for about a distance of five feet. The Southampton lads called it a short flight and were pleased, but I broke one of their beautiful foam and glass-fibre propellers.

I thought I'd have the muscle to pedal it, but after testing the power output at a cycling velodrome, with a fancy crankset and dashboard measuring the power, we found out, after my initial burst of pedalling, I was nowhere near powerful enough. While the plane builders were creating the plane, I was training like mad to make sure I could produce 400 watts of power for four minutes. That takes a lot of doing, but if I couldn't, the thing would never fly.

The event we made the attempt at was the annual Icarus Cup, for human-powered aircraft, near Northampton. Our goal was to be the fastest; we weren't going for duration or distance. I might have the power, but I was too heavy, much heavier than the world record holder, a German with less meat on him than a butcher's shoe.

The conditions at the Icarus Cup suited our design, and I got the plane off the ground, this time for a proper flight, not a hop, skip and a jump. Our air speed was 29 mph with a 10 mph headwind. It wasn't enough to break the world record, but it was the quickest at the competition. I had done a fair bit of cycle training to be able to get this thing into the air, and afterwards some of the students from the university tried pedalling and they couldn't get it off the ground, so the training paid off.

The hydro-bike was another dangerous scheme. The idea was to aquaplane a motorbike across a lake. A 450-cc motorcrosser was modified by a couple of switched-on fellas in their fifties, Charlie and Graham. They had a fair bit of involvement with amphibious vehicles, so they knew about lift and thrust. Underneath the engine of the bike was a computer-designed skid plate, designed to act like a speedboat on the surface of the water. The rear wheel was fitted with a sand tyre with paddles, exactly the same as riders use in Californian deserts. We took the bike to a Welsh lake and went for it. Things didn't go according to plan. Well, I say that, but the plan was so hare-brained that perhaps it did.

I was told to ride at 50 mph into the lake, so Charlie and Graham could work out what angle the skid plate needed to be set at, and so the scuba divers knew where the bike would land on the bottom of the lake and they could practise retrieving it. The rescue team wanted me to crash time and time again in the shallows to see how I'd crash in the deep water. The motorcycle had a small float attached to it so the divers could locate it when it sunk, but there was a risk that the rope would tangle around my leg and drag me down. It did once in the practice, so they strapped a knife to me.

I asked Spellman, 'Is this dodgy?' He told me that plenty of BMXers do jumps into lakes. I thought, 'Right!'

I was hitting the water at over 50 mph, hung off the back of the bike, trying to get it to take off and lift out of the water, so the rear paddle tyre would dig into the water, but the bike would start see-sawing and I'd go over the handlebars at 50 mph, hitting the water head first. There was no lack of commitment on my part. I look back now and think, 'Was it a good idea to ride into a 25-metre-deep lake on a motorbike?' If I sat and thought about it I would've talked myself out of it.

In the end I rode across Bala Lake in North Wales for a distance of 64 metres. It wasn't the 100 metres we were aiming for, but it was still some achievement.

The challenge I was most nervous about was the toboggan speed record in Austria. I'd nearly knocked myself out practising for it. I was on a skateboard, well a longboard, lying down, riding down a hill, but the trucks – the skateboard's axles – weren't tight enough so it started tankslapping. When I tried to correct it, the thing chucked me off. It left a right scar on my hand and scratched my face, and that was just before the 2013 TT. I had a pushbike helmet and some gloves on, but I wasn't about to ride a skateboard in leathers. Course not.

We went to test a few variations of the sledge at the indoor snow dome in Castleford, West Yorkshire. The slope there is 11 degrees, but from the top it looked steep enough. We had consultants from Sheffield University doing the maths who said, 'At this angle of slope and this density of snow; the weight of the sledge; the weight of you, you'll probably do 34 mph.' And I did 34 mph and that was enough for me. When I walked over to the brains of the operation they said, 'That's all right, that's all going to plan. The slope in Austria is 45 degrees and if everything goes to plan you'll do 177 mph.' And they said it all with straight faces!

We cut it really fine to attempt the record. Two of the weekly shows had already been aired, before we drove out to Andorra in early January, 2014. The weather in Europe hadn't been suitable and things were tight. In the end we settled on a speed skiing slope in Grandvalira. I drove out with a carbon-fibre sledge that had been designed by Terry Senior and Nick Hamilton. The design had undergone all this advanced fluid dynamics testing until the designers came up with a canopy for me to hide behind. Then it was made by EPM Technology, the same way F1 racing car bodies are made. It was a trick thing. But I still crashed it ... The second time I went down the slope it got all out of shape when I started to brake, then it flipped, cracking the bodywork. Not an ideal start, but luckily we had a replacement body.

Again, like all these attempts, the time comes when it's shit or bust. We hauled the sledge up the mountain, and after a last pep-talk from Olympic gold medal skeleton bob racer Amy Williams, I climbed on further up the mountain than I'd attempted before.

This time there were no mistakes. The sled ran as straight as an arrow, and the dragster-style parachute deployed without fault, slowing me down. We'd smashed the record. The run of 84.39 mph was over 21 mph quicker than the previous record, set by Rolf Allerdissen in 2010 in Austria.

People have talked about banning real road races like the TT, because riders are sometimes killed, but the racers would simply find something else dangerous to give them their buzz. Attempting these records made me think that the kind of people who race on the roads wouldn't be happy just watching TV or walking the dog when it came to the weekend. It's not how we are wired up.

In 2012, I got involved with a TV show presented by the bicycle stunt rider Danny MacAskill. The mountain-bike-trials rider had become famous when the film of him riding his bicycle around and over obstacles in Edinburgh went onto YouTube. It was filmed by a friend and shows Danny riding along the top of a iron railing spikes, using a tree as a ramp for a backflip, bunny-hopping to the moon ... The film had over 30 millions views. He did a brilliant follow-up, *Industrial Revolutions*. When he does a 180-degree jump from one train track's rail to the other, it blew my mind. Danny ended up leaving the bicycle shop he worked in and getting Red Bull sponsorship, advert appearances, opportunities, travel and injuries. He's a self-made man. I was, and still am, a massive fan. He's a legend.

MacAskill was making a TV show called *Daredevils: Life on the Edge* for Channel 4. It was about 'risk takers' and what drives them. Danny would go out and meet people in the extreme sports world, like people who walk between cliffs on slack line ropes, wing-suit fliers ... and me.

The plan was for me to take him for a pillion ride on my 1000-cc Superstock bike around Kirkistown race track, a short circuit in Northern Ireland. Danny, my mechanic, had fitted a road bike's twin seat and pillion footrests to my 1000-cc Superstock race bike.

It was all touch and go, because MacAskill was still recovering from a broken back. His surgeon wasn't happy with his plan of going for a ride, but he was well up for it. Also his collarbone had been surgically pinned not long before and seemed to be uncomfortable as he pulled on some one-piece leathers he'd borrowed for the day.

He said he'd been interested in the TT for a long time, and had started noticing me specifically in the last couple of years. He thought we were on the same wavelength.

While the film crew were fitting on-board cameras to the bikes we were chatting. We were talking about wheelies. I'm crap at them. He told me he once wheelied his pushbike for two miles. I'd struggle to wheelie the length of the garage we were stood in.

He explained that he was calculating about the risks he took, and how he can picture things in his head, see a specific set-up, whether it is something in the streets of Edinburgh or a dam in the middle of the Highlands. After he visualised them, imagined what he'd like to do, then he would push for it. Obviously he doesn't just fling himself off stuff. He's riding within his capabilities.

While he crashes a lot, he reckons he actually takes very little risk. He reckoned I'd jumped further on my race bike, at 160-plus mph, than he'd jumped on his pushbike, and maybe he had a point, but I'm as blown away by what he does as he seemed to be by what I do.

The TV show wanted to describe some of the psychology of so-called risk takers, so they had a psychologist called Dave Collins, PhD along for the day to monitor heart rates and give his view on stuff.

He said that he didn't agree with the idea that people like Danny and me don't think of the consequences of what we do. He said we just don't dwell on what could go wrong. Danny obviously has a very good sense of what he can and can't do; it's just that his limit, on a bicycle, is very different to yours and mine. The psychologist went on to confirm what I already know, that I'm not a psychopath – someone who ignores the consequences of his actions.

Collins debunked a lot of the crap that is talked about people like TT racers or extreme sports folk. He reckons people who take risks have a lower susceptibility to the stress hormones, so it takes more to make them worried than someone who is nervous. He added that there is a psychological effect, that people in these sports have an identity that is tied in with their dangerous activity. We don't see it as dangerous, because we are in control and see being on top of it as an important part of who we are. He also reckoned that there is a social effect, that risk takers gain social status because they behave in a certain way. There are a lot of things humans do that can be accounted for by an interaction of these three areas.

The psychologist said, 'The brain and the body do very, very clever things when you push them to extremes, when you force them to function at a different level. And it is very addictive – people feel really alive in the flow state: "This is me, this is what I am."'

The 'flow state', he said, is when the challenge and the expertise needed to carry it out are roughly balanced. If the challenge is greater than your ability, you're nervous or anxious; if it's less, you're bored; the flow state is a space in between. I can definitely relate to that.

Collins went on to say you couldn't race the TT unless you were really in the moment. You don't have the time or space to be thinking, 'Ooh, hell, I might crash.' He's right about that, too.

It's hard to say if MacAskill gets the same kind of buzz from what he does as I do from racing. He said that if he was doing tricks he'd never attempted before or a line that needed a lot of speed, jumping into a lot of air, as he put it – the kind of jump, that even if he landed it perfectly, would leave him with sore wrists and ankles – it would take him a while to get over the fear. Sometimes, he said, he'd get a block in his head, thinking he was going to crash, but it only took him one attempt, whether he crashed or not, to keep going at it till he achieved what he was trying to do. His pay-off was not getting beaten. He'd have a dream scenario in his head, sometimes thinking about a jump or trick for months while he was injured, then he'd go and make it work. After it, he said, he'd get the feeling of satisfaction and relief that he didn't get skewered by the spiky fence or break his neck. He reckoned what he did was more about achievement than adrenaline.

Collins the psychologist also talked about people experiencing different levels of 'super-perception in moments of extreme pressure'.

Listening to that made me think of the way I dealt with the slide that led to my crash at the 2010 TT. It all happened in the blink of an eye, less than two seconds from the front tyre beginning to slide to me admitting defeat, but I tried a few different things to save the crash so it felt like so much longer.

Whatever Danny's surgeon and his personal trainer had said to him went in one ear and out the other, because he climbed on the back of the Suzuki GSX-R1000 as the tyre warmers were taken off.

'I want to be scared for my life,' he said.

The crew pulled out a special belt to fasten around me with handles for Danny to hold on to, but I didn't think he needed it. 'Just hold on round me, you'll be right,' I told him. Then we rolled out into the damp and windy Irish weather.

Danny had never been on a motorbike before, not even on the back of a Honda Knobber 90, so he was stuck to me like shit to a blanket. He did well, though. We had the bike wound up to 150 mph or so. It was wheelie-ing with both of us on, and the wind would catch the front wheel when it was off the ground, pushing us a bit off line.

We did ten laps before pulling in, and the first thing Danny shouted was, 'That was ace!' Then he reckoned it didn't feel scary, just fun and exciting. He couldn't stop smiling. He said the braking was ferocious and that it was over too soon. He definitely is on the same wavelength.

As I said before, if road racing didn't exist, the people who raced at the Ulster and the TT would find something else that gave us the buzz, whether it be BASE jumping, downhill mountain biking, slackline rope walking or some other dangerous sport or pastime. We wouldn't be stamp collecting.

CHAPTER 21

WHERE NEXT?

'But I've brainwashed myself into needing to work on trucks'

SO WHERE NEXT? It's a big question, but not one that keeps me awake at night. You've probably got the picture that I'm not much of a forward planner. When I first started working on this book I was thinking very hard about packing in the trucks, because it was getting harder to fit everything in. If I manage to get on an endurance team it will become even harder.

The biggest problem with the truck job is, the tail wags the dog. And I'm the dog. The hours are unsociable. I can work with my boss, Mick Moody, to slot trucks in for their six-weekly checks and pre-MoT work, but the trucks still have a window of time within which they need to be seen. Race meetings go in the diary first. Then I put all my MoTs in for the next three months.

Finally, the TV fits in around all that. Of course there are truck breakdowns to deal with too.

I had an idea that I would like to start my own workshop and build bikes. If I was building bikes for people, I could choose my own hours and only work from eight till five for customers, and outside that time I wouldn't answer the phone. It would be me doing the work, not just someone else working under my name. A one-man band to start. With Moody's I'm there from six or six-thirty in the morning till five in the afternoon, and I regularly work Saturdays and Sundays to get caught up. The thing that's stopping me leaving the job is simple: I love it.

I like the pressure of having to have everything done yesterday. It keeps me honest. The truck driver who's having a go at me because he has a ferry to catch isn't bothered if I won a race two days ago or a TV show I'm on is going to be shown that night; he just wants me to finish his truck so he can be back on the road and earning a living. Spannering trucks is dealing with the real world and I need to do that. If I don't, I miss it too much. It's hard for some people to understand, but it's just the way it is.

I see it as good honest work. I've been doing it since I was 12 years old and I still can't get to work quick enough. I get a lot of job satisfaction from it. My dad's the same, but my brother, Stuart, isn't. He's good at his job, but he doesn't have the same passion for truck-fitting as I do. He does his work, then goes home and doesn't give it another thought till he gets back the next day, but I'm always thinking about it. Most people would say that Stu has the balance right: it's a job, concentrate on it when you're getting paid and forget about it when you're not. That's his attitude.

The bits of truck-fitting I like is seeing the whole job through. I like fault-finding and finishing the job off right. Making sure all the bolt heads are lined up and the washers are the right way around, the cables are routed tidily and the cable ties are cut off neatly. A truck I was repairing for Moody to sell had a damaged mirror adjustment unit. A replacement costs £400, because it has CANBUS ECU receiver in it, like a mini computer in the door. I took the broken one to bits, built it up with Araldite and fixed it. I don't cost Moody much money and I'm good at my job. He's flexible with me, so it all works. We suit each other. I think he likes the soap opera of my life.

I prepare the trucks for MoT, and I didn't have a failure all through 2013 and I'm proud of that. Racing sometimes gives me the same feeling of a job well done, but very, very rarely and it's nothing to do with winning. Winning the Gold Cup doesn't. The first Senior TT, back in 2004, did. As did the 2006 Ulster Grand Prix, the 2013 Southern 100 and the 2013 Ulster Grand Prix. I'd won at the Ulster before, but I still got a lot of satisfaction from winning that one. The 2013 Le Mans gave me a load of satisfaction too.

The TV work is getting better all the time. I enjoyed making *How Britain Worked* more than *The Boat That Guy Built* and I enjoyed *Speed* most of all, but it isn't the real world and I definitely don't want to become a full-time TV presenter. I'm afraid it's going to change me. I used to say that TV didn't give me any opportunities that I couldn't probably sort out myself if I really wanted to, but that's changed. I've done plenty now, and they've been experiences that money couldn't buy.

I'm not meaning to be disrespectful to the TV people I worked with. The directors and cameramen graft, and there are dozens behind the scenes working hard to keep everything on the rails, and I enjoy working with them, but I still don't see it as a proper job. I've been brought up with trucks, and even though I've had my eyes opened to all these other things, I still love going back to them after racing or filming.

I'm not so into the TV job or the money it pays that I'll do everything they push in front of me. I get about ten requests from TV shows and nearly as many sponsorship offers a week, but they all go to Andy Spellman, who deals with that side of stuff so I don't have to. I don't know why they think I'd want to do a cookery show ... but never say never.

Channel 4 have a big series, that might be out by the time you read this, about classic cars – restoring them, driving them, rating them – but it's all been done before. Or I felt it had, so Andy let them know I wasn't interested. This, I'm told, is not the done thing. Andy told me they were a bit miffed I had turned it down. I don't think it computes with most of the TV folk, because nearly everyone else they deal with is desperate to be on TV, chomping at the bit for every opportunity. My problem with the classic car series was that they already had the idea planned out, and then they decided who they thought would be interesting to present it – and I'd rather be doing ideas that they've come up with for me to do. That's what *Speed* was, and that was definitely a bit of me.

Becoming a full-time motorcycle racer is even further away from becoming a reality than being the next presenter of the BBC's *Question Time*.

I do love racing motorcycles, but I have never seen it as a career; and as I get older, and there is more attention on the events I used to love the most, like the Isle of Man TT, it means I'm not as into it as I was ten years ago.

When the hassle surrounding racing does outweigh the buzz, I'll pack it in. I know I've made a rod for my own back by doing interviews and all the TV stuff. People rightly point out it that if I say I don't want to be famous in a TV, radio or magazine interview, it doesn't add up, but I really don't want to be famous. It's not what drives me.

I'm still happy to do interviews with the right person, but it's getting me in the right situation. I sometimes enjoy doing an interview, if I like the person who is doing it. Now, though, so much stuff has been changed and twisted that I think I just won't bother. I'm sometimes not the sharpest tool in the box when it comes to talking to journalists. I think they're just having a yarn with me to pass the time of day, but then something I've said in passing ends up on the front page of a motorbike paper.

If I'm being encouraged to do interviews because the team want me to, then I do what I can to get out of it. I make arrangements with the teams I race for that I won't take their money and they won't ask me to do PR stuff I don't want to do. It was their idea in the first place and it suits me fine. The problems starts when people, whether it is sponsors or the organisers and promoters of races, put out press releases saying that I'm going to be doing this or that before they've even spoken to me to confirm it. Then, when I say I can't do it, it's me who looks like the dickhead.

I still love racing bikes, there's no doubt about it. The kind of race I like the best is one like the Southern 100. It's organised with military precision – and I like how the schedule says stuff like '18:46 – bikes to pre-grid'. I like the way the organisers hand out vouchers to the racers for a cuppa at the tea hut over the road from the paddock. The track is hardcore and the weather's normally good. Also I can go on a Monday, be back for work on Friday, so I'm not too long away from work, compared to the TT, and I'm getting a lot more races than during a BSB weekend. I'm not bothered about what make of bike I'd race. I've been using big four cylinders for all my racing life and they're all pretty much the same, the throttle is on the right. Some are better at one thing, but worse at another. I wouldn't be bothered what I'm riding, unless it's a Britten. That's a dream.

Ideally, I'd have one motorbike and one mechanic and be working out of the back of the van. I'd arrive in a Transit. Well organised, with a small generator, a toolbox, a couple of sets of wheels. Some people want a best mate or their missus, with them, but I don't. Racing has to be fun, but I take it seriously when I'm there and want the best results, without distractions.

I used to say I would win a TT before I went to the grave, and when I said it, it was the right thing to say. It's what I believed. I don't regret it. If it comes, it comes. If it doesn't, so be it. But the amount of attention that has been brought by me not winning one is almost driving me away.

I don't enjoy the whole experience of the TT now. The time I'm on the bike is the best thing. Money could not buy the feeling, but as soon as I get off the bike, the shit I have to do nearly outweighs it. I get asked the same questions I've been asked for years. That's why I love getting back to Moody's. When those gates are closed, no one's getting in.

For a time I thought there was a mental block stopping me from winning a TT. I've seen a pit board, when I was leading the Senior, and it said P1 +7 – meaning I was leading the race by seven seconds. It was skin-of-my-teeth stuff, bouncing off kerbs and skimming walls. When I saw the next pit board and read that the lead had decreased, I genuinely thought to myself, 'At least I won't have a load of hassle at the end of the race.' I remember I was at the Guthrie's Memorial section. I didn't want the grief and all the interviews. Once that thought entered my head, the race was over. I was never going to win it that day.

When I leave a TT disappointed with the results, I think, 'It's only motorbike racing. Stop mincing around with them and go back and do your proper job, fix some trucks.'

I've always got an excuse. I can always say, 'It's not my job. I've got a proper job. I might be a shit racer, but I've got a proper job to go back to. I'm only a truck mechanic.' It's not a lie, but I say it out loud so I don't ever get above my station. I'm not suddenly, at 32 years old, going to become a professional motorcycle racer. That's the last thing I want to become. I think it's a joke. What are you really doing? Going around in circles for 15 weekends a year? Get a grip.

I truly don't give a monkey's what people think or say about me, but there are plenty who are spouting about me being too busy with the TV job, or that I'm not focused on racing because of this thing or that thing. I won at 2013 Southern 100 and Ulster Grand Prix, where I won three races, out of five starts, beating good riders at the top of their game, on good bikes. I really had to race for them. Nothing was gifted to me through breakdowns. I had to catch the leader, pass him, and then I pulled away from him. I don't give a damn about the critics, but I knew I'd given the competition something to think about. I think some had been starting to believe I was a soft touch. That if they put a hard move on me, they wouldn't see me back again.

I'm different to some of the riders I race. All the boxes have to be ticked for me to really push, but when they are, I'll give it my all. Sometimes that's still not enough. I've done that and still come second, but on that day, with the bike and tyres I was on, I can look at myself in the mirror and know I couldn't have done anything more.

I've always said – and over ten years since my first real road race it's still the case – that I'm not afraid of dying, but if it happens I want to be at lap record pace and battling for the lead. I don't want to risk everything while splashing around in the wet on the wrong tyres. Some lads will hang their balls out, whatever the conditions, and I admire that, but it's crackers. Tomorrow's another day. I was once told a saying: 'There are plenty of old riders. And there are plenty of bold riders. But there aren't many old, bold riders.'

There are still other motorbike boxes to be ticked. I want to build a few specials – mega motorbikes, then race them at places like the Pike's Peak International Hill Climb in Colorado. I would like to race the Suzuka 8-hour Endurance in Japan, the Bol d'Or if it goes back to Paul Ricard in the South of France, and I want to race the Daytona 200, too.

I have, I must admit, a weird relationship with money. The TV job pays well, but it all goes into a company bank account. My truck money is what I live on day-to-day. I don't feel like the company money is mine really, because I haven't got my hands dirty earning it. The company paid for, and owned, the Aston, but I can have that car, that cost over a hundred and thirty grand, sat round the corner and still feel skint, like I did when I stopped working with my dad and I didn't have a job. I thought I needed a car, so I bought a 12-year-old Astravan. Driving the Aston didn't cross my mind.

And I know I can wake up on a Monday, out of work, and have a job by Wednesday because I'm not afraid of graft. It doesn't matter if it's fixing lorries or shovelling shit – if you're not shy of work, you'll never be short of work.

Money from the truck side and barrow jobs, tuning or building bikes for people, is right money. The money from racing and TV is different. It's easy come, easy go. I lost £60,000 on the Aston. Looking at it another way, it cost me £20 a mile. That's 3,000 hours of Sunday double-time overtime, but then I'll try to get 100,000 miles out of the Transit's brake pads and do my nut if it's not delivering the mpg numbers I expect. I lost a 12 mm socket, a £10 Snap-On part, and it broke my heart. I turned the garage upside-down looking for it.

I've always thought trucks were the long-term plan. It came, in part, from seeing other racers get to their mid-thirties, not be as competitive as they were and have no plan B. The trucks were what I always could rely on. Now, though, I have the TV job and all those opportunities. I could do it for a couple of years and be set up for life if I took everything I was offered. But I've brainwashed myself into needing to work on trucks, so I can't turn my back on them, even though, financially, I don't need to work on them. I've also half convinced myself that truck-fitting is an either in or out job. If you leave it for too long, the technology moves on and you're left behind.

I also fear that if I didn't work on the trucks I'd turn into just another bike racer, with the hat and the sunglasses, thinking I was a rock star or something. I'm afraid I'd start to believe the hype, so I don't want to risk it.

One thing is for sure, I'm just going to keep doing my own thing, because, as Voldemars said, 'When you dead, you dead.'

ACKNOWLEDGEMENTS

Gary Inman for his help with this book; The Martins of Kirmington for keeping me in line; The Farmer's Daughter; Trellis; Mad Nige for keeping the ship afloat; The Moores; Sam Finley for starting the whole thing off; and Andy Spellman for joining up all the dots.

CAREER RESULTS

2003 – TEAM RACING SUZUKI

Southern 100

Solo Championship ... ... DNF (crash at Iron Gate)

Scarborough Steve Henshaw Gold Cup

Superbike 1st

2004 – UEL DUNCAN RACING/ROBINSON CONCRETE

North West 200

Superbike 15th
Production 1000cc 10th
NW200 Superbike ... ... DNF

Isle of Man TT

Formula One 12th
Production 1000cc ... ... DNF
Junior 600cc ... ... DNF
Production 600cc 21st
Senior ... ... 7th (winner of the Newcomers Trophy)

Southern 100

Solo Championship ... ... DNF (crash at Church Bends)

Ulster Grand Prix

Production 1000cc 9th
UGP Superbike 6th
Supersport ... ... DNF

Scarborough Steve Henshaw Gold Cup

Superbike 1st

2005 – UEL DUNCAN RACING/ROBINSON CONCRETE/WILSON CRAIG/BARRON TRANSPORT

North West 200

Superbike	11th
Supersport 1	DNF
Superstock	...
7th Supersport 2	11th
NW200 Superbike	5th

Isle of Man TT

Superbike	6th
Superstock	5th
Supersport A	5th
Supersport B	4th
Senior	3rd

Southern 100

Solo Championship

Ulster Grand Prix

Superstock	3rd
Supersport 1	10th
UGP Superbike	6th
Supersport 2	DNF
Superbike	2nd

Scarborough Steve Henshaw Gold Cup

Superbike	1st

Macau Grand Prix

Superbike	12th

2006 – AIM YAMAHA

North West 200

Superbike ... ... DNF
Supersport 1... ... ... 6th
Superstock 4th
NW200 Superbike 5th
Supersport 2... ... ... 9th

Isle of Man TT

Superbike ... ... DNF
Superstock 4th
Junior 600cc 13th
Senior 5th

Southern 100

Solo Championship 2nd

Ulster Grand Prix

Superstock 2nd
Supersport 1... ... ... 1st
UGP Superbike ... ... 1st (Recorded the first official 130mph lap of the Dundrod course)
Supersport 2... ... ... 1st
Superbike 1st

Scarborough Steve Henshaw Gold Cup

Superbike 1st

Macau Grand Prix

Superbike 5th

2007 – HYDREX HONDA

North West 200

Superbike 4th
Supersport 1... ... ... 3rd
Superstock 3rd
NW200 Superbike 2nd
Supersport 2... ... ... 8th

Isle of Man TT

Superbike 2nd
Superstock ... ... DNF (ran out of fuel)
Supersport 600cc 3rd
Senior 2nd

Southern 100

Solo Championship 2nd

Ulster Grand Prix

Superstock 5th
Supersport 1... ... ... 1st
UGP Superbike 2nd
Remainder of meeting cancelled due to torrential rain

Scarborough Steve Henshaw Gold Cup

Superbike 1st

Macau Grand Prix

Superbike ... ... DNS due to crash in practice

2008 – HYDREX HONDA

North West 200

Superbike 2nd
Supersport 1... ... ... 7th
Superstock 4th
NW200 Superbike ... ... DNF
Supersport 2... ... ... DNS due to crash at Black Hill

Isle of Man TT

Superbike ... ... DNF
Superstock 3rd
Supersport 1... ... ... DNF
Supersport 2... ... ... 6th
Senior ... ... DNF

Southern 100

Solo Championship ... ... DNF

Ulster Grand Prix – Meeting cancelled due to torrential rain

Scarborough Steve Henshaw Gold Cup

Superbike 1st

Macau Grand Prix

Superbike ... ... DNS due to crash in practice

2009 – HYDREX HONDA

North West 200

Superbike 6th
Supersport 1... ... ... DNF
Superstock 5th
Supersport 2... ... ... Race not held (adverse weather)
NW200 Superbike ... ... Race not held (adverse weather)

Isle of Man TT

Superbike 3rd
Supersport 1... ... ...
2ndSuperstock 2nd
Supersport 2... ... ... DNF
Senior ... ... DNF due to broken chain at pit stop

Southern 100

Solo Championship 1st

Ulster Grand Prix

Superstock 4th
Supersport 1... ... ... 5th
UGP Superbike 3rd
Supersport 2... ... ... DNS
Superbike 1st

Scarborough Steve Henshaw Gold Cup

Superbike 1st

2010 – WILSON CRAIG RACING HONDA

North West 200

Superbike	DNF
Supersport 1	DNF
Superstock	7th
NW200 Superbike	4th
Supersport 2	DNS due to machine problems in first race

Isle of Man TT

Superbike	4th
Supersport 1	2nd
Superstock	5th
Supersport 2	4th
Senior	DNF due to crash at Ballagarey

Ulster Grand Prix

Superstock	6th
Supersport 1	4th
UGP Superbike	4th
Supersport 2	5th
Superbike	5th

Scarborough Steve Henshaw Gold Cup

Superbike	DNF

2011 – RELENTLESS BY TAS SUZUKI

North West 200

Supersport 1... ... ... 8th

Remainder of meeting cancelled due to torrential rain and oil spill

Isle of Man TT

Superbike ... ... DNF

Supersport 1... ... ... 3rd

Superstock 3rd

Supersport 2... ... ... 3rd

Senior 2nd

Southern 100

Solo Championship 2nd

Ulster Grand Prix

Superstock 2nd

Supersport 1... ... ... 5th

UGP Superbike 2nd

Supersport 2... ... ... 4th

Superbike 1st

2012 – TYCO SUZUKI

North West 200

Superstock 1 ... ... 9th
Supersport 1... ... ... DNF due to crash at Dhu Varren
Did not compete after the opening Supersport race due to injury

Isle of Man TT

Superbike 4th
Supersport 1... ... ... DNF
Superstock 5th
Supersport 2... ... ... 8th

Southern 100

Solo Championship 2nd

Ulster Grand Prix

Superstock 3rd
Supersport 1... ... ... 5th
UGP Superbike 1st
Supersport 2... ... ... 7th
Superbike 2nd

Scarborough Steve Henshaw Gold Cup

Superbike 1st

2013 – TYCO SUZUKI

North West 200

Supersport 1... ... ... 3rd
Superstock 4th
Supersport 2... ... ... 5th
Remainder of meeting cancelled due to torrential rain

Isle of Man TT

Superbike 4th
Supersport 1... ... ... 6th
Superstock ... ... DNF
Supersport 2... ... ... 8th
Senior 5th

Southern 100

Solo Championship 1st

Ulster Grand Prix

Supersport 1... ... ... 1st
Superstock ... ... DNS
UGP Superbike 1st
Supersport 2... ... ... DNS
Superbike 1st

Scarborough Steve Henshaw Gold Cup

Superbike 2nd

Moody International

Truck MoTs... ... ... 100-per-cent success rate

INDEX

ABOUT THE AUTHOR

Christopher Pike was born in New York, but grew up in Los Angeles, where he lives to this day. Prior to becoming a writer he worked in a factory, painted houses and programmed computers. His hobbies include astronomy, meditating, running and making sure his books are prominently displayed in his local bookshop. As well as being a bestselling children's writer, he is also the author of three adult novels.

Spooksville

1 The Secret Path
2 The Howling Ghost
3 The Haunted Cave
4 Aliens in the Sky
5 The Cold People
6 The Witch's Revenge

Spooksville

THE WITCH'S REVENGE

Christopher Pike

Hodder
Children's
Books

a division of Hodder Headline plc

First published in the USA in 1995
as an Archway Paperback by Pocket Books
a division of Simon & Schuster Inc.

First published in Great Britain in 1996
by Hodder Children's Books

10 9 8 7 6 5 4 3 2

A Catalogue record for this book is available from the British Library

ISBN 0 340 66118 6

Typeset by Avon Dataset Ltd, Bidford-on-Avon, Warks.

Printed and bound in Great Britain by
Cox & Wyman Ltd, Reading, Berks.

Hodder Children's Books
a division of Hodder Headline plc
338 Euston Road
London NW1 3BH

One

The argument was old. Was Ms Ann Templeton, Spooksville's most powerful and beautiful resident, a good witch or a bad witch? There was no question whether she was a *real* witch. Adam and his friends had seen too many demonstrations of her power to doubt that. But whereas Adam and Watch liked to think she was a nice person, Sally and Cindy were certain she was dangerous.

The argument started in the Frozen Cow, Spooksville's best known ice-cream parlour. The owner would only serve vanilla, so they were all having vanilla shakes when the idea of visiting the witch's castle came up. Of course, later, they would blame each other for the idea. Later, that is, when they couldn't find their way out of the castle.

It was a hot summer Wednesday, ten o'clock in the

morning, a perfect time for a milk shake. School was still a few weeks away. As was often the case, they were trying to decide what they were going to do with the day.

'We can't go to the beach because of the sharks,' Sally said as she listed the various possibilities. 'We can't go to the lighthouse because we burned that down. We can't go to the reservoir because we burned that up as well. And we can't go to the Haunted Cave because it's haunted.' She paused. 'Maybe we should try to contact Eckweel and go for another ride on a flying saucer.'

Watch shook his head. 'We forgot to get a communication device from him. We have no way to contact him.'

But he promised to call us some day,' Adam said.

'Yes,' Sally replied. 'But he's an alien. They have a different perspective on time. Some day might be ten thousand years from now for him.'

'I thought you didn't like Eckweel,' Cindy said to Sally. 'You kept calling him Fat Head.'

'I called him that because he had a fat head,' Sally said. 'That does not mean I disliked him. I call you plenty of names and I still like you. Most of the time.' Sally added.

Cindy was not impressed. 'I am *so* relieved.'

'What if we didn't do anything special today?' Adam suggested. 'What if we just hung out and relaxed? We could play checkers or chess or something.'

Sally stared at him as if he had lost his mind. 'Are you all right, Adam?'

'I'm fine,' he said. 'Just because I want to have a relaxing day doesn't mean there's anything wrong with me.'

'But this is Spooksville,' Sally said. 'We don't relax here. That's the first thing that will get you killed. You always have to be on your guard.'

'I don't see how playing chess could be dangerous,' Adam said. 'Even in Spooksville.'

'Ha,' Sally said, turning to Watch. 'Tell him what happened to Sandy Stone.'

Watch frowned. 'We're not sure if the game did it to her.'

'Of course we are,' Sally said. 'She was playing on the witch's chess board when it happened.'

'What happened to her?' Cindy asked.

Sally shrugged. 'She turned to stone. What would you expect with a name like Sandy Stone?'

'Is that true?' Adam asked Watch.

Watch appeared uncertain. 'Well, we did find a

stone statue of Sandy not far from the witch's castle. And the statue was sitting in front of a mysterious looking chess board.'

'I don't understand,' Cindy said.

'Chess was Sandy's favourite game,' Sally explained. 'She was a master of it. She could beat anyone in the city. The trouble is, she boasted about the fact, and apparently Ms Witch Ann Templeton heard about it, and didn't like it. The witch plays chess herself, and sent out a challenge to Sandy, which Sandy accepted.' Sally paused and shook her head. 'And that was the last time any of us saw her alive.'

'Are you saying the witch turned her to stone because Sandy lost to her?' Adam asked.

'It may have been because Sandy beat the witch,' Sally said. 'The witch is a well-known bad loser.'

'Is the stone statue still there?' Cindy asked.

'No,' Watch said. 'It was made of soft stone, like compressed sand. After the first good storm it was gone. Down the gutter.'

Cindy glanced at Adam. 'Do you believe this?' she asked.

Adam shrugged. 'Ms Ann Templeton never seemed that bad to me.'

Sally snorted. 'Just because she's pretty and she

smiled at you, Adam, you're willing to forgive a dozen years of murder and genocide.'

'What does genocide mean?' Adam asked Watch.

'Unpleasant behaviour towards many people,' Watch said uncertainly.

'I can't believe she would murder anyone,' Adam said.

Sally threw her head back and laughed. 'You are too much! What about those friendly bodyguards of hers we met while we were in the Haunted Cave? Have you forgotten how they tried to spear us for dinner? Do you think they were just playing? Do you think she didn't approve of their hunting habits?'

'But it was Ann Templeton who gave Bum and me the clues for how to find you guys while you were trapped in the cave,' Watch said.

'Yeah,' Adam said. 'She also gave Watch the magic words that helped us rescue the Hyeet from the Haunted Cave. How do you explain that?'

Sally replied with exaggerated patience. 'She told Watch how to get into the cave because she thought there was no way he would get out. She probably told him the magic word because she was hoping we would all get trapped in another dimension.'

'But when the Cold People attacked,' Adam said,

'she was one of the few people who really tried to fight them off.'

'She was trying to save her own skin,' Sally said. 'Nothing else.'

'For once I have to agree with Sally,' Cindy said reluctantly. 'I saw those trolls she keeps in her basement. She must be an evil witch to have such monsters in her castle.'

'Not necessarily,' Adam said. 'She might just feel sorry for them. I would imagine trolls have trouble finding places to live.'

Sally stared at him. 'I can't believe you just said that. Her castle may be many dark things but it is not a refuge for homeless trolls.'

'I have never actually seen her hurt someone with my own eyes,' Watch said.

'Yeah, but you're half blind,' Sally said. 'You have never actually seen the sun come up.'

'I can see the sun,' Watch said quietly, perhaps hurt by the remark. 'I can see the moon, too, as long as I have my glasses on.'

'A lot of these stories about people dying and disappearing might have nothing to do with her,' Adam said. 'They might be caused by natural creatures, like aliens and ghosts and things.'

‘But if she isn’t evil,’ Cindy said to Adam, ‘why is everyone so afraid of her?’

Adam shrugged. ‘People believe all kinds of nasty rumours.’ He added, ‘You know, she invited me to her castle once.’

‘But even you were not stupid enough to accept her invitation,’ Sally said. ‘Which just proves my point. Deep inside you know she would just as soon eat your heart out as smile at you.’

‘That’s not true,’ Adam said. ‘The only reason I haven’t visited her at her castle is because I’ve been too busy since I moved here.’

‘You’re not busy today,’ Sally mocked.

‘I wouldn’t mind visiting her at her castle,’ Watch said softly, almost to himself. ‘I have heard she has the power to heal. I wonder if she could do something about my eyes.’

To everyone’s surprise, Sally reached over and squeezed Watch’s hand. ‘Your eyes are fine the way they are,’ she said. ‘You don’t need to be healed by that witch. I shouldn’t have said what I did about your vision. I’m sorry, Watch.’

Cindy glanced at Adam. ‘I can’t believe she just apologised,’ she said.

‘I’ve seen her do it once before,’ Adam said.

Sally spoke seriously to all of them. 'No one's going to the castle. There're alligators and crocodiles in her moat that would eat you alive before you could even get inside. Believe me, the place is a death trap.'

'But there's a drawbridge,' Watch said. 'If she wants us to enter, she'll let it down.'

Adam studied Watch. 'You really do want to go, don't you? Do your eyes bother you that much?'

Watch looked away, out of the window of the ice-cream parlour. 'Well, you know, I don't like to complain.'

'Complain,' Adam said. 'You're with friends. How are your eyes?'

'I don't know,' Watch said. Briefly he removed his glasses and cleaned them on his shirt. When he put them back on, he squinted into the distance. 'I think they're getting worse.'

Cindy was concerned. 'Can't you get stronger glasses?'

Watch spoke reluctantly. Clearly the subject embarrassed him. 'The doctors say no. You see, it's not just a focusing problem. Everything seems to be getting dimmer, like it's always evening-time.'

'How is it at night-time?' Adam asked.

'I can't really see then at all,' Watch said. 'Not any more. I just bump into things.'

Sally was worried. 'You never told us.'

Watch shook his head. 'There's nothing you guys can do.'

'But you should have told Eckweel,' Cindy said. 'Remember the way he fixed my ankle with his healing machine?'

'They weren't as bad then,' Watch said. 'And I didn't want to bother him.'

'Watch,' Adam said, frustrated. 'He's our friend. He would have been happy to help you.'

Watch lowered his head. 'Well, he's gone now. And we don't know when he'll be coming back.'

'But maybe Ann Templeton can help you,' Adam said. 'I think it's worth the risk to ask her. Why don't we do that now?'

'Do what?' Cindy asked.

'Go to the castle,' Adam said simply.

Sally and Cindy looked at each other. 'The boys have lost their minds,' Sally said.

'They're looking for help in all the wrong places,' Cindy agreed.

'You two don't have to come,' Adam said. 'If you're scared.'

'I'm not scared,' Sally said. 'I am just a reasonable, thinking, human being. Calling on evil witches – even in the middle of the day – is just plain stupid. She won't heal Watch's eyes. More likely, she'll carve them out with one of her long red nails and have them in her evening soup.'

'She wouldn't have such a terrible reputation if she hadn't done something bad,' Cindy added.

'I trust my own instincts,' Adam said. 'I think she's a good witch. What do you say, Watch?'

Watch nodded enthusiastically. 'I want to visit her. I think she'll welcome us, especially since she's already invited you.'

'This is going to be a long day,' Sally said darkly.

Two

The walk to Ann Templeton's castle was not long. The group had been near the place before, of course, while fighting the Cold People. The castle was located on a hill overlooking the cemetery. From its front porch one could see the ocean as well. As they approached, Adam imagined that Ann Templeton had a wonderful view up and down the coast from the top of her highest tower.

From the outside, it appeared a medium-sized castle, but Adam knew from experience that its basements ran deep. Made of mostly large grey blocks of stone, it was surrounded by a wide moat that at first glance looked like a pleasant pond. But if one stared long enough, large dark shapes could be seen moving beneath the water.

There was no doorknob or bell on the outer wall.

Adam wondered how they were supposed to make their presence known. He said as much to the others but Sally thought that was the least of their concerns.

'She knows we're here,' Sally said. 'No one gets near her place without her knowing.'

Cindy gestured to the moat. 'Has anybody ever fallen in there?'

'I have heard she pushed a few kids in the moat from the top of her tower,' Sally said. 'You could hear their screams miles away.'

Cindy turned to Adam. 'I still think this is a bad idea,' she said.

Adam was getting annoyed at the girls' gloomy outlook. 'We told you that you and Sally should stay at home.'

'Yeah, but you accused us of being cowards,' Sally said. 'So in a sense you forced us to come.'

Cindy jumped suddenly. 'What's that?'

That was the sound of the drawbridge slowly lowering. The group all backed up. The wide wooden plank creaked as it descended; the metal gears sounded as if they hadn't been used in ages. Adam wondered if Ann Templeton had another route for leaving the castle.

The drawbridge came to a dust-shaking halt a few

metres in front of them. It was made of thick boards. Obviously it could support their weight. Yet as the drawbridge settled, they noticed that the crocodiles and the alligators came closer to the surface. Adam saw several pairs of hungry eyes peering at him.

'She might try to raise it the second we step on it,' Sally warned.

'We would slide straight into the water,' Cindy agreed.

'I think she's welcoming us,' Adam said, stepping on to the edge of the drawbridge. 'I think it would be rude to ignore her welcome.'

'Better to be rude than to be dead,' Sally said.

Watch stepped all the way on to the bridge. 'I don't care about the rest of you. I'm going to go talk to her.'

Adam stopped him. 'Before we go inside, I want you to know there's probably only a small chance she can help with your eyes. I mean, I just don't want you to get your hopes up.'

Watch smiled faintly. 'I know that, Adam. You don't have to worry about me. I always get by.'

Sally looked at Cindy. 'Stop them.'

'How am I supposed to stop them?' Cindy asked.

'I don't know,' Sally said. 'You always get Adam to do what you want.'

'Adam, don't go inside,' Cindy said. 'Please.'

'I have to go,' Adam said. He tugged on Watch's arm. 'Come on, we'll go alone. There's no reason for the girls to risk it.'

Cindy turned to Sally. 'That didn't work.'

Sally came alongside Adam. 'No reason for the girls to risk it? There you go again, another sexist statement. Cindy and I can take whatever risks you guys are taking.'

'I wish you wouldn't drag me into your feminist philosophy,' Cindy said, even though she also hurried to catch up with them.

The front door was huge. Had the four of them stood on each other's shoulders, they would have been unable to reach the top of it. There was no doorbell but instead there was a huge gold skull-shaped door-knocker. Sally did not like the design of the knocker.

'When have you ever seen a skull on the door of a good witch?' she said.

'It's decorative,' Adam said as he reached up to use it. He knocked gently a couple of times, and then took a step back. He did not know what sort of creature would answer the door, or if it would be Ann Templeton herself. But he was sure somebody would answer. That was why he was so surprised when the door slowly began to swing open all by itself. As a group, they stared into the vast dark interior. They could see a fire place burning in a grate in the distance, but little else.

'Hello!' Adam called.

His voice echoed as it trailed off into the distance.

No one called back.

'Could the castle be empty?' Cindy wondered aloud.

'If it's empty, then who opened the door?' Watch said.

'It could be a magic door,' Sally said.

'I don't think the place is empty,' Adam said. 'You don't just go and leave a castle without someone to guard it.' He gestured to the open door. 'I think we're being invited inside.'

'Why isn't she here to make the invitation in person?' Sally said. 'This feels like a set-up to me. As soon as we step inside, the door will close at our backs. Then the trolls will come, and then we'll be dead meat.'

Adam stuck his head through the open door. Beside the distant fireplace, he could see a row of burning torches lighting a long hallway. But the actual walls of the room, the furniture it may have held, were hidden in the shadows.

'I don't see any trolls,' Adam muttered.

'You don't see a butler in a tuxedo either,' Sally said. 'This is too weird. I say we turn around now, have another vanilla shake at the Frozen Cow, and consider ourselves lucky we listened to me.'

Watch stepped forward. 'I've been in darker places. I don't mind doing a little exploring.'

Adam followed him. 'If she wants to hurt us, she could have hurt us already.'

Sally chased after them. 'If she wants to hurt you, you don't have to make it easy for her.'

Cindy also followed them inside. 'We don't even have a flashlight,' she fretted.

They were barely inside when the door slammed shut at their backs.

The noise made them jump.

'I'm not going to say I told you so,' Sally whispered in the dark. 'But I did.'

Three

The entrance room was vast; it also seemed to be made largely of grey stone. As their eyes adjusted to the dim light cast by the fireplace and the torches in the nearby hall, Adam saw that the place was empty. There was no furniture, no ornaments or paintings of any kind. He wondered if Ann Templeton ever came into this room. Although it was free of dust and other signs of age, it felt as if it had been deserted for a long time.

'It's cold in here,' Cindy said, shivering.

'It is a psychic chill you feel,' Sally said. 'Your soul realises it has entered a place of great evil, from which there is no escape.'

'I kind of like this place,' Watch said, squinting in the dark.

'It's good to be out of the sun,' Adam agreed.

'You guys are in a state of denial,' Sally snapped.

'We're already in danger and you refuse to admit it. Where is Ms Ann Templeton? She knows we're here. The only reason she hasn't appeared is because she is playing some weird game with us. And her games are always dangerous.'

'I wouldn't mind leaving now,' Cindy said, glancing nervously round.

'I want to see what's at the end of this hallway,' Adam said, gesturing to the torch-lit passageway. He and Watch stepped into the narrow stone hallway. The girls followed a few steps behind, whispering to themselves about how stupid boys were.

'Can you see where you're going?' Adam asked Watch.

'I'm OK,' his friend said. 'Do you think she's here?'

'She must be here,' Adam said.

'I hope we meet her before we run into one of her trolls,' said Watch.

'I think she keeps them in the basement,' Adam replied.

'I wonder what else she keeps there,' Watch said.

The hallway was long. It wound left and right. Finally they entered another large room. This one was also lit by torches and a single massive fireplace, but it was decorated like an ancient castle chamber should be, with over-sized gold-framed furniture, and giant paintings of forgotten battles. There was even a throne inlaid with gems at the far end of the room. But that was not what caught their eyes.

In the centre of the chamber was a huge hourglass.

In place of sand fell sparkling jewel dust.

The dust glowed like stars, as it dropped, counting the seconds.

'We've seen this before,' Adam said, touching the hourglass. It was twice their height, and was supported with a shiny stand made of gold and silver.

'Where?' Cindy asked.

'On the other side of the Secret Path,' Sally said. 'In the evil witch's castle. We didn't tell you about her, but she was a real pain. Except on the other side of the Secret Path the sand flowed upwards – probably because time flowed backwards in that dimension.' Sally paused. 'In fact, the evil witch said that Ann Templeton had a similar hourglass. It was as if she wanted us to know. Do you guys remember?'

'I do,' Watch said. 'I also remember that her evil sister's hourglass was the main source of her power.'

Sally rested her palm on the hourglass, her face lit with colour from the sparkling dust. 'I wonder if this is the source of Ann Templeton's power,' she said, a mischievous note in her voice. 'If we hold it all in our hands.'

'I think you two are forgetting something,' Adam said. 'When we broke the other hourglass, the whole place went crazy. Everything started to fall apart. We have to be careful with this hourglass. Who knows what would happen to our world if we damaged it?'

'I wasn't thinking of breaking it,' Sally said.

'We believe you,' Watch said.

'It's incredibly beautiful,' Cindy said. 'I wonder what this sand is made of. It looks like stardust.'

'It might be *real* stardust,' Watch said. 'It definitely has some kind of power.'

'But that brings me back to my original questions,' Sally said. 'Why does she let us find these things? Why isn't she here to explain what we're looking at? I still think this is some kind of set-up. We have to be careful.'

Adam pointed to another narrow hallway. 'Let's check down there.'

'If we take hallway after hallway,' Cindy warned, 'we'll end up lost.'

'She has a point,' Sally said. 'You notice we haven't really gone underground, and yet we've already covered a lot of ground, more ground than the castle seems to cover from the outside.'

'What are you saying?' Adam asked.

Sally spoke seriously. 'We might be in another dimension already, and not know it.'

'I think you're jumping to your usual grim conclusions,' Watch said.

'We'll see,' Sally said.

They walked down the next hallway, and soon came to another room. This one was not as large as the previous one, nor were there as many decorations or furniture. But there were another two blazing fireplaces. With all the fires, Adam wondered that the castle was not shrouded in smoke on the outside. Yet in spite of the fires, the room was as cold as the others.

In the centre of the chamber were four necklaces.

They rested on a white sheet. Each held a different coloured precious stone: a green emerald, a red ruby, a blue sapphire, a yellow topaz. The jewels were exquisite, perfectly polished, and large – Adam decided they must be worth a fortune. They were each attached to a fine gold band. The gold also wrapped around each stone, like a miniature claw, and held the gem in place. In front of each necklace was a small card with a single printed word on it.

Before the emerald was the word IMMORTALITY.

Beside the ruby was the word STRENGTH.

In front of the sapphire was the word MATURITY.

Next to the yellow topaz the card said BEAUTY.

The stones seemed to shimmer with a light of their own making. As the four of them approached, they found they could not stop staring at the stones. Adam in particular was drawn to the blue sapphire. He didn't know why, but he felt as if Ann Templeton had laid it out specially for him. Being on the short side for his age, he had always wanted to be older, more mature. He had no doubt that each stone was capable of giving the quality listed beside it. For some reason, he immediately assumed they were magical necklaces.

Adam went to touch the sapphire when Sally stopped him.

'Don't,' she said. 'It's a trap.'

Adam had to blink to clear his head. He realised, in a space of a few seconds, that the stones had almost hypnotised him. 'What are you talking about?' he asked.

'She wants us to put these on,' Sally said.

'I don't want to put one of them on,' Cindy said.

Sally eyed her suspiciously. 'Aren't you attracted to one of them, Cindy?'

Cindy seemed embarrassed. 'Well, the yellow topaz looks nice.'

'Which one do you like, Watch?' Sally asked.

'The red ruby,' Watch said.

'Adam?' Sally said.

'I like the blue one,' Adam said. 'But so what?'

'I like the green emerald,' Sally said. 'I was immediately drawn to it. Like you, I went to reach out and put it on. But then I remembered where we are, who we're dealing with.' She paused. 'The necklaces have been placed here to tempt each of us. They're designed to do that.'

'I still don't know what you're talking about,' Cindy said.

'The witch knows us,' Sally said. 'She can probably read our minds. For example, she knows that you, Cindy, are obsessed with your appearance.'

Cindy was insulted. 'That's ridiculous! I'm not vain.'

'You're as vain as a Persian cat,' Sally said. 'You're not attracted to the topaz because you like the stone. You like the idea of what it can do for you. Listen, I'm not singling you out. You guys are always talking about how I am obsessed with death. Well, what I'm really interested in is living forever.'

'Sally might have a point,' Adam said. 'I'm drawn to the sapphire, and I think it's because it can make me older and wiser.'

Cindy shook her head. 'It never occurred to me to want to look more beautiful.'

'Fine,' Sally said. 'Then there's no need for you to try the topaz necklace on.'

'I can try it on if I want,' Cindy said.

Sally snorted. 'I bet you put it on the second I look away.'

'You could be right,' Watch said. 'I am drawn to the ruby. I think if it gives me strength, it will probably make my eyes and ears stronger as well. I want to try it on. I think I'm going to in a second, just to see if it does work.'

Sally was exasperated. 'Are you crazy? You think we will get these qualities for free? The witch will make us pay for whatever these stones can do for us.'

'How do we know they can do anything for us?' Cindy interrupted. 'They might just be pretty pieces of jewellery.'

'Because we're in a witch's castle,' Sally said. 'Not a shopping mall. The witch has got magic, I never said she didn't. But it's black magic. I say we get out of here now.'

'As you've said before,' Adam muttered.

'Good advice cannot be repeated too often,' Sally said.

'But if we leave now,' Watch warned, 'we'll never know what these necklaces might have done for us.' He reached for the ruby. 'I'll try this. Just me. The rest of you can see if anything happens to me.'

Sally quickly grabbed his arm. 'No! What if you turn into a frog?'

'I have never seen a strong frog,' Cindy remarked.

'Maybe she does want to trick us,' Watch said to Sally, who continued to hold on to his arm. 'But maybe she wants to help us. We've had this argument already. The only way we can know is for one of us to put on one of these necklaces.' He reached down and gently removed Sally's fingers. 'Don't worry, if I turn into something gross you can always put me in the creek. I sort of like the place.'

Sally shook her head and took a step back. 'It's your life.'

'And I'm not getting any younger,' Watch agreed.

He reached down and put the ruby necklace over his head.

He paused and looked round, blinking several times.

The rest of them held their breath.

'Interesting,' Watch finally muttered.

'Do you feel strong?' Adam asked.

Watch flexed his arms, squeezed his fingers.

'I feel slightly different,' he said.

'But do you feel stronger?' Sally demanded.

Watch continued to flex his muscles, to look around. 'Yes. I feel just a tiny bit stronger. And I think I can see slightly better.'

'You might just be imagining the changes,' Cindy warned.

Watch stretched out his arms and took a few steps around the room. 'I don't think so. I could barely see this room at all a few seconds ago. Now I can see the walls, the details on the brick-work.' He paused. 'The effect is growing as time passes. Already I can see better than when I first put on the necklace.'

Adam laughed nervously. 'If you keep getting stronger so fast, soon your muscles will bulge out of your clothes.'

Watch smiled, which he rarely did. He fingered the necklace lovingly. 'I like this thing. I think you guys should try on the other ones.'

Cindy reached for the topaz. 'All right. But I can't imagine that I could look any more beautiful than I already do.'

Sally grabbed her arm. 'Wait a second! This has been no experiment. We have to observe Watch for a while, see how he changes.'

Cindy shook her off. 'But we can see already that the change is for the better. If I want to try on the necklace, I can. You're not the boss, you know.'

'I should be,' Sally said.

'Maybe I should be the next one to try a necklace,' Adam said, staring at the sapphire again. 'Let us guys take the risks.'

'Ha,' Cindy said. 'Let you guys get to enjoy all the magic is what you mean. Let's try on the necklaces together. That's fair.'

Sally continued to shake her head. 'You're all going to turn into toads. I'm going to have to go down to the creek every day just to see you guys.'

Adam and Cindy ignored her. Together they put on the necklace they were most drawn to. Adam liked the feel of it as it went over his neck. He stroked the sapphire as it hung close to his heart. He glanced over at Cindy who beamed back at him.

'How do I look?' she asked.

'The same,' Sally muttered. 'Like a stick-in-the-mud.'

'No,' Watch said, stepping closer to Cindy. 'I think you look better. Adam?'

Adam studied Cindy. 'Yeah. She looks more radiant. Like she's glowing.'

Cindy grinned and rubbed her bare arms. 'I feel more beautiful. I feel – it's hard to describe – like I'm filling up with light.'

'I feel like I'm getting a headache,' Sally moaned. 'How about you, Adam? Are you older and wiser?'

Adam frowned. 'It's like Cindy said. It's hard to describe. I feel some kind of change – a little stronger, a little smarter maybe.'

'I think you look a little taller,' Watch said.

'Yeah, he's definitely not as short,' Cindy said enthusiastically.

Adam was taken back. 'I didn't know you thought I was short to begin with.'

Cindy patted his shoulder. 'I didn't mean you were short-short. You just weren't . . . as tall as Watch.' She paused and burst out laughing. 'But what does it matter now? You're going to be taller than all of us. Hey, Sally, go ahead, put on your necklace.'

'Yeah,' Adam said. 'If it does work, and it makes you immortal, then nothing's going to hurt you anyway. What do you have to lose?'

Sally glanced at the emerald necklace. 'Are you sure you guys feel better?'

Cindy began to dance about the room. 'I feel like a beautiful princess. I *am* a princess!'

'I can definitely see better,' Watch said, taking off his glasses.

'And I definitely feel less like a kid,' Adam said.

Sally reached out and touched the necklace, but then withdrew her hand. 'But don't you like feeling like a kid?' she said.

'I think these necklaces are gifts,' Adam said simply.

'I guess I'll have to trust you guys,' Sally said.

And with that she reached down and lifted the emerald necklace and placed it over her head. For a moment she stood fingering the beautiful green stone. Then she looked up and let out a laugh.

'Now I feel more like a kid,' she exclaimed.

Another wave of laughter sounded. But it did not come from any of them. This laughter was older, deeper and darker, and maybe a little wicked. It came from the direction of yet another hallway, that none of them had noticed at first because it had been unlit. But now a tall figure in a black cloak was walking their way, clasping a burning torch in her hand. Her green eyes glimmered in the stone passageway, even before she entered the room, and Adam was reminded of the emerald in Sally's magical necklace. For right then

Adam was convinced they were in the presence of great magic. But whether it was white or black, he was not yet sure.

'It's the witch,' Sally whispered, scared.

'Shh,' Adam warned. 'Don't call her that.'

'But I don't mind,' Ann Templeton said as she stepped into the room and threw back the cape on her cloak. She smiled as she said it, even laughed, but in her green eyes was a light more dangerous than any light they had ever seen before. Cold as the glow of a frosty dawn, but as powerful as the light of a distant star. She added, 'I'm your favourite witch.'

Four

'What do you want?' Sally asked suspiciously. Instinctively, they had all gathered together. Cindy was, in fact, holding on to Adam's arm. They even backed up a step as Ann Templeton came further into the room. She was like Adam remembered, beautiful with her long dark hair and her piercing green eyes. She was also as pale as he recalled; it did not seem like she often saw the sun. She smiled slyly at Sally's question, as she stood tall and in command in front of them.

'Shouldn't I be the one to ask that question?' she said. 'You four are the ones, after all, who came here looking for something.'

'We don't want anything from you,' Sally snapped.

Ann Templeton was amused. 'Oh, Sara. Then why have you tried to steal my necklaces?'

Adam stuttered. 'We didn't intend to steal anything, ma'am. We just wanted to try them on. We can put them back now if you want.'

Ann Templeton continued to wear a smile. 'Do you think you can just put them back, Adam?' she asked. 'Do you think it's that simple?'

'I'll put mine back if you don't want me to have it,' Watch said. He took hold of the necklace and began to pull it back over his head. 'We thought maybe they were gifts, but we're sorry if we made a mistake.'

Then Watch froze, the necklace half way over his head.

He looked stunned with surprise.

'What is it?' Sally asked nervously.

'I can't get it off,' Watch said.

'What do you mean you can't get it off?' Sally asked. 'Just take it off.'

'You try taking yours off,' Watch said.

Sally reached down and started to pull the necklace over her head. But she could only get halfway there. The fine gold band that carried the stone refused to pass all the way over her head.

'Oh no,' Sally whispered.

Adam and Cindy tried to take off their necklaces.

But they couldn't get them over their heads.

Ann Templeton laughed softly to herself.

'Do you still think it's that simple?' she asked.

Sally took a step forward. 'You tricked us.'

Ann Templeton shook her head. 'No. You tricked yourselves. I didn't make you put on the necklaces. If you had come here not wanting anything, you wouldn't be in this situation right now.'

'Are we in trouble?' Adam asked. 'I mean, I kind of like this necklace. If it's stuck around my head, I don't mind.' Then he added, 'As long as you don't mind that I keep it?'

Ann Templeton stared at him. 'That is sweet of you to say so, Adam. Actually, I made these necklaces for each of you. Certainly you may keep them. If you meet just one condition.'

'What is that?' Sally asked suspiciously.

'My condition is simple,' Ann Templeton said. 'You just have to find your way out of my castle. If you do, then you may keep your necklace. You can even take it off and put it back on whenever you wish.' She added in a more menacing tone, 'But as long as you're in my castle, you can't take off the necklace. No matter how hard you try.'

'But we know how to get out of here,' Watch said. 'We just have to walk back to the hourglass room, and then through the hallway on the right, and then we'll come back to the front door.'

'Where is the hourglass room?' Ann Templeton asked in a slightly mocking tone.

'It's just over . . .' Watch began, before his voice trailed into silence.

The hallway through which they had entered was gone.

'Am I confused?' Watch asked Adam.

Adam shook his head. 'No. The hallway's vanished.'

'It disappeared the moment all four of you had put on your necklaces,' said Ann Templeton.

'It's just as I thought,' Sally said bitterly. 'This has all been a set-up to trap us. I told you guys she was an evil witch.'

Sally's outburst caused Ann Templeton to laugh heartily. 'The necklaces are not here to trap you, Sara. They're here to test you.'

'How?' Watch asked.

'You will see,' Ann Templeton said as she turned to leave. 'Now I have to get back to my own affairs. I will give you only one piece of advice while you stumble around trying to find your way out of here.' She paused. 'Watch out for my boys.'

Cindy gulped. 'Who are your boys?'

Ann Templeton. 'My boys are like boys everywhere. Full of fun and mischief. But their idea of fun might not be the same as your idea of fun.' She laughed at that. 'Try to stay out of their way!'

With that Ann Templeton strode back up the hallway from which she had emerged. As her torch began to fade in the long darkness, they noticed that the opening to the hallway had vanished – leaving them trapped in a room that seemed to have no way out.

Five

'Now what are we going to do?' Sally grumbled.

'She said this is a test,' Adam said. 'That means there must be a way out of this room. What do you say, Watch?'

Watch continued to flex his arms and hands. 'I hope that's true. But if it's not, it won't matter anyway if I keep growing stronger like this. I'll be able to tear down these walls.'

Adam nodded as he studied his own body. The floor definitely looked further away. 'I'm changing fast as well,' he said. 'I think I must be thirteen years old by now.'

Sally, who looked an inch shorter, made a sarcastic swooning sound. 'Oh, an older man. How exciting.'

'I'm not ready to panic yet.' Cindy said. 'I'm still

excited about my necklace.' She paused. 'I wish I had a mirror. Do I look as pretty as I feel?'

'You look very nice,' Adam said honestly.

Sally squinted at Cindy. 'I don't know if you're prettier or not, Cindy. But I think you're beginning to glow. I mean really glow, like a light bulb.'

It was true. As Cindy stepped away from the fireplaces and into the shadows, she seemed to cast a shadow of her own. Her skin was emitting a faint radiance, almost as if she were radioactive. But the effect did not disturb Cindy. She appeared excited about it.

'I can be a movie star,' she said. 'I don't just have sparkle in my eyes. I have it everywhere!'

'Do I need to remind you that we are in a life and death situation here?' Sally said in a slightly squeaky voice. 'We are surrounded by stone walls, and we have nothing to eat or drink.'

Watch gestured to the ceiling. He had been staring at it for the last minute. 'I think I see a hole into the attic.'

'What are you talking about?' Adam said. 'I don't see anything.'

'And castles don't have attics,' Sally added.

'It doesn't matter what we call it,' Watch said,

removing his glasses and rubbing his eyes, before pointing to one spot on the dark stone ceiling. 'It looks like a way out to me.'

'But we could never get up there,' Cindy said.

In response, Watch jumped off the floor. But it was not an ordinary jump that an ordinary boy might make. He flew up almost two metres before coming back down.

'Wow,' he said. 'I can't wait until the next Olympics. I'll clean up on the gold medals.'

'But even if you're feeling stronger,' Sally said, 'that ceiling's ten metres high. You can't reach it.'

Adam gestured to the table where they had found the necklaces. 'But what if we take this table, break it in half, and set the two halves on top of each other? If Watch jumped from the top of that, he might be able to reach the hole in the ceiling.'

'But what about us?' Cindy asked. 'We'll still be stuck.'

Watch pulled the long white sheet off the table top. 'I'll take this with me. And once I'm up there, I'll lower it for Adam to grab. And you two can hold on to Adam's feet and I'll pull you all up at once.'

Sally smirked. 'Right. You can lift all of us at once.'

Watch spoke with a straight face. 'I think I can. I know for sure I can break this table into two pieces.

Stand aside, I don't want any of you to get hurt.'

To their amazement, they watched as Watch cut the table in half with one sharp karate chop. Or perhaps Adam was not that surprised. It had been his idea to begin with, and he was growing smarter all the time, not to mention taller.

Not needing their help, Watch piled the two pieces of the table on top of each other. Then he tucked the tablecloth in his belt, and jumped up on the very top of the tables. The gang moved back even further as he made a desperate leap for the hole in the ceiling. His first effort failed, and he came crashing back on the table top. The wood shuddered, as if he weighed a ton, and they feared the whole structure would come crashing down.

But Watch was not fazed. He made another supernatural leap, and this time he managed to catch on to the rim of the hole. In two seconds he had pulled himself up and out of view. But his head reappeared a moment later.

'This hole is like a heating duct,' he called down. 'It looks like it goes way back.' He began to feed the edge of the sheet down. 'Hurry, grab hold of the cloth. We should get out of here before Ann Templeton comes back.'

'But what if you drop us?' Sally asked as she climbed up on the split table tops.

'You're the last person who has to worry about that,' Watch said. 'You're immortal now.'

Sally frowned. 'I don't know about that. I just feel . . .' She suddenly stopped. 'Hey, is my voice getting higher?'

'Yeah,' Cindy said. 'And you're getting shorter, too.'

'You're not just getting shorter,' Adam said, studying Sally. 'You're getting younger.'

Sally was stunned. 'You mean you guys get to be older and stronger and more beautiful? And I have to turn into a baby?'

'Looks like it,' Adam said. 'But I'm not surprised the witch gave you the worst necklace. You're always rude to her.'

'Right now we don't know which necklace is good,' Watch warned them from above. 'And which necklace might be bad.'

Cindy giggled. 'I'm not worried about becoming too beautiful.'

Sally gave her a hard look. 'I think we should all be worried.'

The three of them finished climbing up on the second of the table tops. But it was only Adam – who was now taller than the rest of them by several centimetres – who could reach the sheet Watch fed down to them. For that reason, Sally and Cindy ended up holding on to Adam's legs as Watch pulled them. It was a strange sensation to have in such a strange place, Adam thought. To have his friend slowly tugging him into the air as if he were a balloon while the girls hung on to his ankles.

'That wasn't so bad,' Adam said, when they were all huddled in the hole in the ceiling. Below them they could still see the massive fireplaces, and the many burning torches. Too late he realised they should have brought one of the torches with them. The hole Watch had lifted them into looked long and dark.

'It's too bad we don't have a flashlight,' Cindy said, peering into the dark.

'I don't think I need one,' Watch said, as he put his glasses in his pocket. 'My eyes are getting more sensitive with each passing minute. I can practically see in the dark.'

They crawled forward, with Watch leading the way, Cindy at his back, Sally behind her and Adam at the rear. The tunnel did not stay even. For a while it headed down, then back up. It seemed as if they had been crawling forever when Watch finally told them to halt. Adam thought he heard metal scraping across stone, but he could not see his friend at the front of their group.

'There is some kind of grid over the space in front of us,' Watch said.

'Does it look like a way out?' Sally asked.

'It might be,' Watch said. 'But I can't see any floor below it. I think it would be risky just to jump down.' He paused and sniffed the air. 'There's this strange smell coming from below the grid.'

'What's it smell like?' Cindy asked.

'I'm not sure,' Watch said. 'But it's not a pleasant smell.'

'Can the grid support our weight?' Sally asked.

'That's another reason I stopped,' Watch said. 'It's pretty rusted. I think we had better go over it one at a time.'

'Good,' Sally said. 'You go first.'

Adam heard Watch moving on to the edge of the grid. The metal creaked loudly, and Adam realised his heart was pounding. 'Be careful, Watch,' he whispered.

'It's bending already,' Watch said in a tight voice. 'We'll be lucky if we all get across.'

'Well, don't bend it too much,' Sally said. 'I don't want to be trapped in here for the rest of my life.

Especially when it was not my idea to come here.'

'I thought you weren't going to say I told you so,' Adam said.

'It goes without saying,' Sally replied.

'I'm almost on the other side of the grid,' Watch whispered.

'How far across is it?' Adam asked.

'A long three metres,' Watch called back. He seemed to shift in the darkness ahead of them, perhaps as he was turning around. 'There, I've made it. Come, Cindy, but be sure to move slowly.'

'I'm scared,' Cindy whispered as she moved on to the grid. Once more Adam heard the creaking metal. 'What if it breaks?'

'Then you will probably fall screaming to your death,' Sally said in her most helpful manner.

'You won't die,' Adam said in an encouraging tone. 'You're a beautiful princess. The beautiful princess never dies in fairy tales.'

'The only trouble with that analogy is that Spooksville is as far from a fairy tale as you can get,' Sally said.

'Would you shut up?' Cindy hissed. 'You're making me nervous.'

'How do you think I feel?' Sally asked. 'I have to go

after you and Watch, and you two guys have bent the grid all out of shape.'

'I can hardly wait until you regress to an infant,' Cindy muttered. 'To before you could talk.'

Adam sighed. 'Isn't it amazing how we all band together at the times of greatest danger?'

Cindy made it across. They heard her celebrating on the other side with Watch. Now it was Sally's turn, and she too sounded scared as she crawled on to the grid.

'It smells like death down there,' she whispered.

'Try not to look down,' Adam said.

'Try telling that to my nose,' Sally said, obviously sweating with every move as she crawled over the grid. For Adam, she was a blur – even though he was only a metre behind her. The darkness seemed to press down upon all of them as the stink below grew stronger.

Adam thought he heard something moving far below.

Wicked licking sounds.

He prayed the grid didn't break when it was his turn.

Finally, he heard Sally call from up ahead.

'I made it,' she said. 'Just pretend you're as light as a hot air balloon, Adam, and you'll have no problem.'

'The only problem with that is I think I've gained ten kilos in the last five minutes,' Adam said, feeling for the edge of the grid. 'I wonder how old I am now.'

'I wonder when you'll stop ageing,' Watch said darkly.

Adam moved on to the grid. Immediately it sagged way down. It was unfortunate – had he been his normal size and weight, the grid would have supported him fine. Now it was creaking painfully. It sounded as if its many metal wires were desperately straining to hold together. Adam felt desperate. There was definitely something moving far below, and it wasn't human. Adam could hear the creature licking its chops, as if expecting a fresh meal. Had the witch just given him the necklace to make him into a bigger piece of meat? It was a terrifying thought.

'You're almost there,' Sally whispered on the other side.

'I've barely climbed on to the blasted thing,' Adam whispered back.

'I know that,' Sally said. 'I was just trying to be supportive.'

The grid suddenly let out a loud creak.

It dropped down half a metre.

'Adam!' Cindy screamed.

'I'm still here,' Adam gasped, trembling badly. He was clutching the grid for dear life, barely able to squeeze his fingers between the interlaced metal. Behind him, he believed, the grid had already torn loose. If he were to let go for a second, he knew he would slide off into the creature's lair. Clearly there was no chance of going back.

'You have to move carefully,' Watch advised.

'But you have to hurry up and do it,' Sally said. 'I can feel the edge of the grid on this side. It's ready to pull away.'

Adam could feel the grid slowly sinking beneath him. He feared if he moved it would just collapse. 'I think I'm stuck,' he said softly. 'I think this is it.'

'Hang on,' Sally pleaded. 'I have a plan.'

'I am all ears,' Adam whispered, feeling the sweat drip into his eyes, the perspiration sliding over his palms, making them slippery.

'Watch,' Sally said, 'do you still have the sheet you used to pull us up here with?'

'Sure.' There was a rustling in the dark. 'Are you going to throw it down to him?'

'Yes,' Sally said. 'Adam, in a moment you'll probably feel the sheet on your face or your hands. Grab hold of it and we'll pull you up.'

'Are you pulling me up or is Watch?' Adam wanted to know.

'Watch can't squeeze past Cindy to get to where I'm sitting,' Sally said. 'It will have to be me. But don't worry, I'm stronger than I look.'

'For a five year old,' Cindy muttered.

'I'm not five yet,' Sally snapped.

'You sound like it,' Cindy said.

Adam felt the edge of the sheet brush the side of his face. 'Are you sure you can hold on to me?' he asked. 'I'm going to make a grab for the sheet right now.'

'I will try my best,' Sally said. 'Cindy, you hold on to me. Watch, you hold on to Cindy.'

'We'll probably all end up going over the edge,' Cindy muttered.

'I'm going to do it now,' Adam said again.

'We're ready for you,' Sally whispered, tense.

In a single swift move, Adam let go of the grill with his right hand and grabbed at the sheet. He could feel exactly where it was, lying against his cheek, and had no trouble getting hold of it. The only problem was that his sudden move made the grill sink even deeper. He had one hand on the grill and the other on the sheet and if he let go of either he was sure he was doomed.

'Can you pull me up?' he gasped.

'Can't you crawl up?' Sally gasped back. It sounded

as if she was straining as hard as she could to hold on to him.

'I don't know,' Adam said, feeling himself slipping down, slowly, bit by bit. 'Can't you help, Watch?'

'Unfortunately the sheet isn't long enough,' Watch said. 'Whatever you're going to do, you better do it now. I don't think Sally can hold on much longer.'

'Ain't that the truth,' Sally whispered.

Using the taut sheet for support, Adam desperately tried to pull himself up. But now the grid was a mass of scary creaks. Adam could actually hear the individual wires snapping as the grid sunk so low that for all practical purposes it was hanging straight down. Far below, the waiting creature seemed to giggle. A wave of putrid air floated upwards, making Adam swoon.

'I can't hold on,' he cried.

'You have to,' Sally said. 'You can't die just when I've become immortal. I'll be bored for the rest of eternity without you to bother.'

Both the sheet and the grid were slowly slipping from his hands. 'I can't do it,' he moaned. 'I'm falling.'

'You fall and I'll kill you,' Sally said anxiously.

'You have to try harder,' Cindy pleaded.

'Just make one big jump for it,' Watch said. 'It's your only chance.'

'All right,' Adam said as he struggled for air. 'I'm doing it on the count of three. One . . . Two . . . Three!'

Using both his arms, Adam yanked up as hard as he could. Unfortunately, the edge of the grid was too far gone to take the shock. Still, he almost made it. He was actually able to grab hold of Sally's hand. He grabbed it hard, as if his life depended on it, which it did. But in a way it just made the situation worse.

The whole grid gave away.

It fell crashing below.

There was a high pitched cry from below – the complaint of an inhuman monster.

Adam dangled in mid air, holding on to the sheet with one hand, and Sally's hand with the other. Above him, he could feel Sally being pulled over the edge.

'I have to let go!' he cried.

'I won't let go of you!' Sally screamed.

'You must!' Adam shouted. 'You'll be pulled over the edge with me.'

'No!' Sally cried.

But Adam was right. He was already doomed, and because Sally refused to let him fall, she too was pulled over the edge. The tension broke all at once. The two of them were fighting with every last drop of strength they had, then they were suddenly falling. Into a black abyss where a pair of hungry red eyes waited to eat them alive.

Six

Cindy and Watch sat in darkness, inside and out. Neither could comprehend what had just happened. The shock was too great. Sally and Adam – their best friends – were just gone. Everything in the whole world seemed hopeless.

'Can you see anything?' Cindy whispered to Watch as he knelt at the edge of the torn grill.

'I'm having trouble seeing past you,' Watch said. 'But it wouldn't matter if I was sitting where you are sitting.'

Cindy's voice cracked. 'Because they're dead already?'

Watch spoke heavily. 'I'm afraid so. They couldn't have survived that fall, or whatever it is that's down there.'

Cindy winced. 'Do you think it's going to eat them?'

'We shouldn't think about that. They're already beyond feeling any pain.'

Cindy felt cold tears wash over her face. 'We should never have come to this evil place. I didn't want to come.'

'I know and you were right,' Watch said. 'It was my fault. I was just worried about myself.' He sighed. 'And now I have killed my best friends.'

Cindy patted his arm. 'You can't blame yourself. You just wanted to be able to see better. There's nothing wrong with that.'

Watch hung his head. 'I would trade both my eyes just to see Adam again, and to hear Sally's voice.'

After sitting for a few more minutes in mourning, they continued to crawl up the stone tunnel. There was nothing else they could do. Cindy wept as they crawled, but Watch kept his tears inside, where he kept most things.

After maybe twenty minutes of plugging along, the passageway took a sharp turn downwards. Fortunately metal rungs appeared on the sides, and they were able to hold on to them for support. Pretty soon they were climbing straight down, as if they were on a ladder. As they did so the temperature increased. A faint red glow appeared below and it seemed as if they were coming to the end of the passageway.

'We've been going down for a long time,' Cindy said as they paused to catch their breath. 'That's not good. We must have entered the witch's basement. That's where we ran into the trolls before.'

Watch nodded, hanging on to the metal rungs below her. 'I'm sure when she was talking about her boys, she meant them. Do you think it's possible she told the trolls not to eat us?'

'I doubt it,' Cindy said bitterly. 'It was she who forced us to crawl through this stone hole. I blame her for Adam and Sally's deaths. When we get out of here, I'm going straight to the police to report her.'

'The police won't do anything about it,' Watch said. 'They're afraid of Ann Templeton.' He shook his head as he stared down below them. 'I didn't think she would do anything really to hurt us.'

'Sally was wiser than all of us,' Cindy said in a sad voice. 'And I was always so mean to her.'

'You were never mean to her,' Watch said. 'You were just always annoyed with her.' He gestured to the red light below them. 'We can't hang here forever. We're going to have to try our luck with the trolls. I just wish we had a weapon of some kind.'

'Do you think you're strong enough to beat up one yet?' Cindy asked.

'No matter how strong I get,' Watch said, 'I don't think I'll be able to take a spear in the chest.' He paused and stared at her. 'You keep getting brighter. We're going to have trouble hiding you from the trolls.'

Cindy studied her body. Watch was right. With each passing minute the flesh on her arms and legs was shining with more light. Indeed, it was almost as if her skin was becoming transparent.

'If it comes down to it,' she said, 'you save yourself. You don't try to save me as well.'

Watch shook his head. 'Did you see how Sally refused to let go of Adam? She held on to him even though she knew it would kill her. How can I leave you behind?'

Cindy wiped away another tear. 'She was very brave.'

They climbed down the remainder of the passageway. The dull red light was their guide. As they climbed out, they found themselves in a wide stone cave. It stretched in both directions, and appeared empty. But the red light was only coming from the right. The left was completely dark.

'This reminds me of the Haunted Cave,' Cindy said.

'But it isn't,' Watch said. 'We can't be that deep. This tunnel was built.'

'But that's an idea,' Cindy said. 'If we could go even deeper, we could make it down to the Haunted Cave. And we know how to get out of there. We've done it before.'

'I wouldn't mind going that way,' Watch said. 'But I don't know which way it is.' He nodded in both directions. 'Do you want to go towards the light, or do you want to go towards the darkness?'

'I just want to go home,' Cindy said. But she pointed in the direction of the red glow. 'But we have to go that way. Even if you can see in the dark, I can't.'

'I agree.' Watch studied his shirt sleeve. 'The material is beginning to tear. My arms are swelling in size.'

Cindy nodded. 'You're not getting taller but you are getting more stocky. I bet pretty soon you'll be able to handle a dozen trolls.'

'Don't even say it,' Watch cautioned.

They started forward, in the direction of the red glow. It grew in brightness as the temperature continued to increase. Up ahead, through a haunting red haze, they glimpsed a huge room, a cavern of some kind, filled with metal equipment and dark moving shapes. Even as they saw the creatures, the creatures saw them. Cindy and Watch heard a bunch of loud howls, and then the creatures were running towards them.

They carried spears.

And they were not human.

Seven

In reality, Adam and Sally were not dead. Not yet.

They had fallen a long way, far enough to break every bone in their body. But they had landed on the softest of all cushions, some kind of huge net. The only trouble was that it was not a net but a sticky web. They were alive but stuck. The net's slimy fibres stuck to them like glue.

And they could hear the spider getting closer.

'It must be a big creature to make a web like this,' Adam said.

'It's probably poisonous as well,' Sally said grimly. 'Can you move?'

'Not much. How about you?'

'I'm slimed. It's all over me – in my hair, on my arms and legs. Can you see the spider yet?'

'No,' Adam said. 'But it's definitely getting closer.'

'That's bad,' Sally said.

'That's putting it mildly. Hey, I want to thank you for holding on to me when I started to fall. That was very brave of you.'

'Thank you. But I think it was awfully stupid of me.'

'Most brave acts are stupid,' Adam agreed. He had landed on his back and there he remained – no matter how hard he tried moving on to his side. The odour he had smelled from up on the grill had grown a dozen times stronger. The stink was like rotten eggs – it made it hard to breathe.

It was dark, pitch black.

They heard a slobbering sound off to their right.

They heard a munching sound off to their left.

'Oh no,' Sally cried. 'There're two spiders.'

'Maybe they'll begin to fight over us,' Adam said hopefully.

'They live together down here,' Sally said. 'They're not going to fight over us. We're doomed.'

'Don't say that. It depresses me.' Adam suddenly had an idea. 'Hey, do you have your Bic lighter in your pocket?'

'Yeah. Why?'

'We can use the flame to burn away the web,' Adam said. 'It's worth a try. Can you reach it in your pocket?'

'I think so,' Sally said as the slobbering sounds grew louder. 'But if I burn away the web, we might fall further.'

'I would rather be falling than be eaten,' Adam said.

'That's a good point.' Sally flicked on the lighter. In the light of the tiny orange flame they could see the approaching spiders. They were hideous to behold. As big as fat sheep, they had a bunch of slimy black legs and arms, and two sharp pinchers. The fire seemed to puzzle them. They stopped and stared at it with wary red eyes. But they did not turn and flee, as Adam had half hoped. Green poison dripped from their ugly mouths.

The web was erected only a metre above a black floor.

If they could burn free, they would be able to stand up and escape.

'Put the flame under the web,' Adam said. 'See if you can get it smoking.'

'I'm trying,' Sally said, manoeuvring the flame beneath the piece of web that gripped her right arm. To their delight, and surprise, it immediately caught fire, as a hair would when put close to a lighter. The web wrinkled up quickly and went back out, but in doing so it released Sally's right arm. She moved the flame to the web that gripped her left arm. The spiders made shrill angry sounds, and began to move forward again.

'Hurry,' Adam said. 'They're coming.'

'I am well aware of the fact,' Sally gasped. Her left arm came free, and then she was hanging above the floor by her feet. As she reached up to free her entangled ankles, the nearest of the spiders reached over with its pincher.

'Watch out!' Adam cried.

'Take that you ugly creature!' Sally yelled as she suddenly pulled off her shoe and smacked the spider in the face. The spider retreated a step and screamed at the other spider. In the meantime Sally freed both her feet and dropped down to the floor, actually landing on her outstretched arms. Adam only noticed then that she looked about six years old.

'You're shrinking,' he said.

Sally hurried to his side. 'Do you really want to insult me at a time like this?'

'Sorry,' Adam said.

Sally moved a flame to his wrists. 'Pull back on the web. It burns easier when it's tight.'

Adam nodded in the direction of the spiders, which had moved close to each other. It was as if the two monsters were plotting a strategy. Adam didn't want to hang around and see what surprises they came up with. He pulled the web as tight as he could as Sally licked the flame over the slimy thread.

'I should carry a lighter myself,' he said. 'It's saved our lives a few times already.'

'You get three in a packet for less than two dollars,' Sally agreed.

Suddenly the spiders turned back in their direction. As a team the monsters rushed them. Adam struggled uselessly, just covering himself with more web.

'Get a stick!' he cried. 'They're coming.'

'We're in a dungeon. There are no sticks.'

'Then get a stone!' Adam shouted as the monster moved within three metres. 'Anything! They're going to sting me with their poison venom!'

Sally looked round. A couple of loose bricks lay against a nearby wall. Grabbing them she whirled on the spiders and let fly with the stones. One hit the closest spider in the eyes. The second brick struck the other spider's stinger. It broke it, in fact – the spider let out a loud miserable screech. Sally returned to melting the web as the spiders retreated to the far corner.

'I owe you one,' Adam said.

'You owe me a dozen,' Sally replied.

A minute later Adam was free of the sticky web, and

able to stand upright on the floor beside Sally. They realised that they were not in a real dungeon. There was a wide tunnel off to the right that led out of the spiders' lair. As they ran away from the web, Sally turned and shouted back at the spiders.

'Next time I'm going to bring bug spray!'

The tunnel led to a stone ladder, which was carved into the wall. The tunnel also continued further along, but they both thought it was a good idea to head upwards. But Sally was shocked to find she could hardly climb the ladder.

'It's because you're getting shorter,' Adam said as he came up behind her.

'I know that. You don't have to keep rubbing it in.' She paused. 'Hey, your voice sounds a lot deeper.'

'Yeah. I sound like a teenager.'

'Don't be coy,' Sally said. 'You sound like a man.'

At the top of the stone ladder – which had been a long climb – they came to another stone tunnel. But this one was different from the others. Lit with a haunting violet light, it was much cleaner than the place they had left behind. There was also a pleasant smell to it, as if someone had recently burned incense. Moving in the direction of the wonderful light, Adam felt as if they were entering a place of ancient magic.

'I have never seen this coloured light before,' Adam said.

'Yes. It's enchanting.' Sally paused. 'We have to be careful of another trap.'

They entered a large dome-shaped chamber, filled with bushes and trees and grass. The violet glow seemed to come out of the ceiling itself. There was even a circular pond in the room. And sitting in the middle of the tiny lake was a girl of about ten, with long curly black hair. She opened her eyes as they entered, as if coming out of deep meditation. Her eyes were as green as Ann Templeton's, but the smile on her incredible face was filled only with kindness.

'Hello,' she said in a gentle voice. 'My name is Mireen. Who are you?'

Eight

Cindy and Watch were captured by a gang of big ugly trolls. The beasts carried spears and swords, arrows and knives. They dragged Cindy and Watch kicking into the large cavern where still more trolls slaved over clanging machines that made heaven only knew what. All the trolls stopped to stare as Cindy and Watch were forced to stand beside a pool of boiling lava. It was the lava that gave off the red light, and perhaps helped fuel the big machines.

Cindy and Watch exchanged worried looks. They had no doubt they would be thrown into the lava, or else cooked over it.

'Can you break free?' Cindy asked in a quiet voice.

Watch shook his head. 'There're too many of them.'

'Silence!' one of the trolls shouted, putting the tip

of his sword to Watch's throat. 'No one gave you permission to speak.'

'I'm sorry,' Watch said. 'I didn't know you trolls could speak English.'

The comment seemed to amuse the monster, for he smiled widely, as slobber fell over his breastplate of stainless steel. Like his partners, his face was blunt, his thick nose hairy, and his skin scaled, like that of a lizard. But he was bigger than his partners, and maybe that was why he was their leader. He strode in front of them as if they were his trophies.

'Our boss has taught us to speak your human language,' the troll said. 'She says we will need it in the future, when we go out into the world, and make all of you our slaves.'

'It won't happen,' Cindy said. 'We humans have a group called the Marines. They'll kick your ugly behinds.'

The troll paused in his pacing. 'Who are these Marines?'

'They are the proud and the few,' Watch said. 'They have much better weapons than spears and swords. If I were you I would stay down here. The Marines would wipe you all out in one day.'

'But are these Marines human?' the troll asked.

'They are human soldiers,' Cindy said. 'They always win, and don't quit until the enemy has been defeated.' She added hopefully, 'They are good friends of ours. If you hurt us, they won't like that.'

'Yeah, you should just let us go,' Watch said. 'If you eat us alive, our friends will become your enemies.'

The troll sniggered at their threat. 'Nobody is going to save you here. We will have you for dinner, that is certain. It only remains to see how you are to be cooked.' He added, 'My name is Belfart, by the way.'

'I'm Watch and this is Cindy,' Watch said.

'Pleased to meet you, Belfart,' Cindy said. 'Do you have to eat us? If you let us go, we promise to bring you back fresh steak from the grocery store.'

Belfart scoffed. 'We don't even like cows. Human meat is much more tasty.' He lightly poked Cindy's side with the tip of his sword. 'I think I will eat you myself.'

Cindy shoved aside his sword and spat on him. 'Then kill us both and get it over with. Your bad breath is giving me a headache.'

Belfart wiped away the spit with his long purple tongue. 'Not so fast. We have to have a vote. We are a democratic group of trolls.' Belfart turned to the gathered monsters. To Cindy and Watch's surprise, he continued to speak in English, perhaps to torture them all the more. 'How do we cook them?' Belfart called out.

Clearly it was an important question, at least as far as the trolls were concerned. Immediately half a dozen of the monsters yelled out that the humans should be roasted. Just as quickly another half dozen said that the humans should be broiled. Still others wanted them boiled, while a couple of trolls wanted them skinned alive. Soon there was a big argument going on, and Belfart had lost all control of his group. Indeed, several of the trolls drew their swords and looked ready to die to defend their choice of how the humans should be cooked. Cindy looked over at Watch and sighed.

'This is worse than being eaten,' Cindy said.

'I don't know about that,' Watch said. 'They can argue as long as they want as far as I'm concerned.'

'We need a plan of action,' Cindy said.

'I was going to suggest that they at least kill us before they eat us.'

'That's no plan. If Adam and Sally were here, they wouldn't give up without a fight.'

'If I try to fight them all,' Watch said, 'we'll both end up dead.'

'I have an idea,' Cindy said. She called over to the

troll leader. 'Belfart! There's something I must tell you guys before you make a decision as to how we are to be cooked.'

Belfart shouted for the group to shut up, and because it was one of the humans who wanted to speak, they did. Cindy addressed the group as a whole.

'Now I know you are hungry,' she said. 'And I know nothing would taste better to you than roasted human right now.'

'Boiled human would taste better!' a troll shouted.

'Grilled!' another troll yelled.

'Satéed!' a troll at the back screamed.

'Whatever!' Cindy yelled back. 'You want to eat us and I can understand that. But there's something we've got to tell you.' She paused for effect. 'Me and my partner are sick. If you eat us, you'll get sick too.'

Belfart took a step closer and sniffed her. 'You don't smell sick.'

'But I am,' she said. 'So is Watch. We have the measles.'

'I already had the measles,' Watch said.

'And now you have them again,' Cindy said quickly. 'In case you think we're lying, you just have to wait a few hours and we'll get these red spots all over our bodies.'

Belfart seemed unconvinced. 'But we're hungry now.'

'Yes,' Cindy said patiently. 'But you don't want to get sick. The measles are awful. If you catch them, all the girl trolls won't even want to get near you.'

That sent a stir through the room. Belfart put his scaly hand to his fat jaw and appeared thoughtful. 'How long does it take you to get the red spots?' he asked.

'We'll have them within six hours,' Cindy said confidently. 'Wait that long and you'll see.'

'Let's wait and then fry them!' a troll shouted.

'We wait and then we bake them!' another yelled.

'No!' a bunch at the back said. 'We put them in the microwave!'

'Where did they get a microwave?' Watch muttered.

'Shut up all of you!' Belfart screamed. 'We will first lock them up and see if they get sick. If they don't, then we can argue about how to cook them.'

Cindy leaned over and whispered in Watch's ear. 'I have just bought us time.'

Watch nodded grimly. 'But they're just going to come for us later.'

Nine

'I'm Adam. This is Sally,' Adam said to the strange girl. 'What are you doing here?'

'This is where I have always been.' Mireen stood up in her place at the centre of the pond. With a slight nod of her head a series of stones appeared in the water, providing a pathway for her across the pond. As she approached, Adam noticed she was wearing a dark grey cloak, similar in design to Ann Templeton's. Mireen asked, 'What are you doing here?'

'We've been trapped in this castle by the witch,' Sally said angrily. 'Has she trapped you as well?'

Mireen appeared puzzled. Her face, although very beautiful, was as pale as Ann Templeton's. It seemed almost as if it were made of marble; it did not have a blemish on it.

'Who is this witch you speak of?' she asked.

'Ann Templeton,' Adam explained. 'She gave us these magic necklaces and now we can't get them off. We can't find our way out of here either.'

Mireen smiled. 'Ann Templeton isn't a witch. Why do you call her that?'

'What would you call her?' Sally demanded in her now squeaky voice. Sally was down to the size of a four year old. In a sense, Adam was not doing much better. Sally was wrong – he was no longer a teenager. In fact, he seemed to have skipped his twenties altogether. He was getting really old, in his mid-thirties at least. Pretty soon he would have arthritis and not even be able to walk properly, like most older adults.

'I call her Mother,' Mireen said.

They were stunned. 'You're Ann Templeton's daughter?' Sally asked.

'Yes. Don't I look like her daughter?'

Mireen did indeed resemble the witch. Yet there was an otherworldly character to her face that even Ann Templeton didn't have.

'Who's your father?' Adam asked.

A trace of sorrow touched Mireen's face. 'His name is supposed to be Faltoreen. But I have never met him.'

'Why not?' Sally asked. 'Did your mother kill him?'

'No,' Mireen said. 'Why would my mother kill him?'

'She's trying to kill us,' Sally said.

'No, my father is alive and well,' Mireen said. 'He just doesn't live here.'

'Where does he live?' Adam asked.

'On another planet,' Mireen said. 'Circling another star.'

Sally laughed out loud. 'I hate to tell you this, Mireen, but that's an old excuse. Your father just took off one day and didn't bother coming back. Not that I can say I blame him after seeing the creeps that are running around this castle.'

'I'm not too sure of that,' Adam said. 'Remember how Bum said that Ann Templeton and her family were connected to star people who live in the Pleiades star group?'

'Pleiades,' Mireen said, her face shining with pleasure at the sound of the word. 'That is it. That is the name of the star group where my father lives.'

'But you say you've never seen him,' Sally said. 'How come he never visits you? Doesn't he have a spaceship?'

'He commands a whole fleet of ships,' Mireen said. 'But my mother says it is not time for him to return here.'

'I don't know if you can believe everything your mother says,' Sally said.

'We have explained how she's trapped us here,' Adam said carefully. 'You can understand that we have good reason to distrust her.' He paused. 'But you're more our age. We would like to trust you.'

'But you're much older than me, Adam,' Mireen said. 'And Sally is much younger.'

'We weren't when we started out the day,' Sally muttered.

'What Sally means is that these necklaces that we can't get off are making me older and her younger,' Adam explained. 'They have magic stones in them.' He paused. 'But maybe you know how to get them off?'

'I can certainly try,' Mireen said, stepping closer. Touching Adam's necklace, she closed her eyes and went perfectly still. Under her breath she whispered a chant. Adam and Sally didn't understand a word of it. Then Mireen opened her eyes and tried to lift off the necklace. But once more the gold strand would not pass over his head. Mireen added, 'These are bound with powerful magic. I can't undo it, but I know my mother could.'

'If she was ever in the mood,' Sally muttered.

'Your mother said these necklaces will not come off until we find our way out of here,' Adam explained. 'For that reason, we have to get out of here right away.

Soon Sally will be in nappies and I'll be in my forties and unable to get around properly.' He paused. 'You do know how to get out of here, don't you?'

Mireen blinked. 'No.'

'But you live here,' Sally said, exasperated. 'You said so yourself.'

'But I have never been outside,' Mireen said.

'Why not?' Adam asked.

'My mother says it is not time for that either,' Mireen explained. 'She says the outside is a cruel and barbaric place.'

'What about the trolls in your basement?' Sally asked. 'I've run into them before. They're not exactly warm and fuzzy kinds of characters.'

'They are always very polite to me,' Mireen said.

'What about the huge poisonous spiders?' Sally asked, trying again. 'Don't tell me they like you as well.'

'No, they can be troublesome. You just have to stay out of their way.'

'Look,' Adam said. 'We don't care if you like trolls and spiders. We just want to find our friends and get out of this place.'

'Where are your friends?' Mireen asked.

'We don't know,' Sally said. 'We got separated

above the spiders' lair. The trolls could have got them by now for all we know.'

'The trolls are not easy to control when they're hungry,' Mireen admitted. 'Come, we'll look for them. And after we find them, we'll search for a way out.'

Ten

Belfart locked Cindy and Watch in an unpleasant cell. It was damp and smelly, and there was a skeleton chained to a wall in the corner. From the size of it, they figured the trolls had feasted on a kid their age earlier in the year. Perhaps as a favour, Belfart had chained them to the wall in the opposite corner.

'I wonder if it was James Hatterfield,' Watch mused. 'He was supposed to have disappeared in the vicinity of this castle.'

'Did you go to school with him?' Cindy asked. She had yet to start school in Spooksville.

'Yeah, he was in the same grade as Sally and me. He was a nice guy but kind of chubby.' Watch added, 'The trolls probably liked that about him.'

'I still can't get over how you guys take it for granted that people disappear in this town,' Cindy said.

Watch shrugged. 'It happens every other day. You get used to it.'

Cindy sighed. 'My mother's going to be really upset if I get eaten by a troll. She wanted me home early for dinner.'

'I haven't had dinner with my mother in years,' Watch said quietly.

Cindy studied him in the poor light. Watch seldom talked about his family. All that Cindy knew was that they were scattered across the country. She did not know why.

'You miss her, don't you?' she asked.

Watch lowered his head. 'Yeah, I do. I miss my father and sister too.' He raised his head. 'But I can't worry about them now.'

'We can talk about them later if you like,' Cindy said gently. 'But first we have to get out of here. Can you break your chains?'

'I was just about to try.' Watch took a deep breath and tugged at the binds as hard as he could. But even though the iron pin that held the chains to the wall groaned as it moved slightly, the chains refused to come loose. Watch finally gave up straining. 'Let's wait a while longer,' he suggested. 'I keep getting stronger. I might be able to pop them loose before the trolls come back for us.'

Cindy nodded at the iron door. 'But will you be able to get through that? I don't know if ten super-strong men could.'

Watch paused. 'I think I hear someone coming.'

'But it hasn't been six hours,' Cindy said. 'It's been less than an hour.'

'Maybe trolls don't know how to tell the time,' Watch said.

Belfart appeared on the other side of the thick metal bars. He had a large black key with him, which he used to open the door. Stepping inside, he set aside his sword and spear, like he wanted it to be a friendly meeting.

'It hasn't been six hours,' Cindy said quickly. 'You can't eat us yet.'

Belfart waved away her remark. 'We'll get to that later. I've come to make you a proposition.'

'What kind of proposition?' Cindy asked.

'I want more information about these Marines,' Belfart said. 'You give it to me and I'll make sure you die painlessly.'

'I have a better idea,' Cindy said. 'We tell everything you could ever want to know about the Marines and you help us escape.'

Belfart shook his head. 'That's not possible. The

boys are all riled up. If I let you go, they'll eat me instead. But if you do help me, at the very least I can make sure you're not satéed.'

'That's something,' Watch said.

'That's ridiculous,' Cindy complained. 'Why should I care if I'm satéed or barbecued if I'm dead? I'm not telling you anything about the Marines unless you let us both go. It's that simple.'

'Why do you want to know about them anyway?' Watch asked.

Belfart scratched his hairy nose and paced the cell. 'This is kind of hard for me to admit, being a troll and all. But when you were talking about the Marines, something stirred deep inside me. They sound like a powerful group of boys. "The proud and the few." I kind of liked the sound of that.' He paused. 'This is strictly confidential, you understand, but I would like to find out how I could join their organisation.'

'The Marines would never accept a troll,' Watch said.

Belfart stopped pacing. His ugly face seemed to fall. 'Are you sure?'

Cindy spoke quickly. 'What Watch means is they would never accept a troll with bad breath. It's against article two-three-zero of their secret code. But if you learn to brush your teeth, gargle and floss regularly, they would be happy to take you on board.'

Watch was not so sure. 'Are you certain, Cindy? How would they find a uniform that fits Belfart?'

'I'm positive,' Cindy said, catching Watch's eye. 'In fact, why don't you give Belfart that brochure you have on the Marines.'

'Which brochure is that?' Watch asked.

'The one in your back pocket,' Cindy said. 'If Belfart unlocks your chains, you can get it for him. Can't you, Watch?'

Watch finally caught on. His new muscles seemed to be making him a little slower upstairs. 'Yes, I remember now. My brochure on how to get into the Marines. I would be happy to give it to you if you just loosen these chains a little, Belfart.'

Belfart paused. 'This wouldn't be some kind of trick, would it?' he asked.

'What can Watch do to you?' Cindy asked. 'He's just a boy, while you're a big strong handsome troll.'

Belfart puffed himself up. 'So you think I'm handsome?'

'I noticed it right away,' Cindy said.

Belfart studied her a bit closer. 'Why is it that your skin is glowing?'

'It's another sign of measles,' Cindy muttered. 'Just open Watch's chains and let him show you the best way to sign up to serve your country.'

Belfart nodded enthusiastically as he took his keys back out. 'I'd like to get out of here, and travel a bit. Don't get me wrong, Ann Templeton is great to work for. It's just that I'm tired of all the back-stabbing that goes on around here. I mean, just last week an old friend tried to put a knife in me while I was taking my afternoon nap.'

'There's nothing worse than a disloyal troll,' Cindy said sympathetically.

'You'll find this brochure very informative,' Watch promised as Belfart worked on the lock.

'Could you read it to me?' Belfart asked. 'I sometimes have trouble understanding promotional literature.'

'I'll make sure the information gets into your head,' Watch said when his hands were free. He nodded to the chains on his feet. 'Could you unlock those as well? It's hard for me to get to my back pocket while I'm still pinned to the wall.'

Belfart was in a trusting mood. 'No problem,' he said, bending over. 'You guys are more polite than most of the humans we've seen around here. Most of them refuse to stop screaming and begging. It gets on your nerves after a while. You just want to put them in the pot even if it means in the end you don't get the meat flavoured exactly the way you want it.'

'We are very polite,' Cindy said, nodding to Watch.

'You can trust us with your life,' Watch said as he brought his hands up above Belfart's head. The troll had just snapped the ankle chains free, and was glancing up, when Watch brought his fists down hard. Watch was strong enough by now. It was a loud blow. He almost took off the troll's head.

Belfart crumpled unconscious to the floor.

'Grab his keys,' Cindy said, excited. 'Undo my chains. We can be out of here before he wakes up.'

Watch reached for the keys. 'I have a better idea. Let's take him as a hostage.'

'Do you think you can handle him?' Cindy asked.

'If I keep a sword to his throat I can. He may even know a way out of here.'

Cindy looked down at the sleeping troll and frowned. 'I don't know. He doesn't look as if he gets out much.'

Eleven

The power of the magic necklaces was still at work. Adam was now an old man, at least fifty, and Sally was as small as a two year old. Adam had to carry her in his arms as Mireen led them through the castle, just so they could both keep up. Sally did not like being carried. She kept bothering Adam about his nappy remark.

'I'm not wearing them,' she said. 'I don't care how young I get. And you're certainly not changing them.'

'You might have to wear them,' Adam said. 'Look at you now. You've slipped out of your pants. Your shirt is the only thing covering you up.'

'I like this shirt,' Sally said. 'It's one of my favourites. But I mean what I say. I don't want some senile old goat taking care of me when I'm a baby.'

'I'm not senile yet,' Adam said.

'But you're getting close. Your hair's almost white.'

'It's silver, it's not white.'

'See,' Sally said. 'You're too far gone to know there's no difference.'

'Do you two always argue like this?' Mireen asked.

'Yes,' Sally said.

'No,' Adam said, then sighed. 'Sometimes. Look, do you know where you're going?'

'I know my way around the castle,' Mireen explained. 'But it's a big place, and I have no idea where your friends might be. I'm just looking everywhere.'

'Let's try searching the trolls' basement,' Sally said. 'Knowing Cindy and Watch, they're probably being roasted alive as we speak.'

'We can look there if you'd like,' Mireen said, stopping in front of a stone wall and muttering a few words of magic. There didn't seem to be many real doors in the place. Mireen was forever materialising passageways out of nothing. This time was no exception. A narrow doorway suddenly appeared before them and they hurried inside. Glancing over his shoulder, Adam saw the wall reappear where it had been. The path before them was dark but that did not seem to bother Mireen.

'Do you have any idea where your mother is?' he asked Mireen.

'If she is in the castle, she is hiding from even me,' Mireen said, troubled. 'I can usually find her just by thinking about her.'

'She might be testing you as well as us,' Adam said.

'Testing me?' Mireen said. 'I don't understand.'

'The witch . . .' Sally began. 'I mean, your mother said she was testing us with these necklaces.'

Mireen continued to appear troubled. 'Are all the kids outside afraid of my mother?'

'Most of them,' Adam admitted. 'She is supposed to have murdered a lot of them.'

Mireen laughed, but it sounded forced. 'My mother would never murder anyone. How can those kids be so foolish?'

'They've lost too many brothers and sisters?' Sally suggested.

Mireen shook her head. 'My mother's powerful, but she never abuses her power. There is a reason behind everything she does.'

'I hope you're right,' Adam muttered.

'Tell me what it's like on the outside?' Mireen asked.

'In Spooksville or in the world as a whole?' Sally asked. 'The reason I ask is because Spooksville is unlike any other place. Other cities don't have castles like this.'

'What do you do each day for fun?' Mireen asked.

'Before I moved here from Kansas City,' Adam said, 'I used to go swimming and fishing in the lake. Sometimes I would ride my bike and play baseball.'

'But since he got here he's been struggling to stay alive,' Sally said. 'We wrestle with ghosts, fight with aliens, destroy cold creatures from the past, get lost in haunted caves. We have all kinds of fun. It's a laugh a minute. You should play with us some time. You're more than welcome.'

'Perhaps some day I will,' Mireen said in a soft, maybe sad, voice.

'Do you have anyone to play with?' Adam asked gently.

'I have learned to play in my imagination,' Mireen said. 'My mother says that's the best place to play. There are more possibilities inside us, she says, than outside.'

'Hmm,' Adam muttered thoughtfully. 'Those are beautiful words.'

'And of absolutely no use to us now,' Sally said. 'Sorry, Mireen, but if we don't get these necklaces off soon, you won't be playing with us. You'll be baby-sitting us.'

'I will do everything I can to help you,' Mireen promised.

They passed from their narrow passageway into a wider tunnel lit with a sober red glow. In the distance they could hear frantic steps, two or three people running their way. But beyond that, a little further away, they could hear what sounded like a small army of trolls in battle gear. Adam strained his eyes in the gloomy light. One of the approaching figures seemed to be glowing. Adam realised who he was looking at.

'Cindy!' Adam called. 'Watch! We're over here!'

Twelve

Cindy and Watch caught up with them a few minutes later. Adam was surprised to see they had a troll with them. Watch guarded the monster by holding the sword to the troll's throat, but for his part the troll didn't seem to mind. In fact, he offered his hand.

'I'm Belfart,' he said. 'I'm a Marine.'

'I'm Mireen,' Mireen said to Cindy and Watch.

'She's the witch's daughter,' Sally said.

'Wow,' Watch said. 'I didn't know Ann Templeton was even married.'

'Belfart wants to be a Marine,' Cindy explained impatiently. 'But let's drop these introductions. We can do that later. What are you guys doing here? You're supposed to be dead.'

'Don't count the dead in this town until you've seen the bodies,' Sally said.

'I'll never do it again.' Cindy hugged them both. 'I'm just so happy to see you guys are all right.'

'Yeah, this is great,' Watch said with unexpected emotion in his voice. He reached over and hugged them too. But they just ended up crushing little Sally. She pushed them away.

'This is not great,' she said. 'I can hardly walk any more. And you, Watch, you look ready to burst out of your clothes. Adam's got the same problem, mind you. Mireen had to find him a sheet to keep him covered. And you, Cindy, you're so radiant you're on the verge of disappearing.'

'I know that,' Cindy said. 'We have to get these necklaces off.'

'First we have to get away from these trolls who are chasing us,' Watch said. 'We just escaped from their prison and they're really mad.'

'I'll talk to them,' Mireen said. 'They won't hurt you.'

'If I may beg to differ, my lady,' Belfart said. 'You won't calm them down by talking to them. I know my boys. They want human meat and they want it now. They don't even care how it's cooked, and that tells you how upset they are.'

'But can't you calm them down?' Mireen asked.

Belfart rubbed his head and glanced at Cindy and Watch. 'They think I helped these guys escape. They're hot for my bones as well.'

'Can't you lead us into a secret passageway?' Adam asked Mireen.

'Can't she just lead us out of here?' Cindy asked.

'That's what I asked,' Sally muttered.

'There is no secret passageway here,' Mireen said. 'We have to go further up the tunnel.'

'But we just came out of a secret passageway,' Adam said.

'Yes, but it was a one way passageway,' Mireen explained. 'Come, let's hurry. I know a place to take you where you will be safe.'

'Will there be a bottle there for Sally?' Cindy teased.

'Shut up,' Sally grumbled.

They ran up the tunnel as best as they could, but the trolls continued to gain on them. Adam had handed Sally to Watch to carry, but he was still slowing down the group. He definitely had arthritis now. His knees and hips ached, plus breathing was hard. Running a few steps winded him. He estimated he was seventy years old.

Cindy was also having trouble running. It was as if her disappearing feet couldn't get a grip on the ground.

She bounced in the air as she ran, as if she were on the moon.

Behind them, the troll army became visible, with dozens of burning eyes.

'The boys are full of life tonight,' Belfart said wistfully. 'Better get us to a passageway quick, my lady, or they'll tear us apart in this very tunnel.'

'We still have a way to go,' Mireen said anxiously.

'You're a witch's daughter,' Sally said. 'Do some witchcraft. Scare them away.'

Mireen stopped. 'There is a spell I know that might slow them down.' She put her hands to her head as if she was thinking deeply. 'But I can't remember exactly how it goes.'

'Is there a pocket witch dictionary or something you can look in?' Sally asked.

'Let her concentrate,' Adam said. 'There's no hurry, Mireen. Take your time.'

'But don't take too much of it,' Belfart said.

Cindy nodded to Watch. 'He's definitely Marine material.'

'I've got it!' Mireen said, excited. 'I think I've got it. All of you, stand back.'

They cleared a space for her as she stepped into the centre of the tunnel and faced in the direction of the approaching army. The trolls were clearly visible now, and they were not a pleasant sight. They already had their swords drawn, and even the sight of their boss's daughter didn't slow them down a step. Unless Mireen was able to stop them, Adam realised, the horde would be on them in a minute.

'Katuu Shamar Plean!' Mireen called as she lifted her arms.

Nothing happened.

'Try another one,' Sally said anxiously.

Mireen closed her eyes and drew in a deep breath. She raised her arms. 'Katuu Shamar Klean!'

The tunnel burst into fire. The flames exploded out of thin air in front of the attacking trolls. Adam was not sure if any of them got burned, but the whole bunch of them definitely got scared. They turned and ran the other way.

But then the flames went out.

'Do it again!' Sally called from her place in Watch's strong arms.

'I can only do it once,' Mireen said wearily as she turned and stumbled up the tunnel. 'That was enough to drain all my power.'

'That won't hold them for long, my lady,' Belfart said. 'Best we find that secret passageway quickly.'

Belfart was right. Already a few of the trolls looked as if they were having second thoughts about leaving their dinner. Several were still staring their way, calling to their partners to come back. Adam braced himself for another exhausting dash. If the trolls didn't get him, he thought, a heart attack would. He had never realised how miserable it could be to grow old.

They hurried up the tunnel, Adam staggering, Cindy bouncing, Mireen stumbling, and Sally complaining. Only Watch seemed in good shape. In a sense, his necklace had done him the most good. At least he seemed to be experiencing the fewest side effects.

Behind them, the trolls regrouped and started after them again.

'Is it much further?' Adam gasped.

'We're almost there,' Mireen called. 'I think.'

Another exhausting five minutes went by. Adam struggled on as best as he could, but invariably he began to fall behind the others. But faint whistling sounds in the dark gave him an unexpected burst of energy. The trolls were firing arrows at him, trying to cut him down. Adam swore he would not give them the pleasure.

Up ahead, Mireen stopped and faced the stone wall. The gang gathered around her. Adam was just coming up when an opening appeared out of nowhere. As a group, they poured into the magic doorway. Arrows bounced on the stone above their heads.

'Close it!' Adam cried when they were all inside.

'Weeta!' Mireen shouted over her shoulder.

The doorway vanished. The trolls were stopped.

The gang staggered through the passageway.

Then they emerged into a large room.

Adam recognised it. The room with the hourglass.

The witch was waiting for them.

Thirteen

'So you still haven't found your way out,' Ann Templeton said, her back to the magic hourglass. The light of the stardust shone about her, creating a coloured aura over her head. To Adam she didn't even look human any more, more like a powerful being from another solar system. Her green eyes glittered as she spoke, as if with strong emotion, even though her voice remained calm. She added, 'What does this mean?'

'It means you need more doors in this place,' Sally said.

Ann Templeton smiled and gestured in the direction of the hallway through which they had first entered the room. 'Why don't you go that way?' she asked. 'See what you can find?'

Adam took a weary step forward. 'We know we would find nothing. You have us locked in a maze.

There is no way out. Even your daughter does not know how to get out of this place.'

Mireen also took a step forward. 'Why are you torturing these nice kids?'

'Be silent, Mireen,' Ann Templeton said. 'Watch, listen, learn.'

'No,' Mireen replied. 'I can't remain silent while my friends are in danger.'

Her daughter's defiance seemed to surprise Ann Templeton, even to anger her. But she quickly mastered her emotions. She spoke in a quiet voice.

'You just met these people. How can you call them friends?'

Mireen shook her head. 'It's just how I feel. I like them, I care about them.' She added reluctantly, 'I can't let you hurt them.'

Ann Templeton smiled coldly. 'Do I hurt them? I did not ask them to come here. They wanted to. They wanted to see what my castle was like. Now they know. Now they're happy.'

'I wouldn't exactly say that I'm a happy one year old,' Sally muttered.

Adam spoke with effort. He still hadn't caught his breath from the mad dash up the tunnel. 'You must know that we're running out of time. Soon Cindy will disappear, Sally will turn back into an egg, and I'll die of old age. If we've failed your test, then we've failed it. We don't know what else we can do to get out of here.'

'Why, Adam, I'm disappointed in you,' Ann Templeton said in a serious voice. 'You have not even tried to get out of here. Sure, you've crawled into this hole, and explored this cave, and searched through this passageway. But that is not how you escape from a trap. To do that you have to look at how you got into the trap. Then you will know what to do.'

'But Mother,' Mireen pleaded. 'Adam told you. They don't have time for this. They're dying.'

'How do you feel, Watch?' Ann Templeton asked. 'Do you feel like you're dying?'

'No ma'am,' he replied. 'I feel stronger than ever.'

'Somehow I'm not surprised.' Ann Templeton lowered her head and closed her eyes, as if thinking deeply. Then she raised her head and stared at each one of them, including her daughter. Finally she spoke, and there was great power in her words, as if she were passing judgment on them. 'I will leave you now. You will pass the test or you will fail it. It is up to you.' She turned away. 'Come, Mireen.'

'No,' her daughter said flatly. 'I'm staying here with my friends. If you won't help them, maybe I can.'

Ann Templeton paused and studied her. But she seemed unconcerned with her daughter's disobedience. 'You're old enough to make up your own mind, Mireen.' She gestured to Belfart. 'Come with me.'

'See you guys later,' he said casually. 'If I'm lucky. Remember that brochure on the Marines. I still think they could use a few good trolls.'

And with that Ann Templeton and Belfart vanished into the wall.

Fourteen

'She sure makes a stunning exit, doesn't she?' Sally said in her baby's voice.

Adam stepped up to the hourglass and leaned against it for support. 'We're back where we started from.'

'No,' Cindy disagreed, in a voice they could hardly hear. They could see right through her now. Her words were like a ghost's whispers. 'We're worse off than when we started. We have only a few minutes left to figure out what to do.'

Adam sighed. 'I just wish I could think more clearly. I'm definitely getting senile. Does anyone have any suggestions?'

'The witch did not have to meet us here,' Watch said. 'But she did, and I think she did so as a favour.'

'I could do with less of her favours,' Sally said.

'You misunderstand me,' Watch said. 'I think she was trying to give us a hint. Let's think about what she said. "But that is not how you escape from a trap. To do that you have to look at how you got into the trap. Then you will know what to do." ' Watch paused. 'The key must be in those words.'

'But how did we get in this trap?' Adam asked. 'We walked over and walked inside and we were trapped.'

'No,' Cindy said. 'The door closed behind us as soon as we stepped inside, but I don't think we were trapped until we put on the necklaces. The witch said as much earlier.'

'I think we have to go further back than that,' Watch said. 'I think we have to ask ourselves why we came here.'

'For the usual reasons,' Sally said. 'Because we were bored and stupid.'

'We may have been bored,' Adam said. 'But the thing that decided us to come here was Watch's failing eyesight.'

'And Watch is the only one who is not suffering right now,' Mireen said. 'Mother pointed that out. She said that it did not surprise her.'

'But why isn't Watch suffering like the rest of us?' Cindy said. 'Maybe that's the key to this big test.'

'I think he's going to suffer when he tries to buy some new clothes,' Sally said. 'And he looks like the Incredible Hulk.'

'Cindy's on to something,' Adam interrupted. 'We came here because of Watch. Actually, Watch was the only one who had a genuine reason to come. He needed help with his eyesight and now his eyesight is better. Also, he was the first one to put on the necklace. He trusted that he would be all right. He had faith.'

'Thank you for the sermon,' Sally said. 'But how does this help us get these stupid necklaces off?'

'I think it gives us a clue as to why we can't get them off,' Adam said. 'I put the necklace on because I wanted something for nothing. I wanted to be more mature.'

'And I wanted to be prettier,' Cindy agreed. 'Even though I was pretty enough to begin with.'

'And humble enough,' Sally added.

'The point is the three of us were fine to begin with,' Adam said. 'We didn't have anything wrong with us. But still we put on the necklaces.' He paused. 'Could the test be just that. That we took something we didn't need. That we were fine the way we were and we still wanted something more.'

Cindy nodded. 'I think that's it. The test is inside. It's there that we failed it.'

'But how do we get these stupid necklaces off?' Sally demanded.

Mireen spoke up. 'My mother has a saying. It's always been one of my favourites. She says that the things we crave the most destroy us the quickest.'

'Interesting,' Adam said thoughtfully. 'I certainly don't crave maturity any more.'

'And I don't crave beauty any more,' Cindy said.

They all looked at little Sally.

'Well, I'm tired of being a baby if that's what you want to hear,' she said. 'Now I have just one tiny question. I've asked it before. How do we get these necklaces off?'

They stared at each other, searching for an answer.

'Why don't you just try taking them off?' Mireen suggested.

'We tried that already,' Sally said. 'Many times. They won't come off.'

'Try now,' Mireen said gently.

Adam tried first.

Without effort, the necklace passed over his head.

Cindy quickly pulled off her necklace.

Sally took off hers. She smiled a big baby smile.

They all stared at Watch. He fingered his ruby.

'You don't have to take it off,' Adam said. 'It isn't hurting you.'

Watch was doubtful. 'But how can I want to be special when you guys aren't allowed to be? It's not fair.' He pulled the necklace over his head. 'I got by before. I can get by again. Even if I do go blind, there are worse things.'

Mireen went over and put her hand on Watch's chest. 'You're a great person. You have a big heart.'

Watch blushed. 'Thank you.'

'I think this may be the start of something,' Cindy said.

'Excuse me,' Sally spoke up. 'Are you guys forgetting a minor detail? We have removed the necklaces and maybe wc have stopped ageing and shrinking and disappearing. But we are still far from back to normal.'

'I think I may have an answer to that problem,' Adam said, touching the hourglass once more. 'Mireen, has your mother ever spoken about this hourglass?'

'Very seldom,' Mireen said. 'But she did once say its power reached to the stars. That even the stars' paths through the heavens could be influenced by it.'

'What does that mean?' Sally said.

'We already know,' Adam said. 'We were shown on the other side of the Secret Path. This hourglass controls the flow of time.'

'But you said we can't mess with it,' Cindy said. 'You said it could destroy our world.'

'I said we couldn't destroy it,' Adam corrected. 'We destroyed the other one in the other dimension. But what if we perform an experiment. What if we put the necklaces back on, and turn the hourglass upside down, and then see what happens.'

'What will happen?' Cindy asked.

Watch understood. 'Time will begin to flow backwards. The effect of the necklaces on us might begin to reverse itself.'

'It's a possibility,' Adam said. 'I can't guarantee anything.'

'I say we try it,' Sally said. 'I think I'm going to be needing a nappy soon.'

'How sweet,' Cindy said.

'Don't joke,' Sally warned.

'This hourglass weighs a ton,' Mireen said. 'How will we turn it over?'

Watch flexed his muscles. 'No problem. I can lift it up with one hand.'

'But Mireen has a point,' Adam warned. 'If our

experiment works, we'll have to turn the hourglass back round. Then you won't be super-strong any more, Watch. We might get trapped in a time warp, where we have to live our lives backwards.'

'I refuse to go through all my psychological crises over again,' Sally said. 'I just finished with that junk.'

'We can worry about that problem when we come to it,' Watch said.

'I would rather worry about it now,' Adam said.

Watch did something unusual then. He reached out and touched Adam's shoulder. He held his friend's eye.

'Adam,' he said. 'A moment ago you said I had faith. That's why I wasn't hurt by my necklace. Well, I have faith now. If we do this, everything will work out. Ann Templeton will know we have passed our test. She will help us if we need help.'

'You really think so?' Adam asked. 'After all she's put us through, you still think she's a good witch?'

Watch didn't hesitate. 'I'm sure of it.'

'So am I,' Mireen added. 'She may be a witch to you, but she's still my mother. I trust her.'

'OK,' Adam said, putting his necklace back on. 'Let's do it. Let's see if we can't get ourselves back to normal.'

With the exception of Mireen, each of them put

their necklaces back on. Watch approached the glowing hourglass. He was as strong as he looked. In one smooth move, he inverted the magical time keeper.

Now the sparkling stardust began to flow *upwards*.

A wave of drowsiness swept over Adam. He blinked, trying to rub it from his eyes, but noticed he was not alone with his tired feelings. Each of them was slumping slowly to the ground. Now they really were in the witch's hands.

There was nothing Adam could do.

The drowsiness was too hard to resist.

He closed his eyes and blacked out.

Epilogue

That evening, while enjoying milk and doughnuts at their favourite coffee shop, they traded stories about what they experienced after the hourglass had been inverted. But basically all their stories were the same. They had fallen asleep and wakened outside beside the castle, in the same shape as when they entered the castle. They'd had another great adventure, but nothing had changed.

Or had it?

Mireen had not been with them when they had wakened.

'But maybe now her mother will let her come out and play sometimes,' Cindy said. 'I imagine Mireen will want to see us again.'

'I want to see her again,' Watch said quietly.

Sally shoved his side. 'You don't have a crush on her, do you, Watch?'

'No,' he said quickly.

'That would spoil your cool and detached image,' Adam teased.

Watch smiled to himself. '*She* didn't want to change my image too much.'

'Who is she?' Sally asked. 'What are you talking about?'

'Ann Templeton,' Watch said. 'She actually woke me before you guys, when we were still inside the castle. I don't know if she wants me to talk about it, but I guess it's all right.'

'What did she say to you?' Adam asked.

'Not much. She just told me to take off my necklace.'

They all jumped. 'Then you stopped the reversal process!' Cindy exclaimed. 'You can see without your glasses.' She paused. 'But you still have your glasses on.'

Watch nodded. 'I had reversed to almost how I was before I entered the castle. She told me that was for the best, for now. But she did allow my eyes to be improved enough that I won't have to keep bumping into things.'

'That's a miracle,' Cindy said. 'You must be grateful.'

‘I am,’ Watch said shyly.

‘Wait a second,’ Sally said. ‘I would be angry with her. She could have at least wakened you early enough so that you didn’t have to wear glasses at all. For that matter, she should have given you the necklace. She promised it to us if we passed the test. If anyone passed it, Watch, I think it was you.’

Watch smiled and shook his head. ‘She said she didn’t want to do that.’

‘Why not?’ Sally demanded.

‘She said I looked better in glasses,’ Watch said simply.

Sally thought for a moment, as she stared at her friend.

Then she too smiled. It was a happy smile.

‘For once I agree with her,’ Sally said.

Look out for the next Spooksville story
by Christopher Pike:

THE DARK CORNER

Adam, Sally and Watch take the Secret Path again – this time into a world full of demons. And it's impossible to leave the Dark Corner, without being judged by the bloodthirsty Gatekeepers . . .

If you enjoyed THE WITCH'S REVENGE *you'll love Christopher Pike's other Spooksville chillers . . .*

ALIENS IN THE SKY

Bright lights in the sky . . .

Then a spaceship lands near the reservoir.
And creatures come out.
Alien creatures who want Adam and the others
to join them.

But who knows when they'll be coming home . . .

THE SECRET PATH

Adam has never met anyone like Sally before.

She tells him terrifying stories about what happens to kids in Spooksville.
Adam doesn't believe her – would you?

Then he meets Watch who leads them along the Secret Path into Spooksville's other dimension.

A place where fear kills.
A place from which few return.

THE COLD PEOPLE

Why are there huge ice blocks in the forest near Spooksville? Adam and his friends are dying to know what's inside.

So they melt one – a big mistake.

A man steps out of the melting ice. He has cold eyes. An icy touch.

And he wants to turn all the inhabitants of Spooksville into Cold People. Can Adam and the others stop him?